'We are very curious to see mighty folk
about whom great tales are told.'
    – *The Saga of Gisli the Outlaw*

VIKING
MYTHS & SAGAS

Retold from ancient Norse texts

Rosalind Kerven

First published in the UK by Talking Stone 2015

Talking Stone
Swindonburn Cottage West, Sharperton
Morpeth, Northumberland, NE65 7AP

ISBN: 9780953745470

Names in SMALL CAPITALS refer to stories in this book.

Words and names in **bold** can be found in the Glossary.

The original versions of these stories were written in
Old Norse, which contains a number of unfamiliar letters.
For ease of reading, this book follows the conventions of
modern scholars in anglicising the Old Norse names.

The book includes a number of quotes from Old Norse texts.
Sometimes these are based on more than one translation,
and are slightly adapted to improve clarity
whilst still maintaining the original content and meaning.

For Richard

ACKNOWLEDGEMENTS

I would like to thank the following for their invaluable help and advice: Professor Diana Whaley, Newcastle University, who generously gave her time to advise on the Glossary, Introduction and skaldic verse. Professor Gisli Sigurdsson, University of Iceland, who comprehensively answered numerous questions, especially about the sagas. Dr Judy Quinn, Cambridge University, for clarifying various aspects of Eddic poetry and mythology. Dr Terry Gunnell, University of Iceland, for sending me his fascinating articles on Viking religion and the performance of Eddic poetry. Professor John McKinnell, Durham University, for his advice on dating the Eddic poems. I am also immensely grateful to all the scholars from the early 20th Century to the present day who have translated the Old Norse texts on which my retellings are based.

CONTENTS

THE CURSE OF ANDVARI'S RING

TALES OF LOVE AND HATE

TALES OF EXPLORATION

GHOSTS AND SORCERY

'The guest has arrived...
Courteous words, then courteous silence
That he may tell his tale.'
— *Havamal*, **Poetic Edda**

VIKING PEOPLE
AND THEIR STORIES

The people we now call Vikings dominated northern Europe for three hundred years from the late 8th Century. Originally from Denmark, Norway and Sweden, their merchants, plunderers, armies and migrants carried Viking culture far and wide. They established flourishing colonies, particularly in the British Isles, Iceland and Greenland.

What was their world like, and what sort of lives did they lead?

Most of the Viking nations were warrior kingdoms, although Iceland and Greenland were democratic republics. Society was made up of nobles, freehold farmers, paid labourers and slaves. Political power and warfare were exclusively male preserves. However, women enjoyed a fair degree of influence and freedom; they could own land and property and had easy access to **divorce**.

The Viking landscape was overwhelmingly rural and most people worked on farms. Their rectangular houses were built of timber, turf or stone. The main room had broad benches along each long wall, for both sitting and sleeping, and was usually dominated by a large upright loom.

Heating and cooking were from the central fire-pit, which burned wood or peat, whilst oil lamps provided lighting. Wealthy people had additional rooms and small bed-closets for the heads of the household; otherwise, everyone slept on the benches.

Women spent much of their time working with textiles – spinning, weaving, sewing clothes and making sails. In addition they preserved and processed food, especially dairy products, cooked two meals a day, and organised the household or served in it. Some acted as midwives. When men were away fighting or raiding, women ran the farms.

Most men laboured in the fields or herded livestock. Some did smithing, construction work or shipbuilding, either as a sideline or a main occupation. Others were merchants who travelled widely overseas; artisans who decorated their handiwork with exquisite patterns; professional courtiers, soldiers or legal experts. It was not unusual for men to join raiding expeditions, either for a single season or on a regular basis; some of the treasure they looted in this way was for personal use, while the rest swelled the coffers of their chieftain, **earl** or **king**. This, alongside warfare, violent quarrels and ongoing **feuds** entailed skill with weapons such as axes, spears and swords.

In some areas, there were walled towns – such as Hedeby (originally in Denmark), Trondheim (Norway), Sigtuna (Sweden) and Jorvik (modern York, England). Here, small houses lined narrow streets, dotted with stalls selling locally produced wares, and perhaps dominated by a nobleman's hall. Along the waterfront there were fishing boats and superbly made ships used for trade, exploration, raiding, war and emigration.

Entertainment included regular feasts, often lasting many days, with copious drinking, sporting contests, horse fights and board games.

But, most importantly, there were stories.

Viking people were mainly illiterate, so storytelling was an oral, communal activity. Family members shared tales around the fireside; itinerant raconteurs brought the latest news and gossip; professional bards recited grandiose narratives at feasts. There was a huge repertoire to choose from: family and local histories, folk tales, rumours, legends, heroic epics and religious myths.

Even after the end of the **Viking Age**, the most popular stories continued to be passed on through succeeding generations. Eventually, during the 12th and 13th Centuries, many were written down for the first time, and some of these ancient texts have survived. Although filtered through the transcribers' later medieval Christian perspective, they provide an invaluable record of Viking narratives. They reveal both simple and very complex tales, some in the form of heavily stylised poetry.

Two of the most important texts are the *Prose Edda* and the *Poetic Edda*. Together these provide most modern knowledge about the Vikings' **pagan** mythology. They also include episodes from heroic legends which the Vikings had absorbed from much older traditions, rooted in 5th Century central Europe. The antiquity of some of these tales can be verified by scenes depicted in extant Viking Age carvings.

Other texts contain an entirely different kind of narrative. Quasi-historical accounts purport to record the reigns of

Viking **kings**, the original settlement of Iceland and that country's **conversion to Christianity**. The **sagas** are full-length historical novels which claim to be based on true stories of real Viking Age people. Short anecdotes with the feel of folk tales are woven into some of the longer narratives.

Information about all the main sources can be found in the GLOSSARY.

The undisputed centre of Viking stories was, and still is, Iceland. According to the ancient texts, the most highly regarded Viking storytellers and poets – especially those who performed for the Scandinavian kings – were Icelandic. Almost all the oldest texts were transcribed or composed by medieval Icelandic scholars. Even today, Icelanders value their literary heritage so much that, per head, they have more writers, and more books published, than anywhere else in the world. Moreover, Viking narrative traditions have endured into living memory: Icelandic saga expert Gisli Sigurdsson recalls his father and friends gathering each weekend to share tales 'hung up on various branches of their family trees – which they knew by heart, backwards and forwards. They constantly spiced up their stories with rhymed, syllabic and alliterated verse – similar to the oral art of Viking Age storytellers.'

This book retells the best surviving Viking stories, with as much medieval gloss as possible stripped away. They are narrated in a variety of voices, to reflect both their oral provenance and **Old Norse** mannerisms preserved in the surviving texts. It is impossible to say whether they are 'correct' versions, nor does it matter; for oral tales are organic entities, their original forms long forgotten, constantly evolving and developing. The importance of retelling them for posterity and enrichment was recognised as far back as the 13th Century, by an anonymous saga author who pointed out that, 'One man's tale is only half a tale'. In that spirit, this book brings the Vikings' rich heritage of stories back to life and passes them on to future generations.

GODS
GODDESSES
GIANTS
GIANTESSES
&
DWARFS

'The chief centre and holiest place of the gods is by the
ash tree, Yggdrasil, the biggest and best of all trees.
Its branches spread out over all the world
and extend across the sky.
It is supported by three roots, standing wide apart.
One root is with the gods and beneath it
they hold court at the sacred Weird's Well.
Another root is with the frost-giants; under it lies
Mimir's Well, the fount of knowledge and wisdom.
The third root stretches into the freezing mists of Niflheim.
There are many other splendid places.
One is called Alfheim, where the light-elves live;
but the dwarfs live down in the ground.'

— Abridged from the *Prose Edda*

THE ORIGIN OF THE STORIES:
MAGIC MEAD

There was a young giantess called Gunnlod Suttungsdaughter. She was buxom and very beautiful, but she had never lain with any kind of man.

One day her father, Giant Suttung, arrived home pulling a wagon. Inside it were three vats. He beckoned Gunnlod over to see them. They were all filled with a curious liquid, the colour of dark amber.

'What is it?' asked Gunnlod.

'Magic Mead,' said Suttung.

'What do you mean by magic?' said Gunnlod.

Suttung said, 'I mean that anyone who drinks this mead will find their head bursting with knowledge and stories about everything in the world.'

'Who brewed it?' asked Gunnlod.

'Fjalar and Galar,' said Suttung, 'two despicable dwarfs.'

Gunnlod sniffed and said, 'It stinks of stale blood.'

'It's the blood of a man called Kvasir,' said Suttung. 'The gods themselves created him from their own spittle, and moulded him to be wiser than anyone in all the worlds. Fjalar and Galar were so jealous of his talents that they murdered him, stole his blood and mixed it with honey. In this way, they brewed the Magic Mead.'

'How did you get hold of it?' asked Gunnlod.

'It's a long story,' said Suttung. 'Remember how your grandfather, Giant Gilling, was drowned at sea? And how, while your grandmother was still grieving for him, a millstone fell on her head? The truth is that neither of these tragedies happened by accident: Fjalar and Galar killed your grandparents too.'

'So you took revenge on them?'

'Of course,' said Suttung. 'I chucked both the dwarfs down a sheer cliff. But instead of falling into the sea and getting washed away as I'd intended, the little rats landed on a skerry and started cravenly pleading for their lives. In the end we agreed to strike a bargain: I set them free and in return they gave me the Magic Mead.'

'Have you tasted it?' asked Gunnlod.

'No,' said Suttung. 'And I'm not letting anyone else taste it either. It's much too valuable. For now, I'm just going to store it somewhere safe, deep inside a mountain.'

'But if the mead is so precious,' said Gunnlod, 'surely there's a danger of someone breaking into the mountain and stealing it. Who will you set to guard it?'

And Suttung answered, 'You.'

So he led the young giantess down long, secret tunnels to a cave in the very heart of the mountain. There he carved her a bed on a rocky ledge and gave her a pile of soft sheepskins to cover it. He set lamps to burn in crannies around the cold rock walls. He showed her where a freshwater spring dripped from the ceiling, and gave her enough dry biscuits and salted meat to last her many months.

Finally, he set the three vats of Magic Mead in the centre of the floor.

'I forbid you ever to touch them,' he said. 'And if anyone ever finds you here, no matter whether it's a giant, a man or a dwarf, don't you dare let him drink any of it. Protect the mead with your life.'

'But…what is the point of owning it, if you never use the mead or even see it?' Gunnlod asked. If anyone else had been in that lonely place, they would have heard despair in her voice.

'To increase my prestige, of course,' said Suttung. And with those words, he turned his back on his daughter, strode out of the cave, sealed up the entrance and hurried back to the sunshine.

How long did the gentle giantess languish in that dreary, shadowy solitude? How did she pass her time there? Did she have wool to spin or a loom to work at? No one can tell.

But at length she was wakened from restless slumber by a curious sound, creaking and twisting like an auger boring through wood. Soon this gave way to a soft hissing, growing closer and closer. At last, from a tiny hole in the rock wall, a snake slithered out and thrust itself into the cave.

Gunnlod screamed.

The snake rose up, shook itself – and suddenly transformed into a handsome, powerfully built young man.

He spoke softly, soothing away Gunnlod's fear. After a while, he came to her rock bed, lay down beside her and took her in his arms.

They spent three very pleasant nights together. Then the man asked Gunnlod if he had healed her loneliness, and whether she loved him. She said he had, and that she did.

'Then will you give me a gift?' he asked her.

She said that she would like to, only she had nothing to offer.

'But you do,' he said. 'You have the Magic Mead.'

'I can't give you that,' she said. 'I've sworn to my father never to let a single drop of it pass the lips of giant, man or dwarf.'

He laughed. 'What giant can slip through an auger's hole? What man can shape-shift into a snake and back again? What dwarf can love a giantess so sweetly? You won't break your oath, Gunnlod, for the one who asks for this drink is a god.'

She glanced again at her lover – and saw now that his handsome features were mere illusion. There was a dark void in his face where one eye was missing. There were claw marks on his cloak where ravens had roosted.

She gasped and shuddered. 'Can it be?' she whispered. 'Are you...*Odin*?'

'Let me taste it, Gunnlod,' said he.

She dared not refuse. But, desperately seeking a way to avoid her father's anger, she cried, 'Only three draughts, Odin, I beg you – no more!'

Odin nodded. He seized the first vat and emptied it dry in one mouthful. He seized the second vat and did likewise. He seized the third vat and emptied this too in a single draught.

His mouth was awash with the Magic Mead.

Gunnlod was helpless.

In the gloom, Odin seemed to shimmer. Then suddenly he transformed again – this time, into an eagle.

The mountain split asunder, revealing a dark, star-spangled sky. The eagle rose.

Gunnlod saw no more.

In the world outside, in the icy wastes of Giantland, Suttung spied the eagle. He knew that it was Odin; he guessed that his daughter had been seduced and tricked.

Suttung too had shape-shifting powers; he too mutated into eagle form. Then he rose into the sky, winging his way after Odin, heading towards Asgard, closing in fast.

The gods saw them both coming. They hastened out with a great cauldron and placed it in an open spot amidst their golden halls. As Odin sank down to land, he caught sight of the cauldron and disgorged the Magic Mead into it.

However, in his hurry, he spilt some. It trickled down the great walls that surrounded Asgard, and from there fell like dew into our own realm.

These drops of Magic Mead are the liquid seeds from which all great stories are born.

For notes on this story, see page 308.

IN THE BEGINNING

Tell me, grandmother, ancient, all-knowing:
How did the world begin?

This is what I've heard and I believe that it's true.

In the beginning, everything was nothing, just emptiness and dark.

Suddenly, from nowhere, a spring began to flow. Faster and stronger it ran, growing, dividing, spilling its water into eleven great rivers.

From these rivers there rose clouds of poison. They froze into ice and were blown by the wind to the north.

In the south there was fire. Sparks danced up from it and flew at the ice.

Thus cold and hot mingled together. They gave birth to a the first living creature, the giant Ymir.

For a long time, this giant slept, enveloped in dampness and heat. Green things grew all around him. Creatures, both male and female, crawled out from his armpits and the creases of his thighs.

At last Ymir was woken by a cow formed of frost. He found he was ravenous and thirsty, so he crawled beneath her and drank greedily from her gushing udders.

Afterwards, the cow slaked her own hunger by licking salt from some stones. The warmth of her tongue melted the frost and on the first evening a man's hair emerged from it. On the second day this was followed by a head, and on the third day a complete man stepped out, handsome and powerful. His name was Buri.

He begot a son called Bor, who married the giantess Bestla. They had three sons. One was called Vili, one was Ve and the eldest of the three was Odin.

Tell me, grandmother, ancient, all-knowing:
What did Odin do?

He attacked Giant Ymir violently, stabbing him to death. So much blood flowed from Ymir's wounds, that most of the other giants drowned in it. However, one managed to float away on a box with his wife and settle in the frozen lands. All other giants and giantesses are sprung from them.

Odin and his brothers dragged Ymir's corpse to the middle of the void and chopped him into pieces.

From his flesh they crafted the earth.

From his skull they created the sky.

From his blood they made the sea and lakes.

From his bones they raised the mountains.

From his teeth they crumbled stones and scree.

All this time, the earth was floating like a feather. So Odin circled it with the ocean to keep it steady. Then he and his brothers created four dwarfs called East, West, North and South, setting them to hold the sky in place above the world.

Tell me, grandmother, ancient, all-knowing:
Where did the first people come from?

Vili, Ve and Odin created them, on a lonely beach by the sea.

From the waves they hauled two logs and breathed life into them, filling them with consciousness, movement, hearing and sight. They taught them how to speak. They clothed them. They gave them names, calling the man Ask and the woman Embla.

Finally, Odin and his brothers wove Ymir's eyelashes into a strong fence and set it around the edge of the earth, to keep out the giants. They called the land inside this fortification Midgard – the Middle Place – and set Ask and Embla safely inside it. They are everyone's ancestors.

Tell me, grandmother, ancient, all-knowing:
When the world was young, was there always day and night?

No, at first there was only vague, unchanging twilight.

So Odin called up the dark giantess, Night, and her youngest son, Day, giving each a horse and chariot. Night's horse is called Frosty Mane: every morning foam drips from his bit and falls to earth as the dew. Day's horse is Shining Mane, and his brilliance lights up the world. As for the sun and the moon, they were once a youth and a girl who were stunningly beautiful. The gods were so jealous that they snatched them away and tossed them into the sky to be endlessly chased by a pair of fierce wolves from Ironwood.

The gods also caused the seasons to be born: Winter was the son of Wind-Cool, and Summer the child of Sweetness.

Tell me, grandmother, ancient, all-knowing:
What more is there to tell of Odin?
Who are the other foremost gods? Are there goddesses too?

Odin is the All-father, very wise and powerful. He is the lord of wars and battles, and of warriors who die fighting. The valkyries work for him, fetching half of those slain in battle to feast in his hall. Two wolves lie at his feet, and two ravens gather news for him from across all the worlds. Always be mindful of Odin and on your guard, for he often travels through our own world in disguise and meddles in people's affairs.

Odin's eldest son is Thor. He is the strongest of all the gods, and can easily double his power by donning his Girdle of Might and his Iron Gloves. Thor is the arch-enemy of giants and his greatest joy is smashing his hammer against their skulls.

Of the goddesses, Odin's wife, Frigg, is the highest.

However, Freyja is the best beloved and most glorious. She rules over love affairs; yet her hall is called Battlefield, and she shares each day's tally of slaughtered warriors with Odin. She has a brother, Frey, who rules the weather, crops and wealth.

You should also know of Loki, who lives amongst the gods as a trickster and a traitor. He is clever yet crude, handsome yet fickle and sly; he's a shape-shifter, and he's fathered several monsters.

All the gods and goddesses live in Asgard, where each has a magnificent hall with hundreds of rooms and doors, surrounded by wondrous treasures. They often meet together in solemn assembly; but they also love to amuse themselves with contests, games and feasts.

For notes on this story, see page 310.

THE DWARFS' TREASURES

Dark and austere is the realm of dwarfs, damp and airless. Its tunnels stretch far under the ground, deep into the mountains, an endless, murky labyrinth. Caverns open out from them here and there, echoing with the clangour of hammers, stinking of soot and scorched metal. Night and day are meaningless in this place, for the dwarfs take no rest from their work at the forges, their gnarled faces thickly crusted with endless years of smoke. The gloom is overwhelming, broken only by smithy fires and sparse flickers of gold.

An outsider descended into this realm, slipping easily along the low roofed passages like a shadow or a sigh of wind. Each time he reached a cavern, he slipped inside, pestering the dwarfs who inhabited it until they shook their heads angrily and forced him to retreat.

At last he entered a smaller chamber containing only a single smithy. When its two occupants saw him, they wiped their hands on grime-encrusted cloths and shuffled towards him.

'Help me!' the outsider entreated them.

'For what reason should we do so?' the elder dwarf said.

'Because I'll pay you well.'

'What do you want?'

'A head of hair spun from gold.'

'Golden hair: that's a tall order. Who's it for?'

'Sif, a god's wife.'

'Which god is she married to?'

'Thor. He'll kill me if I return without it.'

'Thor! If *he's* after you, there's no escape. What's your name? Why do you need it?'

The outsider fidgeted from one foot to the other. In the glimmering light of the smithy fire, his eyes darted about, his smirking face smooth as a snake.

'I'm Loki. I need it to replace all Sif's real hair because I cut it off while she was asleep, and dumped it in a midden.'

The dwarfs nudged each other and turned away, murmuring. The younger one hissed over his shoulder, 'That's disgusting. Why did you do it?'

'Mind your own business,' Loki snapped. 'But I'll pay you this whole bag of silver – if your skills are up to the task.'

The dwarfs bristled. 'You're not questioning our mastery, are you?' said the elder. 'Don't you realise? We are the renowned Ivaldi's Sons. We can make anything anyone desires and fashion it even better than their most extravagant fantasy. No one can rival our craftsmanship. Stand aside, Loki, while we get to work.'

Loki rooted himself to the floor of the rock chamber and waited. Ivaldi's Sons shut themselves away in their forge. Eventually, they came out bearing an enormous box, overflowing with a drift of finely wrought, golden strands. As they carried it towards Loki, the gold rippled gently, like seaweed under water.

Loki peered at it and slipped his long fingers through its

31

mass, groaning with pleasure at the silky texture. 'It's good. I'll take it. Here's the promised fee.'

The younger of Ivaldi's Sons snatched the bag of silver from him and tipped it onto the floor. The two dwarfs counted it carefully and conferred again. Then the elder said, 'You've paid us generously, Loki. For the same price, we're willing to throw in something else. Say what you want.'

Loki sniffed. He scratched himself and shrugged.

The elder dwarf said, 'You'll be in trouble with the other gods for bringing Thor's wife a treasure and nothing for the rest of them. Who's most likely to vent his anger on you?'

Loki considered. 'Odin,' he said. 'He reckons his wisdom entitles him to even more tribute than Thor's brawn.'

'Then we'll make something for him too,' said Ivaldi's Sons.

They went back into their workshop and hammered feverishly again. When they emerged, they brought out not one more treasure, but two.

The first was a superbly fashioned spear. Its iron head was welded into swirling patterns like the branches of the world tree, Yggdrasil; its oaken shaft, inlayed with silver bands, was so long that even the tallest mortal man would have to crane his head to see its end.

'Give this to Odin. Tell him it's in honour of his dominion over battle,' the elder dwarf said. 'Its name is Gungnir. We guarantee it will never fail him or stop in its thrust.'

Loki took it, then sneered at the younger of Ivaldi's Sons. 'And what's that trinket you're clutching?'

Into Loki's outstretched hand he dropped the perfect replica of a ship, no longer than a mortal's finger, complete with miniature oars and sail.

'Give this to Frey. Mortals are always heaping praise on him, so no doubt he'll feel entitled to a treasure too. Its name is Skidbladnir. Don't be fooled by appearances: this is no plaything but a real ship, folded up for easy carrying. When Frey wants to go sailing, it will immediately transform to a full-sized vessel; and it will always catch a fair wind.'

Loki snatched up the three treasures, balancing them awkwardly in his arms. Then he turned his back on Ivaldi's Sons and staggered away with his load, into the gloomy passages.

However, he could not find a clear route out. He made steep descents, rounded convoluted corners, then climbed a flight of rough-hewn steps right up through the murky heart of a mountain. He saw no glimpse of daylight, only more chambers and caverns.

At last he accosted another dwarf and asked directions.

'I won't tell you,' the dwarf replied, 'until you've told me something first. What's that you're carrying?'

'The best handiwork in any of the worlds,' said Loki.

'Who says so?' demanded the dwarf.

'Ivaldi's Sons,' said Loki.

'And who are you to believe them?' said the dwarf.

'I live amongst the gods,' said Loki. And he told the dwarf his name.

'Well, Loki, you gods' arse-licker,' said the dwarf, 'My name's Brokk and I can tell you unequivocally that Ivaldi's Sons are wrong. My brother and I can make far finer treasures than them.'

Loki raised his eyebrows scornfully. 'Liar.'

'Insulting me, are you?' cried Brokk. 'I tell you what, Loki, we'll get to work in our smithy straight away. The gods themselves can judge us. And if they prefer our treasures over yours, my brother and I will have your head. There, that's a formal wager. Shake hands on it.'

'I can't,' said Loki. 'My hands are full.'

'You're not getting out of this so easily,' said Brokk. 'Whether you agree or not, the wager's on.'

'I can't be bothered to argue,' said Loki. 'But we agreed another deal, before you started drivelling on about unwanted wagers. I told you what I'm carrying, so you've got to reveal how I can get out of this loathsome mountain where you and your kind lurk like slugs.'

Brokk laughed in his face and told him. Loki, still balancing his three treasures, stumbled away. But as soon as he was out of sight, he put the treasures down and transformed himself into a horsefly. Then he flew back into Brokk's cavern and alighted on the lintel of the smithy.

Brokk had gone back inside to tell his brother, Eitri, about Loki and the wager. The two dwarfs discussed it at considerable length, rubbing their twisted hands together as their ideas grew.

Finally, Eitri said, 'Make a start on the hog, brother, while I nip out to fetch some bits of metal.'

He pulled a hunk of rawhide from a wooden chest, muttered some obscure words over it and tossed it into the furnace. Brokk got to work on the bellows. Eitri watched as the fire flared up, then scurried away down a low tunnel.

Loki buzzed down onto Brokk's arm and bit him hard. Brokk swore, brushed the fly away and continued squeezing. Loki crawled down onto Brokk's fingers where they gripped the bellows, and bit him several times more. Brokk didn't react, but just carried on sweating over his work. Loki flew off and perched on the rough cavern wall.

As Eitri returned, Brokk pulled the forged rawhide from the furnace. At once, it sprang to life as a gigantic boar, covered snout-to-tail in gleaming golden bristles.

'I name it Gullinborsti,' he said. 'It can run across sky and sea faster than any horse, and its bristles will light up the night. It's for Frey.'

Eitri nodded approvingly and tossed a nugget of gold into the fire. Brokk set to work on the bellows again, while Eitri went out on another errand. As Brokk blew up the flames, twice as hard as before, Loki flew over and bit his neck – also twice as hard. Brokk ignored him and kept diligently at his work.

As soon as Eitri came back, Brokk pulled a second treasure from the furnace – a splendid golden ring.

'Behold, Draupnir,' he said. 'Every ninth night, it will spew out eight more gold rings, each one equally heavy. We'll give it to Odin.'

'Nice,' said Eitri. 'Now try this.'

He threw a lump of iron into the flames, then sat down on his stool. Brokk got back to the bellows. Loki buzzed around the cavern, then settled on Brokk's eyebrow. He crawled down onto the dwarf's eyelids, first one and then the other, and bit them both viciously. Blood spurted and dripped into Brokk's eyes, temporarily blinding him.

'Keep blowing, brother,' Eitri urged.

So Brokk worked on. At last he drew from the furnace a magnificent iron hammer head, polished as richly as silver, deeply carved with mysterious flowing designs, so heavy he could scarcely carry it. He nailed it to a thick shaft of ash wood.

'I name this Mjollnir,' he said. 'It will never fail to hit its target, and it can be thrown to any distance required, yet always return to its master's hand. We'll present it to Thor.'

The two dwarfs scooped up their handiwork, then hastened out, hard on the heels of Loki.

In Asgard, Odin had hauled Loki up before the gods' assembly. He was accused of stealing Sif's hair and thus desecrating her transcendent beauty. Loki neither feigned his innocence nor admitted his guilt. Instead, he laid the treasures made by Ivaldi's Sons before Odin's feet.

'Inside this box,' he said, 'you will find my vindication for this deed. It contains far better hair than Sif has lost, made of dwarfs' gold. She'll love it and so will Thor. I have a marvellous gift for you too, All-Father; and also one for Frey.'

Odin didn't even glance at the treasures. He said, 'Any gift from you is bound to be treacherous, Loki; and one made by dwarfs will be even worse.'

Loki had no chance to argue, for at that moment there was a great commotion as Brokk and Eitri burst in. They marched up to Odin and bowed deeply before him, laying their own treasures at his feet.

Brokk said, 'My lord, forgive us for intruding, but we have come to help you arrange the perfect penalty for this scoundrel. He has already accepted a wager...'

'I haven't,' cried Loki; but no one heeded him.

'...a wager,' Brokk continued, 'for you gods to decide whether the gifts he's brought are better or worse than ours. Since you have not yet looked at any of these offerings, please permit us to display all six before you without revealing which treasure comes from whom. Then let each god examine his gifts objectively and reach his own decision. If it is decided that any one of Loki's treasures exceeds all of ours, then he will be the winner; and to honour that you must spare him. However, if one of our pieces is chosen as the best, Loki has agreed to sacrifice his own head.'

'I've agreed nothing,' said Loki; but his protest was ignored.

Odin considered the matter carefully and accepted the dwarfs' plan. They said which two treasures were intended for Odin, which for Thor and which for Frey. However, they gave no clue as to which they themselves had crafted, and which were made by Ivaldi's Sons on behalf of Loki.

The three gods considered each item carefully, murmuring amongst themselves.

At last Odin said, 'It's impossible to choose between this spear and the golden ring; for each is equally marvellous.'

Frey said, 'Likewise, this folding ship and the golden boar are both truly exceptional.'

So the casting vote fell to Thor.

He picked up the golden hair spun by Ivaldi's Sons, turned it slowly around and trickled it through his fingers. He nodded approvingly, then walked over to a dark corner where his wife, Sif, was sitting alone, concealed in an enormous shawl. Thor coaxed her out and gently unwrapped the shawl, to reveal that her head was completely shorn. He spread the golden hair tenderly over it. As soon as it touched her, the hair took root and came alive, falling in a dazzling cascade across her shoulders and flowing softly down her back. Sif put up her hand to stroke it, then tossed her head about, swinging the extraordinary locks this way and that. She flung her arms around her husband, her lovely face wreathed in smiles.

The whole assembly broke into applause. Loki let out an exaggerated sigh of relief.

Now Thor picked up Mjollnir, the hammer that Brokk and Eitri had made. He weighed it in his hands, then hurled it carelessly across the hall at the carving on a roof-post. The hammer hit the target square on. Everyone cheered. The hammer spun round – and flew straight back into Thor's hand. The cheers grew louder. Thor turned it over in his hands, admiring its ornamentation.

'A very fine piece of handiwork,' he said. 'But not perfect, for the shaft is rather short for a big fellow like me. A pity.'

He tugged at the ash wood handle in frustration, then shook it… And at once, something extraordinary happened: the hammer extended to enormous size, twice as large as before, and the handle lengthened exactly in proportion. Thor grinned and tried shaking it again. This time, the hammer shrank so small, it fitted inside his clenched fist.

'An ingenious gift indeed,' said Thor. 'I'm inclined to think it's the best one. But what is your opinion, All-Father?'

Odin said, 'Each of the other gifts will be much appreciated by its owner. However, there is no doubt, Thor, that *everyone* in Asgard will be grateful for this extraordinary hammer. For the giants are threatening us. With each day and night that passes, their harassment grows greater and worse. Now, this hammer will enable you to strike them down.'

'You're right, All-Father,' Thor said quietly. 'With this

weapon in my hand, I can swat the giants like flies and be the saviour of all who need my protection. I agree with your judgement. The hammer is certainly the greatest of all the gifts.'

Odin said, 'Speak, Loki. Is the hammer gifted by you?'

Loki snarled and said nothing.

Brokk bowed before Odin. 'My lord,' he said, 'Loki cannot deny that the hammer was made by my brother Eitri and myself. And the forfeit that Loki agreed to pay for losing this wager was his own head.'

'There can be few in Asgard who will be sorry to see it cut from his body,' said Odin.

'Ha! But you'll never catch me,' cried Loki, 'for I'm wearing shoes with power to carry me away faster than the wind!'

Even as he spoke, he was rushing out and launching himself up to the sky. The gods stared after him in dismay.

But Thor shook up his new hammer to its full size and flung it after Loki. It soared into the clouds – found its mark – clubbed Loki hard – attached itself to him – spun round – and wheeled him straight back to Thor's waiting hands.

Thor pulled Loki free of the hammer and held him in an armlock. Brokk drew his knife and moved it towards the trickster's throat.

'Whoa!' sniggered Loki. 'My head is the price of losing this wager – but not my neck.'

Thor gave a roar of exasperation. 'It's impossible to behead him without cutting through his neck. So we can't inflict this punishment without compromising our honour.'

Brokk said, 'True. But the head itself is ours and we can easily subdue it.'

He pulled an awl from his shirt and pierced a series of holes along Loki's upper and lower lips. Then he drew out a leather thong and sewed the lips together – rendering Loki totally speechless.

For notes on this story, see page 312.

THE THEFT OF THOR'S HAMMER

Thor, the great protector, uses his hammer Mjollnir to maintain order and defend all the worlds against the giants. It is the mightiest weapon of all times. No matter how many times Thor thrashes his enemies with it, Mjollnir never breaks or wears out. Hundreds, maybe thousands of giants have felt its deadly power against their skulls.

Once Thor woke up and found that Mjollnir was missing. He never mislaid it. He knew it was stolen.

Who would want to seize it from him? Only the giants.

Asgard keeps its gates strongly barred against them; but Thor guessed at once who had overcome this obstacle and helped commit this terrible theft. It must be that wily, two-faced trickster, Loki.

Thor summoned Loki to his hall and made his accusation.

Naturally, Loki denied it. 'Why would I want your hammer, Thor?' said he. 'I'm not even strong enough to lift it. Only a giant would be capable of snatching it away.'

'Exactly,' Thor roared at him. 'No giant can enter Asgard

unless someone opens the way to him; and the only person treacherous enough to do that is you. Where is Mjollnir hidden, Loki? Fetch it back for me, you snake! Hurry, before the giants start breaking down our defences and overrun us.'

Loki slunk off and sought out Freyja. He whined and bleated at her, hoping her soft heart would help him out of this latest fix.

But when Freyja heard what he had done, she turned white with alarm. 'Loki, you must travel to Giantland at once and retrieve it,' she urged him. 'Without Mjollnir in Thor's hand, we're all exposed and utterly helpless.'

Loki tried to evade his duty with excuses.

But Freyja said, 'You have no choice, Loki. Here, borrow my feather cloak: it will carry you to Giantland in no time.'

She draped the cloak over his shoulders. At once, Loki was transformed into a bird. He flapped his arms, soared into the air and vanished.

But he returned empty handed, and with disturbing news:

'Giant Thrym's got hold of Mjollnir. He's buried it eight leagues deep under the ground. He refuses to return it unless Thor grants him a boon.'

Thor was waiting beside Freyja. 'What does he ask for?' he growled.

And Loki answered, 'Giant Thrym wants Freyja to be his bride.'

'Outrageous!' cried Freyja. 'Never since the beginning of time has a goddess ever lain with one of those repulsive giants.'

'True,' said Loki peevishly. 'Though it's not unusual for giantesses to mate with gods. There could always be a first time.'

'I'm married already,' said Freyja.

'But abandoned by your husband,' Loki taunted her. 'And since then, you haven't been exactly fussy about the men you associate with. There's not a god in Asgard who hasn't at some time shared your bed. What's your problem?'

'The hammer is my responsibility, not hers,' said Thor gallantly. 'Of course, you have no scruples, Loki, but I tell you it is iniquitous to compromise a lady on account of a weapon. Besides, I seriously doubt whether Thrym would even honour the bargain he proposes. I have a better solution. I shall dress up to resemble Freyja myself, and in this guise, I will go to Giantland, pretend to marry Thrym in her place, and thus retrieve my stolen weapon.'

Loki's eyes widened in horror. 'You can't dress as a woman, Thor! Even a mortal man would never do such a thing. You might as well have your balls cut off. You'll be a laughing stock.'

'Unless I take drastic action,' said Thor drily, 'Asgard will be ruined. 'No doubt you had such a scandal in mind when you contrived this catastrophe, eh, Loki?'

The trickster didn't deny it.

'And since you're already knee-deep in the filth,' said Thor, 'don't think you'll get away with it. A bride can't go to her own wedding without at least one maid to accompany her. Loki, that maid shall be you. You can emasculate yourself too and join me in female fancy dress.'

Thor was a true hero. Just as he never flinched from battle against any indomitable enemy, so he did not try to avoid the only action that could save Asgard.

He ordered a woman's silken gown, trimmed with gemstones and fine embroidery, to be fashioned to fit him. He dressed himself in it with relish as if he were donning a suit of armour. His enormous muscles rippled under its pleats as he pinned on glittering beads and golden brooches. He placed a fine linen bridal veil over his head, completely covering his face like a nervous virgin.

He also ordered a much simpler gown for Loki – some might have called it ragged – and forced the wretch to put it on. Then he harnessed the goats to his wagon, and drove in it with Loki at lightening speed, through the air, over earth and ocean, to Giantland.

When they arrived, Giant Thrym was ready and waiting. His feasting hall was bursting at the edges with food, drink and sniggering guests.

'Welcome, Freyja, my beauty,' he greeted Thor. 'What a wonderful day this is for me. Who would have thought that a giant would ever win the most beautiful goddess to be his wife? And who would have foretold that such a giant would be me? How splendidly you are attired. But I long to see your blushing face. Let me lift your veil.'

'Not yet, Thrym,' Thor simpered in a falsetto voice. 'It's not fitting to touch me until we are married.'

'Oh, indeed, indeed,' said Thrym. 'Delay just adds to the thrill of anticipation. But let's get the ceremony over as quickly as possible, my dear. I can't wait to bed you.'

'But Thrym,' squeaked Thor, 'won't you let your beloved rest first and have a bite to eat? I've endured the most terrible long journey all the way from Asgard. And I've been so excited about our wedding, that I've been off my food for days. Now I'm here at last, I can relax – and I find that I'm starving.'

'Of course,' Thrym replied. 'Sit at the table, my dear and I'll get some dainties brought to you.'

'What, only dainties?' said Thor. 'Thrym, I beg you, let's have the full feast before the ceremony. Bring me a proper meal.'

'Anything to make you happy, my dear,' said Thrym. 'Guests, take your seats. Slaves, bring on the food, pour out the drink – and serve everything first to my bride!'

All the giants and giantesses sat down at the long tables. A great barrel of ale was brought in. Before any of it could be poured into his cup, Thor seized the barrel itself and swigged it down in a single gulp. Then a whole roast ox was served. Thor didn't even wait for it to be carved, but grabbed the carcass and gobbled it up. This was followed by eight whole salmon and a cask of strong mead. Thor quickly devoured the lot.

'Ahah,' grinned Giant Thrym, 'a maid with such a lusty appetite for food will surely have a similar appetite in bed. Can I tempt you with some more, Freyja? Or shall we get on with the nuptials?'

'I am ready to proceed,' Thor squeaked back at him.

'Excellent,' said Thrym. He led Thor over to the high-seat. 'Now, let me teach you the wedding customs of Giantland. Our usual ritual is to hallow the bride by laying a hammer in her lap.'

'How lovely,' squeaked Thor.

'Sit,' said Thrym.

Thor sat. Trussed up in his own woman's dress nearby, Loki smirked.

'Bring in the hammer,' Thrym called.

A door was flung open. A team of slaves came in, staggering under the weight of Mjollnir. Thor shifted in his seat.

'This is a very special wedding,' Giant Thrym continued, 'so, in your honour, Freyja, I have obtained a very special hammer to mark it. I hope it will make you feel at home.'

'Goodness,' squeaked Thor. 'But that's *Thor*'s hammer! How come you're using it for my wedding, Thrym? Aren't you meant to return it to Thor, in lieu of my bride-price?'

'Ha! you didn't really believe that, Freyja my dear, did you?' Thrym turned to his slaves. 'Lay it in her lap and let's get this pomp and ceremony over with.'

Thor put his mighty legs astride and arranged his silken bridal gown over them. Slowly, the slaves lowered Mjollnir onto his skirt.

No sooner was this was done, than Thor seized it. He leaped up and, with a roar of mocking laughter, threw back his veil.

'Freyja, my darling,' cried Thrym, 'What are you…? Aagh!' He let out a disgusted howl. 'But…but you are not the most beautiful goddess after all. You have a beard! Your skin is as coarse as a pig's. And that crazy look in your eyes…!'

'What am I doing?' roared Thor in his own voice. 'I'm claiming my own, that's what. See, Thrym, you have put Mjollnir back into Thor's own hands despite your best attempts to deceive me. Now let me tell you about a "usual ritual" with hammers that we practise in Asgard. Thor the

Mighty ritually uses this very hammer, Mjollnir, to smash in the skull of every giant that gets in his way. And I shall honour you at this "very special wedding" by letting your own head experience it. So!'

And with that, he swung his hammer back and struck Thrym dead at a single blow.

For notes on this story, see page 313.

HOW ODIN
WON THE RUNES

Who wended his way
through wild wood and wasteland
to spear his own soul at the murk-rooted tree?

    Only the Raven God,
    Ruler of Asgard:
    Odin All-Father, lord of the slain.

Why did he go there
storm lashed in solitude?
What did he seek there, what did he do?

    Symbols he yearned for,
    speech carved in silence
    thoughts drawn in lines, secrets and spells.

    He hanged himself, dangling,
    speared himself, starved himself,
    cast his own sacrifice, swung from the tree.

How long did he hang there there,
hankering, hungry
whipped dead by wind in the cold, boundless gloom?

Nine nights he suffered,
thirst-scorched, famished
screaming through gales, grappling with death.

Who took his sacrifice,
and answered his prayers?
Who drank his blood those nine nights through?

Odin himself
both gave and consumed blood,
lost himself, won himself,
stretching and grasping
until knowledge came.

What did he find there
hanging in darkness,
dying, delivered on the murk-rooted tree?

From one cut came many words,
from one stain, many signs,
from one deed much was done...

Nine songs sung softly,
blood spawning sorcery,
symbols and runes.

And then, what of All-Father,
self-killed and reborn,
at the end of nine nights on the sacrifice tree?

>His strife brought healing,
>grief spawned freedom,
>foes' blades blunted, arrows repelled.

>He was reborn as rune-master,
>charm chanter,
>wind queller,
>carver of messages,
>thwarter of witches,
>winner of lovers,
>quencher of fires
>subduer of seas.

Remember how the runes were won:
carve them carefully.
Sacrifice unstintingly.
Tell tales truthfully.

For all gifts seek a fair return.

For notes on this story, see page 314.

FISHING UP
THE WORLD SERPENT

There was a giant called Hymir, a hulking, ill-tempered fellow. His house towered above the sea, overlooked by a wilderness of stone and frost.

One day a traveller came by and asked Hymir for a night's lodging. The giant grumbled a bit but did the right thing: he ushered the traveller in, shared his meal and let him sleep by his fire.

The next morning, Giant Hymir said he was going fishing.

'I'll help you,' said the traveller.

The giant snorted. 'I don't want a maggot like you getting in my way, puking up when the sea turns choppy and whining to turn back.'

'I'm tougher than I look,' said the traveller. 'Give me a try.'

Giant Hymir shrugged irritably. 'Ach, suit yourself. But if you want to come, hurry up and find some bait because I'm about to launch my boat.'

The traveller hurried to the pasture where the giant's oxen were slurping up weeds through a grimy layer of snow. A huge bull bellowed and came charging at him.

While Giant Hymir had his back turned, the traveller caught the bull by the horns and twisted its neck, snapping the head clean off. He shoved the head into his bag and carried it down to the beach.

Hymir was already easing out his boat. The traveller leaped in and they rowed off. As soon as the shore was just a thin line on the horizon, the giant dropped the anchor.

'I've decided to make things easy for you, skinny ribs,' he said. 'I've stopped here so you can catch some tiddlers.'

The traveller shook his head. 'Find me something bigger. I want to prove my strength to you.'

'Ha ha, seeking some real man's action, are you?' sniggered Hymir. 'In that case, I'll take you out to the whaling grounds. But watch you don't piss your pants – because there's monsters lurking out there as well.'

They rowed on. Up ahead, they soon saw a magnificent pair of whales spouting and diving. Hymir hurled his harpoon and killed them both without any effort at all. He roped them nonchalantly to the stern of his boat and turned back to the traveller.

'Your turn, weakling.'

The traveller nodded. He opened his bag and tipped out the bull's head. The giant raised his eyebrows in surprise. The traveller fixed the bull's-head onto his hook, tossed it overboard and started dragging it through the water.

The sea began to froth and foam. A thick, dark shape appeared under the surface; but it was impossible to see either where it began or where it ended.

The traveller heaved on his line. The dark thing rippled and flailed. The water seethed. The traveller pulled even harder.

A scaly hump, ten times longer than the boat, burst up through the surface for a moment, then crashed back into the waves.

'Stop, you blockhead!' Giant Hymir roared. 'That's no ordinary worm: it's Jormungand – the World Serpent! The one who circles the whole ocean and keeps the earth from sinking into the depths! Let him go! You don't realise the danger you've unleashed!'

'First you called me a weakling,' said the traveller calmly, 'but I bet *you've* never managed to pull Jormungand up to the surface, eh? Now you're accusing me of stupidity and ignorance – and you're wrong again. It so happens, I set my bait right on target to catch the World Serpent. I've *deliberately* unleashed his rage.'

Hymir lunged forward, trying – but failing – to snatch the traveller's hand and wrench the line from his grasp. 'Drop it,' he spluttered. 'If you pull the World Serpent out, it'll destroy everything. Let him go!'

'I might pay heed if you get down on your knees and beg me,' said the traveller. 'On the other hand, maybe I won't.'

Giant Hymir's jaw dropped open. 'You mean…you actually *want* to destroy the world?'

'I mean, it lies within my power,' said the traveller. 'What more do I have to do before you realise who I am?'

Hymir let out a long breath. He stared at the traveller, noticing for the first time the red hair, the unkempt beard, the bulging muscles, the swagger.

At last he spat, 'Ach! Just my bad luck. It's *you*, isn't it? You bastard – Thor!'

Thor nodded. 'And you know my business as well as my name, don't you, Hymir? – destroying giants. Not even the mightiest of you stands a chance against my hammer. Remember how you mocked me earlier? Well, for a bit of fun before I deal with you, I'll show you how strong I am by pulling Jormungand right out of the sea.'

'Don't!' bellowed Hymir. 'You'll bring the whole world to an end! Listen, Thor, kill me when you're ready to, but in the name of everyone else alive and all those yet to be born – let Jormungand go – I beg you!'

The giant made another grab for Thor's hand. Thor brushed him off like a fly and tightened his hold on the line. He braced his feet against the well of the boat and heaved. Under the surface, the World Serpent gave a great jerk. The boat leaped out of the water, spun round and almost capsized.

Hymir cowered.

Thor steadied the boat and tugged on his line again. The darkness in the water seemed to thicken. Jormungand burst through the surface, sending up a cascade of toxic droplets. The monster's grotesque head stared at them. His fangs gnawed at the bull's-head, gagging on the hook as he tried to free himself.

'Stop, stop!' Hymir screamed.

Thor tugged harder. He dragged the line steadily up until part of the monster's breast was balanced on the gunwale, noxious spittle dribbling from his mouth. Waves washed over the boat. Giant Hymir turned white as bones and vomited. Thor balanced the line and the Serpent in one hand; with the other hand, he pulled his hammer from his shirt and shook it until it swelled to enormous size.

'Which would be better entertainment?' Thor muttered. 'Pull Jormungand right out? Or simply slice off his head?'

Luckily, he never got the opportunity to make his choice. For at that moment Giant Hymir pulled himself together, leaped forward brandishing his bait knife – and sliced Thor's line in two.

Jormungand slithered away. Thor hurled his hammer after him. But it was too late, for the Serpent had already crashed back into the water.

The bowels of the earth rumbled. For a long moment, the whole ocean – the whole world – shuddered and tilted. Waves as high as mountains came splashing over them, engulfing the boat.

'Worried that I really managed to hurt the beast, eh Hymir?' said Thor. 'Then you'd better go down there yourself and find out.'

He punched the giant overboard. Then he stepped out of the boat and waded back to the shore.

For notes on this story, see page 316.

THE EIGHT-LEGGED HORSE

Odin had called everyone in Asgard to an assembly. Only one person was banned from it: that unsavoury misfit, Loki. No matter: he wormed his way into nooks and crannies, and eavesdropped on the whole debate. He listened to the gods railing against the constant harassment of the giants. He heard them agree to build a mighty rampart to encircle Asgard and keep the giants away.

'Milksops!' he muttered to himself. 'Fancy needing to hide their little bums behind a wall.' He sniggered and cocked his ear again – in time to catch a fretful discussion about how to find a suitable builder for the project. 'They're even too helpless to construct it themselves and don't know where to turn for help. What would they do without me?'

Loki slipped out of his hiding place and streaked away to Giantland. There he gossiped openly about the gods' plans.

In no time at all, he was back in Asgard. He smoothed his clothes, composed his features and burst into the assembly. He stepped up lightly to Odin and grovelled before him.

'All-Father,' he simpered. 'You know this wall you plan to have erected around Asgard…?'

'How has news of this already reached you?' said Odin.

'My lord, don't clutter your wise thoughts with trivial questions like that,' said Loki. 'And don't worry about the wall either. I've found the perfect fellow to construct it for you, strong enough to work with the most massive blocks of stone.' He licked his lips. 'A giant.'

'Never!' cried Odin.

But Loki was already running to the door and flinging it open. The next moment a hefty giant came striding into the hall.

The gods all leaped up. Thor flushed and drew out his hammer, brandishing it menacingly.

However, the giant held up his hands to show he was unarmed.

'Calm yourself, Thor,' he said. 'I come in peace.' He turned to Odin. 'Sir, I know you are very wise, so you won't judge me by what I am – but by what I can do for you. Loki's told me about your urgent need for an impenetrable fortification. Let me construct it. I can make it higher and thicker than a mountain, totally unassailable. Once it's completed, you won't be troubled by my people in any way, ever again.

Odin narrowed his single eye and regarded the giant suspiciously. 'This sounds a promising offer – on the face of it,' he said. 'How long would it take you to complete?'

'Hmm. I reckon...around three seasons,' the giant builder answered.

'Why do you want to help us?' said Odin.

'Because you gods irritate my people. Once Asgard's hidden inside this wall, we can forget you even exist.'

Odin snorted. 'And how much do you intend to charge for your labour?'

'Just consider how unique this fortification is going to be,' the giant builder said. 'And according to Loki, it's vital.

In the circumstances, only a fool would accept a low fee. So my asking price is this: possession of the sun and the moon.'

The ravens perched on Odin's shoulder squawked in alarm. The high god himself glared at the giant, holding his shifty eyes in his gaze.

Odin said, 'If you took control of the sun and moon, you'd probably hide them away and plunge all the worlds into darkness. I refuse your offer.'

'Don't be inflexible, All-Father,' Loki called out. 'He may be persuaded to accept an alternative.' He turned to the giant. 'Will you negotiate, my friend? Name something else you would take in payment, instead of the sun and the moon.'

A slow grin spread across the giant builder's face. 'Well now. Yes, there is something else I'd take. In fact, to be honest, I'd far prefer it to the sun and moon. I didn't ask for it, because I was pretty sure the answer would be "no". But since you seem desperate to get this wall into place as soon as possible, maybe you won't dismiss it out of hand?'

'Name it,' said Odin.

'Very well,' said the giant. 'What I'd really like is some regular rumpy pumpy with one of your goddesses...'

A gasp ran round the hall.

'...But not just any one,' the giant finished. 'I want the ravishing Freyja.'

'No,' said Odin.

Freyja jumped up, trembling with fury. 'Throw him out, Odin!' she shrieked. She turned to the giant builder, her bewitching features twisted into a disgusted grimace. 'You filthy, lumbering, oversized numbskull. Look at those coarse labourer's hands of yours. Ugh! how dare you even think of trying to touch me, let alone bed me. Thor, I beg you: destroy him!'

Thor strode forward. But Loki leaped between him and the giant with outstretched arms.

'Calm down. Peace, peace!' he cried. 'Why fight? Why take up extreme positions? Odin, I suggest you send the builder to wait outside for a few moments. We need to discuss this proposal in private.'

He didn't wait for Odin to agree, but ushered the giant builder back through the door. He returned alone, locking the door behind him.

'What right does Loki have to participate in this discussion?' demanded Freyja.

'It's essential that I'm here,' said Loki. 'Only I have inside knowledge of the enemy.' He lowered his voice. 'Freyja, my sweetest, don't worry, I'll get you out of this unscathed.' He flashed her a suggestive smile. 'You know, I always do what's needed.'

Odin said, 'If you have something useful to say, Loki, speak so all can hear it. Otherwise be silent.'

'I've got a brilliant compromise to suggest,' said Loki. 'It'll mean you get the fortification almost completely built without putting Freyja in any serious danger. Firstly, you need to reduce the available timescale drastically. Don't allow him the three seasons he's asked for, but insist the job is finished within a single winter. That's impossible, but you know how arrogant giants are: he'll never admit he can't do it, he's bound to work flat out in the hope of winning his prize. Which is exactly what we want: hopefully, by the first day of spring most of the wall will be in place. But that's not good enough: the giant will have missed the deadline for *full* completion. You'll get the fortification within a squeak of being completed – but he'll forfeit his payment. Which means that the lovely Freyja will be safe. You'll have to finish building the wall yourselves, of course, but the bulk of the work will be done and no harm caused.'

'That's no use at all,' objected Freyja. 'All he needs do to win his…' she shuddered '…his prize, is get a load more giants to help him. They'll be running around all over Asgard. The wall will be finished in no time. And then he'll… Ugh!'

'Hush, hush, don't get so jittery, Freyja,' Loki soothed her. 'That won't happen. Because secondly, Odin must specify that the giant has to do the building single-handed. No one is allowed to help.'

Odin heard him through, then sat very still, pondering. At last he said, 'This does sound like an acceptable solution. However, I have a queasy feeling that there may still be trouble. If that occurs, Loki, I hold you responsible. You will either have to overcome it, or suffer a fearful punishment.'

'That's fine by me,' said Loki.

Odin summoned the giant builder back into the hall, and formally announced the conditions of the contract. The giant weighed them up silently, and agreed to give it a go. Then he went back to Giantland.

On the first day of winter, the giant builder returned, bringing with him a strong black stallion. He took up his position on the boundary and immediately set to work, hacking rocks into building blocks and setting his horse to drag them into place.

Freyja eyed him suspiciously, then went hurrying to Odin to complain: 'All-Father, the terms of the giant's contract specify that he has to work single-handed. He's broken them by bringing a horse.'

Loki sidled out of the shadows. 'There you go fretting again, my darling,' he hissed. 'All this upset is so unnecessary. Since when did a horse have hands? Of course he needs a beast of burden: even a giant isn't strong enough to haul up boulders without one.'

'What's your authority to comment on the law?' she snapped at him.

'Loki has no right to pronounce on any aspect of this,' said Odin, ignoring the trickster. 'But I have warned him that if the wall is constructed too fast, thus putting you in danger, Freyja, *he* will pay a forfeit – with his life.'

The giant and his stallion worked steadily all through the winter. A very impressive structure quickly began to rise around the edge of the gods' realm. It was so thick and so high that it would be impossible for the giants even to spy over the top, let alone breach it. Day by day, night by night, the wall gradually grew longer, snaking around the borders of Asgard like a massive ring.

Both Freyja and Loki watched progress closely, each with good reason to be nervous.

The days lengthened. Buds opened, birds began to sing. The giant and his horse continued to work together at breakneck speed. Only a rapidly diminishing gap remained to be filled in.

It was the last day of winter.

Freyja wept tears of red-gold. She led her cats to Thor's hall and rapped urgently on the door. Thor let her in and gave her sanctuary in his five-hundred-and-forty rooms. He fetched his hammer and iron gauntlets; he polished them grimly.

The giant builder sweated and laboured, spurred on by fantasies of his forthcoming reward.

Loki slipped into the forest.

He padded silently through the trees, dodging under briars and brambles. He nibbled rotting toadstools. He muttered grotesque words.

Weird shocks convulsed him. He fell onto all fours; his handsome face lengthened and turned expressionless. His body stretched and contorted into curves. Short hair sprouted all over it; long tresses grew from his rump and his neck.

Male into female. Barren becomes fertile. Man transforms into beast.

Meanwhile, the giant builder surveyed his work, rubbing his hands together. Only another few loads of rock were needed, then the whole fortification would be finished. With renewed energy, he hitched his stallion to drag up the next batch. But the animal seemed uncannily distracted. He kept turning his head towards the forest. He pricked his ears; and the giant caught the sound of branches cracking, hooves moving over rough ground, a soft but constant whinnying.

Suddenly a stunningly beautiful mare came bounding out of the trees. Her mane seemed to be woven with stars, her thick tail was a river of shimmering silver.

Loki!

The stallion sniffed intently. He gave a loud snort and strained against his harness. The leather straps burst apart. He reared up, kicked his master out of the way and set after the mare at a run. She nickered, then turned and galloped back into the forest, the stallion hard on her heels. The giant builder hurled down his tools and raced after them.

But who can catch a stallion maddened by a wild mare on heat?

Night fell. All through it, the two horses gambolled. Over and over, they mated. The giant builder chased them hopelessly.

When dawn came, it was the first day of spring. And the great fortification was not finished.

The giant builder was incandescent with frustrated lechery and rage. He had never even considered that he might have to accept defeat.

'Loki, where are you, boy?' he yelled. 'Bring me the whore like you promised! I've worked all winter and I'm not going back to Giantland without her. If you don't bring her, I'm seizing her by force.'

Loki made no answer – for he was nowhere to be found.

But Thor heard him. His blood boiled at the giant's profanities.

'Dear lady,' he said to Freyja, 'the time has come.'

He stomped out of his house, marched up to the giant and smashed his hammer with full force onto the brute's head. The giant's skull shattered into a mass of tiny fragments. For a long moment, they hung suspended in the air... Then a soft breeze blew up and wafted them away.

Meanwhile, Loki stayed in hiding. Nobody missed him.

Almost a year passed.

From somewhere very deep in the forest, gut-wrenching moans seared through the air. After this came a series of screams, on and on, like a woman deranged by the agony of childbirth.

But none of the goddesses was with child, none of them had gone missing. What could it mean?

It meant that, at last, Loki came slinking and smirking out of the trees, smeared with blood. Behind him trotted a grey newborn foal, still trailing its umbilical cord.

The foal was beautiful. But it was also a monster – for it had eight legs.

Loki led the foal through Asgard. Everyone stared at them, but nobody hailed them. It was still at Loki's heels as they reached Odin's silver-thatched hall. Loki strutted inside and made his way to Odin's throne.

Odin was gazing out moodily across the distant human realm.

'All-Father,' said Loki softly.

Odin turned. When he saw who it was, he shook his head wearily. 'Loki, what are you troubling me with now?'

Loki winked. 'Sorry it's taken me so long to offer reparation for organising that risky business with the giant builder. Only it took a bit of time to organise this gift.' He pointed at the foal. 'Meet Sleipnir.'

Odin looked at the eight-legged foal suspiciously. 'Where did you find *that*?'

Loki sniggered. 'Where did I find him? Don't *ask*. Can't you guess? Don't you remember that night of mischief I had

with the giant builder's stallion? Phoar! But afterwards...
What an effort it was to carry this little fellow for so long...
let alone to bring him out. But it was worth it, because I did
get that fortification almost completely built for you, didn't
I? *And* I saved Freyja – *and* I created this.'

'It was Thor who saved Freyja in the end,' said Odin
coldly.

'Let's call it a joint effort,' said Loki. 'But never mind.
What happened last year is gone. Just think of now. Enjoy
this young horse I've brought you. You can see his destiny
better than I can, but I promise you he will grow into a steed
that's truly worthy of you, All-Father. I swear he'll serve you
well.'

And, though Loki could rarely be trusted, on this
occasion he proved as good as his word.

For notes on this story, see page 318.

THE MIGHTY WOLF

How bleak the world is tonight! The heavy frost, the cruel east wind stripping the trees, the fields bare and iron hard. It seems that dusk long ago devoured the last dregs of the sun.

Bolt the door. Stoke up the fire. Block your ears, for wolves are drawing closer. Even worse, can you hear that eerie, anguished howling from beyond the edge of the world? It's their monstrous brother, Fenrisulf...

Fenrisulf is a giant of a wolf in every way. He's improbably big, impossibly strong; he's savage and uncontrollable. Where did he come from? Where do you think? He's one of the bastard brats that Loki fathered on the giantess Angrboda – brother to Jormungand, the World Serpent; and to that mistress of sickly death, the goddess Hel.

Odin was deeply concerned when he learned that Loki had brought such a beast into being. He didn't leave anything to chance, but had the wolf abducted from Giantland and dragged into Asgard. He ordered the gods to make a real effort to tame him. But Fenrisulf's temper and fangs put paid to that. And his mother's pedigree soon came through, for with every day that passed, he grew ever more gigantic.

How could the gods be intimidated by a mere wolf? Why didn't they kill him? Or why didn't they just stop feeding him and let him starve until he died? Only All-Father knew the answers, for only he could decipher the omens carved into the runes of prophesy. His orders were, that Fenrisulf must be cared for and generously fed.

'I need a volunteer to be his master,' Odin said.

No one was eager to take this on, but eventually Tyr offered himself. He took on the job of feeding the wolf with live creatures, and stood well back as Fenrisulf enjoyed tearing them apart. He spent long periods talking to the wolf, trying to calm him as one might a dog. But Fenrisulf was as restless and spiteful as his father, the type that's impossible to subdue. As time went by, he became increasingly dangerous.

Tyr warned, 'He'll attack us all unless we tie him up.'

So the gods got together and crafted a strong iron chain for him. When Fenrisulf was dozing, Tyr crept up to him and tried to slip it over his head. But Fenrisulf woke at the sound of the links clanking, aimed his enormous forepaw at it and broke it easily with a single kick.

The gods made a second chain, twice as thick as the first. But Fenrisulf's guard was up after their first trick. He refused to sleep, and when he saw them bringing the chain, he bared his teeth menacingly.

'Friend,' said Tyr coaxingly, 'this isn't a fetter; it's a game to test your cunning and strength. It'll give you the chance to prove how inviolable you are. If you can break this as easily as the first one, think how impressed everyone will be.'

Fenrisulf was flattered. He lowered his head and let Tyr slip the chain over his ears and into place around his great, sinewy neck. No sooner was it fixed, than the wolf began to buck like a startled horse and writhe about and shake himself. In no time, this chain too lay uselessly on the ground, shattered into tiny fragments.

Tyr looked at his charge in horror.

Fenrisulf threw back his head and bayed his joy and conceit – loudly enough to be heard in Giantland. The gods began to fear that none of them, and nothing, could ever overcome him.

Odin called for a messenger: 'Who will descend into that black hole far beneath the earth where the dwarfs lurk? Who will visit them and say, "All-Father orders you to make a fetter so strong that even Fenrisulf cannot break it"?'

At first no one volunteered; the dwarfs are wily and deceitful and their realm is devoid of daylight. But finally Frey's servant, Skirnir stepped forward, for he was used to going on errands in dangerous places. He offered his service for the good of all who lived in Asgard.

He was gone a long time. When he finally returned, he brought a strange object. It was very long, smooth and soft, like a woman's ribbon.

'What use is this?' said Odin dubiously.

'It is not what it seems,' said Skirnir. 'The dwarfs assure me it is stronger than any fetter that has ever been seen in any of the worlds. For they crafted it from

     the sound of a cat's footfall,

     a woman's beard,

     a mountain's roots,

     a bear's sinews,

     the breath of a fish and

     a bird's spittle.'

Odin said, 'As I hoped, it seems that the dwarfs have fashioned a truly exceptional thing.'

Tyr took it to Fenrisulf, saying, 'Your strength has become famous far and wide, my friend. But now many people are muttering, "Fenrisulf has reached his limits. It's one thing to break a bond made by the gods – but he'd never be able to overcome the work of those master smiths, the dwarfs!" How about proving these naysayers wrong? All-Father himself invites you to take up this challenge. He's organising it for you in the heart of an island that stands in the middle of a great lake. Follow me to the shore and I'll take you there in my boat.'

Fenrisulf stood as still as a rock, staring at Tyr with his yellow, unblinking eyes.

So Tyr said, 'Perhaps you're suspicious? But I swear we won't inflict any harm on you. To prove it, and as a mark of our good faith, before we place this fetter over you, I will place my own hand inside your mouth.'

At these bold words, Fenrisulf shook himself and turned to go to the lake shore with Tyr. In fact, he was so eager to win even greater glory, that he actually led the way.

The other gods were already waiting on the island. Odin showed the wolf the silken ribbon that was the dwarfs' fetter. Fenrisulf grinned with scorn and began to play with it, taking it in his mouth, rushing round with it and tossing it into the air like a cub.

Odin said, 'Enough! This game isn't enhancing your reputation, Fenrisulf. Allow us to bind you with the fetter, so you can prove your power by breaking it and making a quick escape.'

By now Fenrisulf was so relaxed from his romp that he

lay on his side, panting and still grinning. Tyr put his right hand between the wolf's jaws, just as he had promised, while Odin wound the fetter loosely around Fenrisulf's four legs. The other gods took hold of the two loose ends, and challenged the wolf to rise and free himself.

Fenrisulf staggered to his feet, gripping Tyr's hand between his teeth. He stretched blithely and strained against the fetter. However, instead of splitting into shreds of yarn as he had expected, it stayed fixed on him. In fact, as he heaved against it, the fetter actually grew tighter. He tried kicking against it, but with each movement, the fetter clinched its hold on him even more. Soon he had no space left to move. The fetter began to cut into the flesh of his legs.

'You are vanquished at last, Fenrisulf!' shouted Tyr. 'But I haven't broken my bargain with you – for the harm you are suffering isn't inflicted by the gods, but by your own straining and kicking.'

If only the gods had not all burst out laughing at this. Then perhaps Fenrisulf would have acknowledged the truth of these words and dropped his master's hand. But their mirth emphasised his humiliation and agony so much that he bit into Tyr's wrist and severed the hand from it.

Tyr yelped in pain. But this vicious act achieved nothing for Fenrisulf, for he was still tightly bound.

The other gods seized a cord that hung from the end of the fetter, threaded it through a stone slab and thrust this deep into the ground as an anchoring peg. At last, Fenrisulf was completely their prisoner.

He spat out Tyr's severed hand with a howl that made the whole earth quiver. Then he lunged at the other gods, gnashing his teeth, spitting at them with blood-stained drool, straining at the fetter as he tried to bite them.

Odin seized a great sword and, while the wolf's mouth was open wide, he thrust this between his jaws. The point wedged into the wolf's palate and the hilt lodged into the gums beneath.

And there it still is. And that is why you may still hear Fenrisulf howling. Weep for the great monster if you will; for his savagery was not his own choice, but foisted on him by his ancestry.

But his ordeal is tempered by savage hope. For it is said that when the world ends, Fenrisulf will at last break free – and take revenge by devouring Odin.

For notes on this story, see page 319.

THE APPLES OF YOUTH

When you think about it, there's not much to distinguish the goddesses and gods from us mortals. Like us they love and hate; some are wise but others misguided; they fight savage battles, then sweeten their wounds with poetry and lust. But they do have one quality that we can never hope to emulate: the blessing of everlasting vigour, beauty and youth.

The source of their eternal youth is a collection of some very rare magic apples. These apples are kept in a certain casket, concealed in a secret sanctuary, guarded by the goddess Idun. Only Idun knows where the tree stands on which the apples grow; only she can maintain their supply and distribute them.

And when one of these apples is eaten – oh, wonders! Any goddess beginning to suffer lethargy or sagging skin will find herself at once restored to the spring-fresh bloom of an eager virgin. Any god who fears his stamina is wasting or his libido dampened, becomes once more dynamic, powerful and hot-blooded.

Not surprisingly, the Apples of Youth are coveted by the giants. One of these giants, a skilled shape-shifter and sorcerer called Thjassi, once worked out a cunning scheme to steal them. You won't be surprised to hear that it involved that duplicitous trickster, Loki.

To be fair to Loki, he knew nothing of Giant Thjassi's plans as he set out alongside Odin and Hoenir on an expedition into Midgard, our own world. The three walked long and far, into a remote range of mountains; and then Loki started staggering about.

'Odin, stop!' he whined. 'I'm so famished, I can't walk another step. Find me something to eat.'

Odin pointed at the valley spread out below them. 'All right,' he said, 'we'll take a diversion, and make a meal of one of those cattle grazing down there.'

They descended to the meadows, killed a cow, butchered it, then dragged it under a great oak tree. Here they built an earth oven, lit a fire underneath, cut a joint from the carcass and set it to roast.

The fire blazed away and the oven became searing hot. However, no matter how long they left the joint to cook, it stayed bloody and raw.

'This isn't natural,' said Odin. 'I smell sorcery.' He gazed around. 'Who's responsible?' he called. 'Show yourself!'

At once there was a loud rustling in the upper branches of the oak tree. An enormous eagle flapped down, perched on top of the earth oven and stared at them unblinkingly.

'Do you really call yourselves *gods*?' it squawked. 'Yet you have so little power, you can't even prepare yourselves a simple meal! Know that this is *my* land and all who enter it must obey me. Let me eat what I want from your kill; then I'll permit the oven to cook the remains for you.'

'Since you give us no choice, we accept your terms,' said Odin. 'Help yourself, eagle, but hurry up.'

The eagle fluttered over to the oven, dragged out the raw joint and pecked at it ravenously. When it had devoured the whole lot, it strutted over to the rest of the carcass and set to work swallowing most of that too.

'You glutton,' cried Loki. 'Stop! By the time you've finished stuffing yourself, there'll be nothing left for us.' He rubbed his belly and started to whine again. 'Can't you see? I'm wasting away with hunger. Get out of here, eagle, before I eat *you* instead!'

'Hold your tongue, fool,' warned Odin.

Loki glowered at him. He grabbed a fallen sapling from the ground, stripped off its branches to form a long pole, swung it back and struck the eagle with it. The eagle yelped and suddenly rose towards the sky, with the pole lodged fast in its feathers – and Loki still grasping the other end.

'My hands are stuck,' screeched Loki, 'I can't let go!'

The eagle glided away down the valley, dangling Loki precariously underneath it. At last, far from sight of Odin and Hoenir, it dived down, trailing Loki just above the ground. The trickster's feet tangled in thorn bushes and scraped over stones; his arms were almost wrenched from their sockets.

'Release me!' Loki screamed. 'Name your price, bird – I'll pay whatever you ask for.'

'Ha! Everyone knows how empty your promises are, Loki,' said the eagle. 'You'll never give me what I want.'

'I will,' said Loki. 'On my life, I'll give you *anything*.'

'Very well then,' said the eagle. 'Bring me Idun and her casket of magic apples. I give you nine days and nights to lure her out of Asgard and into the deepest part of the forest to meet me. If you fail, I'll hunt you down again and my revenge will be far worse than what you've suffered today. '

'Is that all?' said Loki. 'That's easy. I swear I'll do it.'

The eagle nodded. Loki's hands suddenly slipped free of the pole. He tumbled to the ground then jumped to his feet. The eagle flapped away and vanished into the sky.

Loki shrugged and ran back along the valley to his companions. They had managed to roast the remaining meat and he was just in time for the meal. He said nothing about what had happened.

The three gods continued their expedition without further adventure, and then returned to Asgard.

Soon Loki's appointment with the eagle was almost due. He hurried to Idun's hall, beaming with smiles, and invited himself in to share a drink with her. At first they chattered light-heartedly; then Loki skilfully turned the subject to her magic apples.

'Sometimes, Idun,' he confided, 'I lie awake at night for ages worrying about them.'

'Whatever for?' said she.

'Well, supposing you ran out of them,' said Loki. 'I'd go bald. I'd get wrinkled and stooped. No one would ever fancy me again.'

'Don't be silly…'

'And imagine Sif's beautiful golden hair turning grey! As for Thor, his strength would fade, he'd shrink and his muscles would waste away… My dear Idun, then who would protect us all from the giants?'

'You don't need to fuss about that,' laughed Idun. 'I always keep my apple casket full to the top.'

'But supposing next year's crop is a poor one?' wailed Loki. 'Even worse, supposing a giant or a mortal found your secret apple tree, and cut it down? You need a contingency plan.'

'So, my friend, are you going to suggest one?' said Idun.

'It happens that I've recently stumbled upon a perfect solution,' said Loki. 'When I was travelling in Midgard recently, I noticed an apple tree growing there, with fruits that looked exactly like your magic ones. It would be an excellent alternative in case you ever need it.'

'It certainly sounds promising,' said Idun. 'Tell me where to find it, and I'll take a look.'

'I'm useless at giving directions,' said Loki. 'It's much easier to show you the way there myself. Why don't we make it a nice day out? The forest where this tree grows is a delightful place. The animals in it are as tame as cats, and the scent from the flowers underfoot is intoxicating. You'll love it.'

'You tempter!' smiled Idun. 'Is it a difficult journey?'

'No, the way is easy enough,' Loki assured her.

'What do I need to bring?'

'You don't need to bring anything, my sweet – except for your casket of apples.'

'Why would I need those?' said Idun. 'I thought the whole idea was to pick the new apples, not use up the ones I already have.'

'It'll be a waste of time picking them unless you're sure they have exactly the right qualities,' said Loki. 'You need to bring along your usual apples, to compare them.'

Idun couldn't find any argument against that. She slipped away to ready herself, then set off after Loki down the Shimmering Path to the wild borderlands of our own world. She followed him into the forest and along an old elk track deep into its heart. Here Loki suddenly ceased his habitual chatter and strode purposefully ahead.

'Are we near the tree yet?' called Idun.

'Very near, my sweet,' said Loki. 'Just stand still a moment and hush, while I recall exactly where it grows.'

Idun obeyed. Loki gave a long, low whistle.

He was answered at once by a loud rustling of branches, followed by a yelp and a beating of wings. A dark shadow dropped suddenly from the sky – the great eagle.

In a flash, its talons fastened upon its prey: one upon Idun's shoulder, the other upon her casket of apples.

'Oh, you double-crosser, Loki!' screamed Idun. 'You snake! Why was I fool enough to trust you?'

Loki didn't answer, for he was bent double with laughter.

The eagle spun round and rose, carrying Idun and her apples into the sky and across the world. Its destination was Giantland. For – as no doubt you have already guessed – it was no ordinary bird, but the shape-shifted form of Giant Thjassi.

The effect of Loki's treachery was devastating. Without regular helpings of Idun's magic apples, almost overnight the gods and goddesses grew old.

Their backs, once so straight and noble, stooped and bent; their limbs stiffened. Their fingers gnarled, their hips twisted with arthritis. Lines and liver spots mottled their once flawless skins. Dull grey or white hair became the norm, and the gods' hairlines rapidly receded. They were constantly coughing and clearing their throats. Their eyes clouded, they cupped hands to their ears, straining to hear. Thor's fingers trembled as he struggled to grip his hammer. Even Freyja lost interest in love making. Odin became forgetful and took to muttering and sighing. Never had there been such a catastrophe.

Odin called an emergency assembly, with only two items up for discussion. Firstly: What has become of Idun's apples? And secondly: How can they be retrieved?

Loki was quickly identified as the culprit – for several goddesses had seen Idun following the trickster out of Asgard. He readily admitted his guilt.

'But I *had* to take Idun to the giant-eagle, otherwise he would have killed me,' he explained. 'I bet if any of you lot were in that situation, you'd do exactly the same. Well, I suppose now you want me to rescue her and bring the apples back, eh?'

'If you don't,' said Odin, 'I personally will supervise your execution. It will be a slow death, by long drawn-out, excruciating torture.'

'There's no need to go into detail,' Loki interrupted, 'because it won't happen. Leave this to me: I'll sort it out straightaway. But first I need someone to lend me a certain magic object, so I can meet Giant Thjassi on his own terms. Freyja! Where are you hiding, my lovely? Ah, *there* you are – I didn't recognise you with all those wrinkles. Can I borrow your feather cloak?'

Freyja stood up with a groan, brushing a tired straggle of colourless hair from her face. 'Borrow whatever you want, Loki, if it'll cure us of this curse,' she croaked.

She hobbled away, fetched the cloak and tossed it to Loki.

As soon as he stepped into it, he assumed the shape of a falcon. In this form, he flew easily up to the sky and sped out of Asgard, heading for Giantland.

There he located the house of Thjassi, perched by the seashore. Hovering over it, Loki saw that Thjassi himself was out on the open sea, fishing from a little boat. The trickster seized this lucky chance, landing at once and breaking his way into Thjassi's house.

Inside, he found Idun crouching by the fire, nursing her casket of apples like a baby. When she saw the falcon, she guessed that it was Loki and began berating him furiously.

'Hush, my darling,' Loki soothed her, 'don't fret. Everything's going to be fine. I've come to save you. Just keep clasping the apples to your heart like that.'

Before she could scold him any more, he muttered a terse spell. At once Idun was transformed into a nutshell.

'But the apples!' the nutshell cried in a muffled voice.

'They're still safe with you,' said Loki. 'I've turned them into your kernel.'

Loki seized the whole nut in his claws, burst out of the house and soared into the sky. Not a moment too soon! For Thjassi was already on his way home. As soon as he arrived and found Idun and her apples missing, the giant guessed exactly what had happened. In a flash, he resumed his eagle form, flew up and went racing after Loki. His wings beat so hard that they whipped up a mighty gale, turning the sea to foam, blasting ships, demolishing houses.

Within no time at all, the ramparts of Asgard were before them. Loki was only a very short distance ahead. Thjassi was catching up with him – any moment now he would surely overcome him…

But the gods saw their approach. Tottering, groaning, they forced themselves into action, piling up wood shavings behind the ramparts and fetching fire-steels.

Loki flew over the wall with the nutshell and landed safely.

With quivering hands, the gods lit the wood shavings. At once, they burst into a line of brilliant yellow flames – just as Thjassi was trying to breach the wall. The fire sucked the eagle-giant into its mass and burst into a blinding inferno. Thjassi was instantly burned to death.

Loki gave a whoop of triumph, tossed the feather cloak back to Freyja and returned to his true form. He released Idun from her own transformation. The gods and goddesses cheered – then quickly fell upon her casket of apples, shoving each other aside and ravenously devouring them.

At once their decrepitude melted away and all were restored to magnificence and youth.

Well and good. But what about that mischief-maker Loki?

To tell the truth, all the gods and goddesses were so relieved to be back to normal that they put Loki's mischief out of mind. Nevertheless, the trickster did get his comeuppance.

For Thjassi had a daughter, the grim giantess Skadi, and she was determined to avenge his death. To this end, she dressed herself in a mail coat and helmet, armed herself with an array of vicious weapons and marched brazenly into Asgard to declare her mission.

Odin received her with considered courtesy and waylaid her complaint before she could even utter it, saying, 'I'll pay you generously to make amends for your loss.'

'Treasure can't make up for burning my father alive,' she spat at him.

'Of course it can't,' said Odin. 'That's why I intend to offer you something far more valuable – something you have never enjoyed in your life before.'

'Name it,' she said sceptically.

And Odin said, 'The gift of laughter.'

'*Laughter*?' she scorned him. 'Impossible! Since the day I was born, nothing has ever caused me even to smile. Stop wasting my time, Odin. I intend to take my revenge on you at once.' She drew a gigantic axe from her belt and raised it threateningly.

'Wait,' said Odin.

He conferred with his fellows, slipped away, then swiftly returned, leading a nanny-goat and a rope. He fastened one end of the rope to the goat's beard and, at a signal, two of the other gods grabbed Loki. At another signal, Freyja sauntered over and casually stripped the trickster naked. A third god held him in an armlock.

Loki struggled and squirmed.

Odin grabbed Loki's private parts and tied the other end of the rope tightly round them. Then he slipped a halter over the goat's head and led it away. The rope tautened.

Loki began to squeal.

Skadi's mouth twitched.

The gods held Loki tighter. Odin pulled the goat further.

Loki's squeals grew louder, like a stuck piglet or a baby with severe wind. His captors dragged him back and back towards Skadi – then suddenly let go. Loki gave a last, piercing scream – then fainted into Skadi's lap.

And sure enough, Skadi gave up all thoughts of revenge. Because for the first time in her life, the miserable giantess burst out laughing.

For notes on this story, see page 320.

A JOURNEY
THROUGH GIANTLAND

In the old days, they say it wasn't unusual for the gods to show up in our own world. No matter if people were rich or poor, humble or mighty; no one was safe from them.

There were some peasants who farmed out in the middle of nowhere. One evening the wife opened her door and found a wagon halted outside – with a pair of *goats* in the yoke. That was her warning; and when she saw their master, her worst fears were confirmed. For he was a huge, ruddy-faced redbeard with shoulders like an ox – none other than Thor the giant slayer! Another fellow was lurking behind him, finely dressed and handsome, with shifty eyes and a snake-like smile – surely the trickster, Loki.

The poor woman was terrified, but what could she do? The gods pushed past her and made their way into her house. Her husband and two children almost jumped out of their skins at the sight of them. Nevertheless, they managed to stoke up the fire and rustle up some decent ale for their guests. The gods made themselves at home, settling themselves on the ricketty old wall benches. The peasant woman crept back in and, with a trembling hand, started stirring the cauldron that was steaming over the fire.

Loki pulled off his boots, sniffed the pot disparagingly and sighed. 'Seems to me, Thor,' he said, 'we'll be lying awake with empty belly rumbles tonight unless we do something about it. And these good people need fattening up. How about your meat-trick?'

Thor nodded. He nudged the boy and asked his name.

'Thjalfi, sir,' the lad answered boldly.

'Well now, Thjalfi: pop outside, unhitch the goats from my wagon and bring them in here.'

Thjalfi did as he was told. The goats trotted in after him, messing copiously on the floor. The peasant woman pursed her lips but held her tongue. Thor drew his knife and cut the goats' throats. He skinned them deftly, then sliced them into hunks of meat and threw them into the cauldron. When the meat was cooked, he seized the peasant woman's ladle and scooped generous portions into her bowls.

'Eat up, friends,' he said. 'But take care: *don't break any of the bones*, because I need them. When you're finished, just chuck them onto the goatskins over there.'

Fresh goat meat from the gods' own pastures! No one went hungry that night. When they had eaten their fill, the peasant couple and their daughter – Roskva, she was called – all piled the bones neatly on one side, as Thor had ordered.

But Loki caught Thjalfi's eye, winked, and shook his head ostentatiously at the pile of bones. Thjalfi stared at him uncertainly. Loki grinned, and winked again.

Thjalfi stood up, holding the big thigh-bone he'd just gnawed clean. He turned his back and took out his knife. Surreptitiously, he sliced the bone open and sucked out the juicy marrow. When he was finished, he hid the broken bone at the bottom of the pile. Loki never said a word.

Very early the next morning, the family was disturbed from their sleep by the sound of Thor muttering incantations. He was standing over the goat bones, brandishing an enormous hammer carved with patterns and runes. In the gloom the bones seemed to flicker and melt into each other. They sprouted flesh, skin, hair. Now they were living goats again, bleating and struggling to their feet.

The peasants all burst into applause. But Thor cut them short with a furious roar. 'Who has disobeyed me? One of my goats is lamed!'

Loki pointed at Thjalfi. 'It was you, lad, wasn't it?' he sniggered. 'Don't deny it: I saw you.'

There was nothing the boy could do to excuse himself. Thor towered over him: 'You little rascal. You louse! Farmer, I demand compensation.'

'Oh, please sir,' cried the peasant woman, all in a dither, 'I'm sorry...we can't. We've got nothing – you've seen how poor we are. There's no excuse for our son...he's behaved outrageously...and to *you* of all people...but...but...'

Loki smirked. 'Thor, in lieu of payment, let's take the boy.'

'That's no bad idea,' Thor said, calming down a little. 'He might actually prove more valuable than silver. And for good measure, we'll have his sister too.'

The peasant woman's mouth dropped open in dismay.

'Don't worry,' Thor told her. 'You won't lose out, because we'll swap them. You can have my goats and wagon in exchange for your youngsters. They'll make excellent slaves for our journey.'

'Slaves?' said the woman fearfully, 'journey? Where are you taking them?'

Loki gave her a dazzling smile. 'We're on our way to Giantland.'

The gods and their new young slaves walked towards the east until they reached the great ocean. There they climbed into a boat, rowed across the water and stepped ashore on the far side in a land of icy wind and drifting mist. They set off along the only path, which led into a vast, thick forest overlooked by snow-capped mountains. They trudged through the trees, ever deeper and deeper. There was no sign of any habitation. The sun turned orange and sank. The twilight thickened.

Suddenly their way was blocked by a towering obstruction. It was too dark to make out properly, but it seemed to be a very curious building. Its walls were soft and flexible, and the front was completely open from the ground to the roof. When they went in, they found themselves standing in a huge, empty space. To one side there was a short tunnel, but it led nowhere.

Thor ordered Thjalfi to lay out fur sleeping sacks and Roskva to pass round some leftover goat meat. They all ate hungrily, then lay down to sleep.

In the middle of the night they were woken suddenly by an ear-splitting, blood-curdling noise. The ground beneath them was juddering and shaking like an earthquake.

Loki shrieked. Roskva and Thjalfi cowered. The noises and juddering stopped. For a few moments, everything went still... Then the turmoil suddenly erupted again.

'I'll guard the entrance,' said Thor softly. 'Slaves, you may hide.'

Roskva and Thjalfi squeezed into the tunnel – where Loki was already skulking. Thor stood like a sentry before the threatening forest.

The uproar continued in fits and starts. At dawn it finally stopped. Thor led the way out.

A short way off, they saw an enormous giant lying on the grass, fast asleep. The terrifying noises and quaking ground of the previous night had been nothing more than his snores.

Thor clutched his belt. His muscles rippled and swelled. He pulled his hammer from his shirt, shook it until it grew to formidable size and raised it, ready to strike a blow.

However, at that moment, the giant suddenly awoke and leaped to his feet. 'Thor!' he exclaimed in a very friendly voice. He stooped down to their level, holding out his huge hand. 'I heard rumours that you were on your way. Welcome to Giantland!'

Slowly, suspiciously, Thor lowered his hand and shook down his hammer. 'Name yourself,' he said gruffly.

'You can call me Skrymir,' said the giant. He peered at Loki and the two young slaves. 'Have any of you, by any chance, seen my glove? I lost it somewhere round here last night... Hah! There it is.'

He pointed at the strange building they had just vacated. In the daylight, it was plain to see that it was indeed shaped like an enormous glove, big enough for Giant Skrymir's hand. The tunnel was actually the hole for his thumb.

Loki narrowed his eyes and sucked in his lips. 'That's a neat trick, Skrymir,' he said.

'It takes one trickster to admire an even better one,' said Skrymir. 'But you've seen nothing yet. No doubt you're heading to Utgard Fortress, eh? Good for you: you'll find a real knees-up when you get there. But it's a long journey and ant-sized creatures like you need help travelling through the perils of Giantland, so I'll come with you some of the way. I'll even carry that heavy bag of food for you.'

He snatched up their pack and strode off into the trees. Soon Thor, Loki and Roskva were left far behind. However, Thjalfi kept sprinting ahead to check where Skrymir had got to, then back to the others to show the way.

'Tell him to stop for a bit,' called Loki. 'I need a rest. And I'm famished.'

Skrymir didn't argue, but waited for them to catch him up, then tossed the food pack to Thor. That done, he lay down and went back to sleep.

Thor set to work, untying the thongs that held the pack shut. However, the more he tried to loosen them, the tighter they became knotted. Loki's stomach bubbled noisily. Thor growled. He cursed. He bellowed with rage. Then he spun round and glared at the sleeping giant. 'The bastard! He's done this deliberately.' He raised his hammer and struck it down, hard, onto Skrymir's head.

Skrymir opened his eyes, yawned and lazily sat up. 'What an annoying dream,' he said. 'It seemed that someone was tickling me...but it must have been a leaf fluttering down. Enjoying your meal?' Then he lay down and dozed off again.

Loki snatched the pack from Thor and tried to bite through the thongs. Roskva scratched at them with sharp fingernails. Thjalfi tried to cut them with his knife. All their efforts achieved nothing.

Thor cursed, stepped back and whacked Skrymir's head a second time.

'What's that?' Skrymir sprung awake again. 'Oh, just a little acorn falling on me.'

He lay back once more and closed his eyes; but this time he tossed and turned and didn't drop off until dawn. Once he was snoring, Thor crept over and, with phenomenal force, hammered the giant yet again.

Skrymir jumped bolt upright, rubbing his head. 'Ach, now a lump of bird muck's hit me. I've had enough of camping outside, after all this.' He yawned. 'But what about you four? Enjoy your meal last night, eh? Sleep well? Not very talkative this morning, are you? Never mind, it's time to say goodbye, because I'm going a different way from here. I've enjoyed your company. Just watch yourselves when you reach the fortress: the giants there are far bigger and nastier than me. So if you decide to turn back rather than run into more trouble, I won't call you cowards.'

'No one sends me back from my chosen path,' snarled Thor. 'Gods have nothing to fear from mere giants.'

Skrymir shrugged. 'Please yourself,' he said.

And then he vanished.

The gods and their slaves walked on, grumbling with hunger. As the sun rose high in the sky, they finally emerged from the forest into a plain. In front of them towered a massive wooden fortress. Its gate was made of iron bars, each one twice as thick as a warrior's leg. There was no guard to let visitors through, and no latch or key to open it.

Thor smashed at the bars with his hammer, but it didn't even dent them. He put his shoulder to the gate, but it wouldn't budge. Loki elbowed him aside. He held his breath and withdrew into himself like a slug. In this way, he easily slid between the bars, and hauled Roskva and Thjalfi after him. But Thor was so brawny, Loki had to keep slipping in and out, shoving and dragging him, until the mighty giant-slayer was scratched and bruised all over.

But no matter, they were inside Utgard Fortress now. The door into the feasting hall stood wide open. They smoothed their clothes and went in.

The hall was brilliantly lit by hundreds of lamps. All down both sides, giants and giantesses were seated on thickly cushioned benches, stuffing themselves from great tables piled high with delicacies and drinks. There were whole sheep's heads, roast swans with the feathers still on, bear steaks, haunches of elk and venison, bowls full of whipped cream and red berry soup, enormous whole salmon, honeycombs and countless delicious titbits.

Thor and Loki led their two slaves down the hall to the high-seat where the King of Utgard was enthroned.

'Greetings,' bellowed Thor. Against the giants, he seemed smaller than a dwarf.

The Giant King peered down at him in a puzzled way, raised his eyebrows and rubbed the end of his nose. But he didn't answer.

'Where are your manners, king?' boomed Thor. 'Answer me! For I am mighty Thor of Asgard.'

At these words, the Giant King burst out laughing, shaking and spluttering until tears ran down his cheeks. At last he managed to spit out, '*You*? Ha! I've heard all these stories, you know: they claim that Thor is an amazing, fearsome hero... *You* can't be him, you soft skinned, newborn baby!'

Loki scowled and spat on the floor.

The Giant King ignored him. 'Anyway, how dare you come barging into my fortress like this? It's not open house here, you know: only heroes can feast at my tables. If you don't want me to kick you out, you'll have to prove yourselves champions. All of you!' Then he noticed Roskva. 'Except the pretty little lady, of course. Come, sit by my foot, tiny girl-child; help me watch the fun.'

Reluctantly, Roskva went forward and sat on the floor next to the Giant King's outsized boot.

'So,' said the Giant King, 'let's start the contest. Who wants to go first?'

Thor was still beside himself with indignation. Loki slapped a brotherly hand on his back and stepped forward himself. 'I will.'

'You don't look up to much,' said the Giant King. 'Whatever can *you* do?'

'Eat,' said Loki. He grinned and rubbed his stomach. 'I can devour food faster than anyone.'

'We'll try you,' sneered the Giant King. He snapped his fingers.

His own slaves came dashing in. Before the high-seat, they set up a new table with a stool at either end. The Giant King gestured to Loki. He sat down on one of the stools. Opposite him came a truly obese giant with a stomach like a puffed-up ox bladder. In front of each contestant, the slaves placed a wooden plate as big as a wagon wheel, piled high with every kind of roast meat.

'Begin,' commanded the Giant King.

Loki and the fat giant both started to eat. Loki gobbled his meat so fast, his jaws were a blur of movement. He didn't stop once, not even to belch. In no time at all, he had finished off the whole lot: there was nothing left on his vast plate except for bones. He grinned in triumph.

'You've failed, Loki,' the Giant King told him. 'You never stood a chance. Look at your opponent.'

He was right. At the far end of the table, the pot-bellied giant had not only swallowed the meat as fast as Loki; he had also devoured the bones and the plate.

'The giants have won the first contest,' said the king. 'Who's next?'

Loki was convulsed with rage. Thjalfi stepped forward.

'Hmm,' said the Giant King, 'not even a god, but a mortal boy. Still, you can't be any more pathetic than the last one. What do you want to try?'

Thjalfi held his head high. 'A race,' he said. 'I can run as fast as the wind.'

'Can you, now?' said the Giant King. 'Well, I'll pit you against one of my own lads. Hugi!'

A young giant jogged up and bowed. The Giant King led everyone out to a stretch of grass behind the hall. He lined the pair up, clapped his hands – and they were off.

Thjalfi ran faster than any lad had ever done before. It seemed that one moment he was just starting, and the next he was already at the finishing post. But when he looked up, he found that Hugi had got there before him.

'Second contest to the giants too,' the king said loftily. 'Now, Thor, it's your turn. Come on, little one, don't let me intimidate you.' He cupped a hand to his ear. 'Speak up: tell me what you think you can do best.'

Thor flushed even redder than usual. He drew out his hammer and made a great show of expanding and shrinking it, twirling it round his head in a dazzle of dark iron. 'I'm famed in Asgard for my prowess in drinking,' he said.

'You old bragger,' scoffed the Giant King. 'By the sight of you, that's really hard to believe. But it's only fair to let you have a go.'

He led the way back inside and beckoned to his slaves. They came staggering in, carrying an extraordinary drinking horn. It was so long that from its brim, the opposite end was just a blur. It was filled to the top with dark liquid.

Thor smacked his lips. 'Mmm. This looks good.'

'But can you do it justice?' said the Giant King. 'I've seen one or two giants drain it in a single swig; but I don't expect you to manage that, Thor – your throat's far too tiny. Two swigs wouldn't be bad. But the absolute maximum I can allow is three: if you can't empty it by then, you'll have to hang your head in shame.'

'No danger of that,' said Thor. He seized the horn, took a deep breath, threw back his head, and gulped, on and on and on... Until at last he had to stop. He stepped back – and stared at the horn in dismay.

'Still almost full,' remarked the Giant King.

Thor glowered and knocked back another draught. But again, eventually he had to stop and draw a breath. Still, the liquid had hardly gone down at all.

'Last go,' said the Giant King.

Thor drank for the third time. His eyes were clenched shut. Sweat poured off him. At last he could go on no longer.

The drinking horn was still almost overflowing.

'Failed,' announced the Giant King.

'You've tricked him,' hissed Loki. 'Thor's never been beaten by booze before. Let him try something else.'

The Giant King chuckled. 'Why not? This is fun. Let's test that famous brawn of yours, Thor. See if you can pick up my cat.'

'Don't insult me,' growled Thor. 'Even Roskva here could do that.'

'Not my cat, she couldn't,' said the Giant King. 'Even we have a problem with him. Here, puss!'

A huge grey tomcat came slinking out. He sat down in front of Thor, who bent down, and tried to heave the creature off the floor. But the cat was heavier than rock. Thor straightened up, flexed his muscles and had another go. But it was as if the cat had been nailed down: nothing Thor could do would shift him. The cat gazed at him from eerie, sea-green eyes. Thor tugged at him again – and at last managed to wrench a single paw, very slightly, off the ground.

The Giant King raised his eyebrows. 'Well done! That's actually quite impressive. How about testing your legendary strength in another way? Fancy a spot of wrestling, eh? I know just the person who'll be a fair match for you: Elli, my old nurse. Elli, my dear, where are you?'

An aged giantess stood up and hobbled towards them, leaning heavily on a walking stick. Her face was a mass of wrinkles, her back was bent, her shoulders hunched, her limbs twisted with arthritis. She grinned, showing a black, toothless mouth.

Thor said, 'I can't attack a lady.'

The old giantess tossed her stick to one side and held up her fists. 'Try me,' she retorted. 'Go on, go on, I'll soon tell you to stop if you're hurting.'

Thor looked doubtful. Nevertheless, he stepped forward

and gingerly gripped the giantess's wasted arms. She hunched down and gripped him too. They staggered around together, huffing, gasping and straining... Until, at last, the giantess pushed mighty Thor to the ground! She stamped her foot on him so forcefully, that he ended up yelling for her to spare him.

The watching giants gave a loud cheer.

'Enough!' cried the Giant King. 'This has been most excellent sport. I've really enjoyed watching you all do so badly – especially you, Thor. You deserve a reward. Take a seat at my table, all four of you: eat and drink as much as you wish. Then have a good night's sleep. Tomorrow, we'll have a chat. And I'll let you in to some secrets.'

By the morning, after an unbeatable blowout at the Giant King's expense, Thor and Loki had forgotten their humiliation and their bluff good humour was restored. The Giant King led them out of his fortress and back through the forest, with Roskva and Thjalfi tagging eagerly at their heels. Soon they stood once more on the shore of the great ocean.

'My friends,' said the Giant King, 'before we part, I've got a confession to make. I'm not what I seem to be. And your adventures in Giantland were even stranger than you think.'

'Tell us everything,' said Thor. 'We want the truth.'

The Giant King turned to Loki. 'You and I share many of the same bad habits, trickster – and almost the same name. I'm known in these parts as Utgard-Loki; and like you, I can be crafty and sly.'

'Speak for yourself,' said Loki. 'I've done nothing to hoodwink you.'

'Which is just as well,' said the Giant King, 'for my sorcery always beats anything you gods can scrape up. Let's go back over your adventures. Remember Giant Skrymir, who you met in the forest when you arrived? Well, he was really me. Thor, you got in such a tizzy when your hammer blows couldn't damage me – never guessing that I'd moved a whole mountain between us to protect myself. Look, that's it over there...' He pointed above the trees. 'It was your hammer that made those three valleys between the peaks'

'So what?' said Loki coolly.

'So, on to you, Loki. Thanks to the magic thongs I fixed on your food pack, when you arrived at my palace, you were starving. But you still couldn't eat as much as the giant pitted against you. That's because his name means Fire. Naturally, Fire devours absolutely everything in his path at lightening speed. Meat, bones or the plate it's served on – it's all the same to him.'

Thjalfi said, 'Sir, what about that young giant who raced against me?'

'Oh, him,' said the Giant King. 'His name means Thought. You were quick, my lad, very quick indeed – but no one can run as fast as they can think.'

'You rogue!' snarled Thor. 'Who did you set against me?'

'I have to admit,' said the Giant King, 'you're more formidable than I ever expected. When you had a go with that drinking horn, I was astonished you succeeded in swallowing some of the liquid. You must have noticed that the end of the horn was out of sight? Well, that's because it stretched all the way to the sea! I was trying to make you drink up the sea itself, Thor. Even the thirstiest giant could never achieve that. But you had a pretty good try.'

'And the cat?' Thor growled.

'It's really a serpent,' said the Giant King. '*The* serpent, in fact – Jormungand, the World Serpent. The one that lies in this very ocean, encircling and guarding the entire earth.'

'That's total madness,' protested Thor. 'If I'd succeeded in lifting it up, I'd have destroyed everything.'

'True,' said the Giant King. 'I got quite concerned when you forced one of its paws right off the ground. No doubt that caused a nasty earthquake somewhere. And now I suppose you're wondering who Elli was – that old woman who you wrestled at the end.'

Thor said nothing.

'I'll give you a clue,' said the Giant King. 'She is the strongest force in the whole world. No one can overcome her. Every man and every woman dreads her coming; for once she arrives and sinks in her claws, they cannot escape her until they die.'

He turned to Thjalfi and Roskva. 'Any good at riddles? Can you guess her name?'

They shuddered at his description, but shook their heads.

'Elli is Old Age,' said the Giant King softly. 'Even you youngsters will be challenged by her one day. Then you will understand how Old Age conquers even the mightiest people; and you will recall with sorrow how Thor himself could not vanquish her.'

In the sky, storm clouds were gathering.

'So you see, Thor,' said the Giant King, 'your expedition here was a complete waste of time. We giants have made fools of you all.'

Thor growled and drew out his hammer, shook it to size and swung it back, ready to strike him. But as it sliced through the air, suddenly there came a flash of light; and by the time it had cleared, King Utgard-Loki and even Giantland had completely disappeared.

For notes on this story, see page 321.

THE DEATH OF BALDR
and THE PUNISHMENT OF LOKI

Baldr was the son of Odin and Frigg. He was beautiful. His voice was like music; light radiated from him like the sun. And yet...

Baldr had disturbing dreams. The gods are immortal, yet Baldr dreamed of his own death. He told his wife, Nanna, about it, and fearfully, Nanna went to Frigg saying, 'Surely this can't be true? I can't bear to think of it. How can we save him?'

'Leave it with me,' said Frigg.

She went out travelling through all the worlds, begging everyone and everything she met not to harm her beloved son. How could anyone refuse such a mother's request? The gods and goddesses all promised not to harm him, as did the giants and troll-wives, the dwarfs and the elves. All the animals made a similar undertaking; so did the birds and fishes, reptiles and insects. Even the World Serpent and Fenrisulf sympathised with Frigg's desperation and agreed to keep the promise, as did the dragons and monsters of the deep. Fire and water swore they would not touch him; so did stones, sand and mountains, all things made of metal, forests, flowers and seaweed, even the very earth itself, even the air. Frigg also persuaded disease never to touch her son, and poison never to work its effect on him.

When this was done, Baldr's nightmares ceased, and his light shone brighter than ever over Asgard. To celebrate, he organised a special game. He called his fellow gods and goddesses together as if for an assembly, and told them to form a circle around him.

'I want you all to throw spears or axes or stones at me,' he challenged them. 'Attack me however you wish, with whatever weapons you can find – then watch them bounce off me. For my mother has made it impossible for anything to do me any harm.'

In this way, everyone in Asgard enjoyed great sport and uproarious amusement. Baldr laughed loudest of all, for no matter how many times he was struck, no matter how hard, he didn't suffer even the slightest injury.

However, there was one – one alone – who had no affection at all for Baldr. This dissenter was the usual culprit: that ignoble back-stabber, Loki.

Loki disguised himself as a mortal woman and paid a visit to Frigg's hall.

'Wise mother,' he said in a falsetto voice. 'Why are you at home today? Come and enjoy the fun at Baldr's games.'

'It's not to my taste,' said Frigg. 'It pains me to see people hurling weapons at my son, even though I know they can't hurt him.'

'So are the rumours really true?' asked Loki. 'Has everyone and everything in all the worlds really sworn never to harm him?'

'Yes,' said Frigg. 'For I organised this great oath myself.'

'And didn't anyone refuse? Not even someone totally insignificant?'

'Of course not,' said Frigg. 'Who would dare not support Odin's own son?'

'And you didn't forget to include even the tiniest thing?'

Frigg hesitated then said, 'I won't diminish myself by telling a lie. As I returned from my long quest, just by Slain Hall I happened to stumble upon a shoot of mistletoe, a plant that I hadn't noticed before. Its leaves had barely even opened and it was so young and tender, it seemed wrong to burden it with such a solemn vow. I'm sure it's of no consequence…'

But Frigg's last words were spoken to empty air, for Loki was already offering his excuses and making a hasty exit.

The trickster hurried to Slain Hall. In the shadows behind it, he found the mistletoe shoot that Frigg had mentioned. Carefully, he plucked it, tied it to a stick and carried this to the sporting ring where Baldr was still the centre of riotous entertainment. A great crowd of gods and goddesses was circling around, assailing him with missiles that ranged from hunks of bread and berries to boulders and spears. The air rang with cheers and laughter.

Loki sidled through the throng, seeking some poor fool who might unwittingly help him. Soon his eye fell upon Baldr's brother, Hod. He was standing a little apart from the others, smiling yet looking awkward.

'Greetings, friend,' said Loki. 'What's up? Why aren't you joining in?'

'It's you, Loki, is it?' said Hod. 'Well, although I know the game's not dangerous, I can't bring myself to attack my own brother.'

'Nonsense,' said Loki. 'It's not attacking – it's just larking around.'

'True,' said Hod. 'But you know I'm blind, Loki. Even if I wanted to throw something at Baldr, I couldn't see to do it.'

'Let me guide you,' said Loki. 'It seems a shame for you to miss out.'

'Don't bother,' said Hod. 'I'm happy enough listening to everyone else enjoying themselves. Besides, I don't have anything to throw.'

'But I do,' said Loki. 'Here, put your fingers round this stick. Now, let's take aim together... Get ready... throw!'

So Hod, in total innocence, and guided entirely by Loki's hand, hurled the mistletoe stick at Baldr. It struck him full on in the chest. Amidst all the commotion, at first no one even noticed it – until Baldr gave a shriek of pain and swooned to the ground.

As soon as the mistletoe struck him, disaster was instant. There was nothing anyone could do. One moment of treachery from Loki – and Baldr the invulnerable lay dead.

Hod quickly realised what had happened and was overcome by remorse. Nobody blamed him – for as soon as Frigg was told of the tragedy, she cried, 'A curse upon Loki! He has betrayed us all!'

Everyone was totally distraught. The goddesses all wept. The gods lambasted Loki's name and vowed to tear the rogue to shreds. Odin declared that Loki's treachery would come back to haunt him.

Nanna beat her breast in anguish and sobbed bitterly that she could not live without her husband – until she too collapsed and died.

Never before had death encroached upon Asgard; and now it had struck there twice.

The gods held a joint funeral for Baldr and Nanna. It was an ominous but splendid occasion. The mourners arrived to the shrieking of Odin's ravens, led by Freyja mounted majestically on her cat, keening and chanting, surrounded by valkyries. She was followed by her brother Frey in a chariot pulled by his golden boar. Even the giants and troll-wives came to offer sympathy.

Baldr's body was laid out in his own ship, with Nanna beside him and Baldr's horse at their feet. A mighty giantess called Hyrrokkin was employed to draw the ship out to sea, surrounded by berserks, and mounted on a wolf with vipers as reins. At her touch, the ship burst into flames. Thor consecrated this fire with his mighty hammer, Mjollnir; whilst Odin sacrificed to it his most precious treasure, the magic golden ring, Draupnir.

After the funeral, Frigg pulled herself together. She said in a voice of stone, 'My son's body is no more. Yet his soul surely lives on in the dark, frozen wastelands of Niflheim, imprisoned in Hel's house of death. My friends: which of you is brave enough to ride the road there? Who will offer that fearsome goddess a ransom on my behalf, if she will only release my son and return him to Asgard?'

Frigg and Odin had a third son, called Hermod. It was he who stepped forward, saying, 'Mother, I will go.'

Odin said, 'Then I will lend you my own horse, eight-legged Sleipnir, to speed you on your journey.'

Hermod rode Sleipnir out of Asgard onto a long, dreary trail through the wilderness. After nine nights, he came to a golden bridge over a deep, rushing river. As he stepped onto it, a woman, dressed in the corselet and helmet of a warrior, stepped out to block his way.

'Halt!' cried she. 'Only the dead may pass.'

'I am neither dead nor alive, but immortal,' said Hermod. 'I am seeking my brother Baldr, who was killed against the natural order of things. We are both sons of Odin.'

'Since you come in the name of the Corpse-Father,' the warrior woman said, 'I cannot refuse you entry. Follow the road on the far side that leads northward and downward into the freezing mist until you come to a towering wall. If you can break through its gates, you will see Hel's hall before you. Your brother is inside.'

Hermod thanked her and went on, following her directions through swirling clouds of filth and ice, until he stood before Hel's great gates. They were locked and there was no gatekeeper. However, Sleipnir did not hesitate, but leaped straight over them, landing in front of a magnificent hall. As Hermod dismounted, the door swung open to reveal a hideous woman. One side of her body was naked flesh; whilst the other was a cavernous, stinking hollow.

'Are you Hel Lokisdaughter?' Hermod asked her.

'I am indeed,' said she. 'What brings a living god into my realm of death?'

'I am searching for my brother, Baldr,' he said.

'Then you are welcome.'

She beckoned with a long, cadaverous finger and led

Hermod inside. It was exactly like all the halls in our own world, except that the people who inhabited it were as insubstantial as shadows.

When they reached the high-seat, Hermod saw two wraiths ensconced in it – and recognised them as Baldr and Nanna.

'My dear brother!' he exclaimed. 'Frigg has begged me to fetch you from here and bring you home.'

Baldr answered in a voice so faint that Hermod had to strain to hear him: 'Oh brother, you can see that the dreams which once haunted me have come true. I would dearly like to leave them behind and go home with you. However, only Hel can grant this wish.'

So Hermod turned to Hel and asked her, 'What is the price of Baldr's freedom? Our mother Frigg will pay anything you ask.'

'Oh, tell her not to bother with treasure,' said Hel with a gruesome smile. 'All she needs do is persuade everything in all the worlds to show their love for Baldr by weeping for him. If they do, I will set him free. But if any refuse, then Baldr must stay here with me.'

'I know our mother will gladly arrange this payment,' said Hermod. 'But I need a token to prove to her that I have really found Baldr, and that the offer is genuine.'

Hel nodded at Baldr. He pulled the golden ring, Draupnir, from his finger and handed it to Hermod.

Then Nanna held out a beautiful linen shroud. 'Give this to my mother-in-law, Frigg, in return for all her kindness to me,' she said. 'And this…' she dropped a gleaming arm-ring into his hand '…this is for my dear friend, her handmaid, Fulla.'

105

Hermod took the offerings, thanked them and bade them farewell. Then he bowed to Hel, mounted on Sleipnir and galloped joyfully back to Asgard.

Frigg and Odin were greatly relieved to receive such proof that Baldr's spirit lived on. They did not hesitate to organise the weeping of the world that was needed to bring him back. They commissioned messengers to go out and tell everyone and everything – people and animals, plants and water, earth, stones and metal – to show their grief with tears. And all things did.

However, as the messengers made their way back to Asgard, their task fulfilled, they passed a cave they had not seen before. Inside it sat an ancient giantess who, unlike the rest of creation, was not weeping but grinning.

'Hail, madam!' the messengers greeted her.

'What do you want of me?' the giantess answered sourly.

The messengers explained their sombre errand and urged her to join in the mourning.

But the giantess said, 'Why should I? Baldr was nothing to me when he was alive, and he's certainly of no use to me dead. Count me out and let Hel keep what she's entitled to.'

Because of those heartless words, the conditions of Baldr's release were not completely fulfilled. Thus the beautiful god never returned from the dead, but was compelled to stay in Hel's house for ever.

When Frigg and Odin heard what had happened, they guessed at once that the renegade giantess was really Loki. They alerted the whole of Asgard to his crime and ordered his capture.

Loki didn't hang around waiting for the gods to ambush him, but hastened away to a remote mountain. On its highest peak, by a waterfall, he built himself a hut with four doors, so that he could see his enemies approach from any direction. To keep vigil, he spent each night knotting linen threads together into a vast, openwork cloth.

One night while he was thus engaged, Loki saw the gods in the distance, marching towards his hideout. He hurled down his handiwork, dashed outside, transformed into a salmon and concealed himself deep inside the waterfall.

The gods reached his house and broke their way in. Seeing it was empty, they searched it ruthlessly, kicking down benches, tossing furs and blankets aside, rooting through chests. Eventually, they spotted Loki's net, tossed to the edge of the fire-pit – the perfect tool to trap him.

Then Thor pointed and roared, 'There he is!'

He dragged out the net and hammered one end to the rock above the waterfall. His fellows seized the other end and stretched the net across the torrent, all the way to the sea. Now, whichever way Loki swam in his salmon shape, there was no escape.

The trickster slipped into a gap between two stones under the water. But the gods saw him and fastened the net tightly over his hiding place with heavy rocks. Loki slithered beneath them – wriggled under the edge of the net – leaped over it to the very top of the waterfall...

But Thor was ready and waiting for him there. With a roar of triumph, he seized the trickster by the tail.

Loki's punishment was brutal.

The gods dragged him to a cave. Then they summoned his sons, Vali and Nari, to take part in their father's penalty. They turned Vali into a wolf and ordered him to tear his brother, Nari, to pieces. Then they tore out Nari's entrails, twisted them into gruesome ropes and threaded these through three stone slabs to bind Loki tightly. One enclosed his shoulders, another went across his loins and the third around his knees. As soon as they were fastened, the bonds turned to solid iron.

At a signal from Thor, the giantess Skadi stepped forward, carrying a huge, poisonous snake. She nailed this to the cave wall above Loki, in such a way that venom dribbled directly onto the trickster's face. Every time a drop touched him, he jolted violently in pain.

'You've got your just deserts at last, Loki,' Thor said. 'No one will pity you.'

But he was wrong. For Loki had a long-suffering wife called Sigyn, and despite his endless bizarre adulteries, she still loved him. After the other gods had gone, Sigyn went to stand beside Loki. She held a large basin between him and the snake and in this way caught the drips of venom before they reached him.

It is said that she still stands there loyally to this very day. But every so often the basin overflows and she has to turn aside to empty it. Then Loki feels the full agony of the venom, and when a drop strikes him, he jerks so much that it causes an earthquake.

And so it will continue until the world ends.

For notes on this story, see page 323.

RAGNAROK
THE DOOM OF THE GODS

I met a wild woman walking down the road.

Her head was uncovered, her grey hair grimy and unkempt, coiling round her shoulders like winter snakes. Her clothes were in tatters, her bare feet covered in sores, her eyes unnaturally bright.

She hailed me. I made to hurry on, supposing she was just some crazed beggar. But she caught my arm, drew me to a boulder and sat down there beside me. The wind dropped. The sun vanished. The air grew very still, like the hush before a thunderstorm. The wild woman began to speak in a clear, compelling voice.

This is what she told me:

I have disquieting dreams.

Valkyries blacken the sky: Wand-Maid, Battle-Maid, Brandisher-of-Spears. After them, comes the Corpse-Father, Odin with his gouged-out eye. He whispers softly, showers me with rings and circlets; but as soon as I lie with him, the world begins to die.

The North Lands freeze. Field and forest are smothered by ice, lacerated by screeching winds. Spring fails, summer never comes.

Where is the sun? Lost behind the horizon for three long years.

Endless war is raging. Mothers stoop to whoring. Sons kill their fathers, brothers slaughter brothers.

Wind Age, Wolf Age!

Hear the dwarfs groaning before their stone doors, hear the pale-beaked eagles screaming. What use now is Odin's wisdom that he once sucked from Mimir's Well? As for Thor, his girdle and hammer have melted, his might is no more. Even the mountains are crumbling.

Look. Fenrisulf has broken the iron fetters that bound him: the great wolf is gobbling up the moon. His venomous breath has already snuffed out the stars.

Now there is only darkness. We are all blind. Everything is lost.

Yggdrasil, the World Tree itself, sloughs its leaves, then withers. Jormungand, the World Serpent, springs awake, writhing in anger, ravenous for floods and earthquakes. The ground heaves as he rips the world apart. The sky bleeds like virgin flesh gashed by a rapist's sword.

There's nowhere to flee, for the giants have already breached the walls of Asgard. They're surging down the Shimmering Path to Midgard, their armour a mass of flames. Surt is at their head, and behind them rage an endless line of troll-wives.

Gold-toothed Heimdall blows his horn. On a battlefield, giants clash with the gods. The wolf is there too, gnashing his fangs. So is treacherous Loki with his simpering cronies. The thrashing World Serpent comes up behind, belching poison. As they fight, the earth cracks right open…

And the gods are annihilated, every one of them. Even

mighty Thor is poisoned by Jormungand's spittle. Even all-knowing Odin is swallowed by the Wolf's gaping jaws. It chokes and howls no more.

When at last the sun shows itself again, it is shrivelled and charred.

The immortal ones are dead. The world is void.

'And then?' I asked.

The soothsayer's eyes softened.

'I see the waters subside, uncovering green shoots. There are unsown crops ripening, awaiting those who are not yet born to harvest them. The perished sun gives birth to a daughter, who lightens the sky.

I see a single hall still standing, more brilliant than the stars, and the dark dragon rising to fly once more. The undead emerge from their hiding place and drink the morning dew.

They stumble over massive golden gaming pieces in the grass. They remember nothing – yet they say, "These are wondrous things! Surely in ancient days, they were owned by gods and giants?"

And at last, before I wake, I see their descendants inherit the earth.'

Thus spoke the wild woman.

For notes on this story, see page 324.

KENNINGS
THE POETS' IMAGES

What is a bear?
It's a forest-walker, winter-survivor, greedy-tooth, snarler;
dark one, yellow-bum, shrivelled-gut, scratcher.

What words should you use when speaking of water?
A river is a fish-trap forest or the mountains' falling noise.
The sea is a snow-road, land of sea-birds and whales, a
house of sands and seaweed, or the cool land's roaring belt.

And what of the ships that sail upon river or sea?
They are sea-steeds and wave-horses,
twisted-rope-bears and mast-top beasts.

How should you describe fire?
As slayer and destroyer of trees; brother of the wind.

And the wind itself?
That is the sails' enemy and the breaker of trees.

How should one describe the sky above?
It's the world of birds and weather; the sun's helmet, the wide winds' basin, the snow road's hall, the sun's dwelling and the world's high tent.

And the earth below?
That is the floor of the winds' hall, and the sea of animals.

What words should you use when speaking of people?
All people should be known first by their family line and descendants; and also by their actions.

A woman may be described by the wine that she serves; by her clothes and jewellery.

A man, on the other hand, may be classed by his wealth and how much he gives away. The battles he fights are the politics of steel, the iron-game or the true language of swords.

For notes, see page 326.

THE CURSE OF ANDVARI'S RING

'Odin immediately sent Loki
into the Land of the Dark Elves.
There he found the dwarf Andvari,
who had taken the shape of a fish in the water.
Loki caught him in his hands and threatened to kill him
unless he paid a ransom
of all the gold that he kept in his cave.
So they went to the dwarf's cave and
Andvari brought out all the gold he had,
and it was great riches.
The dwarf tried to conceal
one small gold ring under his hand –
but Loki saw it and ordered him to hand it over.
The dwarf begged him not to take this ring,
saying that if he kept it,
this ring would produce new wealth for himself.
Loki answered that the dwarf could not keep anything,
and he seized the ring from him.
However, as he went out, the dwarf cursed the ring
to bring death and ruin to everyone who ever possessed it.'

– The **Prose Edda**

SIGURD
THE DRAGON SLAYER

There was a man called Hreidmar, a sour-faced old brute, who kept a farm out on the edge of the wilderness with his three sons. No wife was ever seen there: the men had fallen into rough ways and sordid habits. Sometimes the sons dabbled in magic.

One night three strangers came knocking at Hreidmar's door. One was beardless and smirking. The second was striking and very tall, but shrouded in silence. The third was an ancient greybeard, wrapped in a vast, dusk-coloured cloak and a wide-brimmed hat that completely concealed his face.

'What do you want?' growled Hreidmar.

The greybeard answered: 'A place to sleep for the night.'

Hreidmar looked them up and down. 'I don't hand out free hospitality.'

The smirking one poked him with a sharply manicured finger. 'We wouldn't dream of asking you to,' he said. He held up his bag enticingly. 'We can pay you well – with food. We passed a waterfall on the way here, and the hunting around it was excellent. I caught a fish and some meat, both in a single blow.'

'All right, then,' said Hreidmar grudgingly. 'You can come in.'

They followed him into his hall. Hreidmar fetched his drinking horn, filled it parsimoniously with weak beer and handed it around. Then he said, 'Right: let's see what you've brought.'

The smirking one opened his bag and drew out a fat, oily salmon. Hreidmar nodded his approval. Then the smirking one winked at his companions – and pulled out a dead otter.

Hreidmar stared at the animal. The colour drained from his face. He let out a strangled gasp. His fingers clutched the air – then flew to his belt and grabbed his sword.

'You *murderers!*' he screeched. 'That otter isn't an ordinary animal – it's the transmuted form of my own son.' He stepped forward, seized the smirking one by the hair and held the sword blade to his throat. 'You've killed my son – you scumbags!'

At that moment, an inner door burst open and two young men rushed in.

'Fafnir,' cried Hreidmar, foaming at the mouth, 'Regin! These rats have just slaughtered your eldest brother. Remember how Otter changed into his animal-shape this morning to go fishing? Well, they stoned him dead – without any provocation – in cold blood. Even worse, they've conned their way in here with Otter's body and they're trying to trick us into eating him. Help me take revenge, boys. Let's kill them in return.'

Fafnir and Regin raised their fists. Hreidmar made to lunge at the strangers with his sword.

But before he could strike, the old greybeard suddenly bellowed: 'STOP!'

The word hung ominously in the air. For an instant, the greybeard's hat shifted – and they glimpsed a hole where one of his eyes should have been; and the other eye sunken like a dark, fathomless well.

'Be still,' he said. 'Listen. We are not what we seem, Hreidmar, not mortal men like you. We are gods. You won't find it easy to kill us.'

The three men froze. Sweat ran down Hreidmar's face. His hand began to tremble. Slowly, he lowered his weapon. At last he said hoarsely, 'I don't care a bull's turd who you are. If I can't kill you, I want proper reparation – a decent payout of blood-money.'

'How much?' said the greybeard.

Hreidmar looked wildly around, then snatched up the dead otter and slashed it open with his sword. The flesh slithered out in a pool of blood. 'Enough gold to fill this whole otter skin... No, more: enough to cover it as well.'

The greybeard nodded slowly. 'You shall keep two of us hostage until you have it,' he said. 'Meanwhile, my companion here, Loki, will fetch it right away.'

At the name 'Loki', the three men blenched. They stared at the smirking one; then turned to the one-eyed greybeard with horrified shudders of realisation.

Loki yawned and stretched lazily. 'Right, All-Father, I'll be off,' he said. 'Don't worry, Hreidmar, you'll get *exactly* what you deserve.'

Then, smooth and quick as a snake, he slipped away.

They waited a long time.

When Loki returned, he came staggering in clutching his

shirt, which bulged and rattled. He lifted its hem carefully and let a pile of fat gold nuggets drop from it onto the floor.

'Here you are, Hreidmar.'

'Where'd you steal this from, trickster?' said Hreidmar.

'Steal?' said Loki. 'You've got a cheek. This is a *gift*. Andvari Oinsson gave it to me. Very fitting, because – just like that son of yours who we killed by mistake – he's a shape-shifter. Andvari was pretending to be a fish. But I easily flushed him out from the underground pool where he was lurking, and coaxed him to turn back into a dwarf. We had a little chat, and he agreed to give me this.'

He started stuffing the nuggets into the otter skin. Once it was full, he stood it upright and used the rest of the gold to cover it.

'There,' he said, 'all done.'

'No it's not,' snarled Hreidmar. 'I said the gold must cover the corpse completely – but there's still an end of whisker showing.'

Loki clapped his hand over his mouth apologetically. 'So sorry! What a shame I've got no more nuggets to give you, Hreidmar. All I've got left is this.'

He reached into his shirt, pulled something out and held it up. 'The very last bit. Andvari's Ring.'

The ring gleamed exquisitely in the lamplight. Hreidmar's eyes widened.

'You can take it if you really want to,' said Loki. 'But let me give you some advice: don't. I didn't offer it initially because, well...you know how risky dwarf smithing can be. This ring's got a dangerous curse on it. It's doomed to destroy anyone who wears it.'

'You liar,' said Hreidmar. 'You're just trying to cheat me.

119

Give me the full payment!'

Loki shrugged and flicked his fingertips carelessly. The ring dropped onto the pile of gold.

'So,' he said. 'Is our debt settled?'

'I suppose so,' growled Hreidmar. 'Now get out.'

The greybeard nodded graciously. Loki guffawed. The silent one said nothing. They went through the door, the night swallowed them up, and they were gone.

Hreidmar shuddered, snatched up the Ring and thrust it onto his finger.

'So,' he said to his sons, 'I did well out of that little adventure.'

Regin said, 'But you've only got this gold because those brutes killed poor Otter.'

His father stroked the Ring. 'Huh! All that weird shape-shifting he went in for: that boy was asking for trouble.'

'Even so,' said Fafnir, 'we'll miss him.' He cleared his throat noisily. 'Now, Father, how about a share-out? Otter was our brother as well as your son, so we're entitled to some of the blood money.'

Hreidmar's face darkened. 'Entitled? Share-out? How dare you!'

'Give it to us, or I'll fight you for it!' roared Fafnir; and he began to slash about his father with his sword.

Hreidmar was no coward: quickly he drew his own sword and fought back. But despite his harsh words, he couldn't bring himself to harm his own offspring. So it wasn't long before Fafnir had won the fight, and his father, Hreidmar, lay dead.

'Two of our family killed in a single day,' said Regin. 'This isn't good.'

Fafnir shrugged and snorted. 'Don't waste any grief for *him*, brother,' he snarled. 'All our lives, he was a rotten, heartless father. He never gave any of us anything.'

He squatted down, forced the ring from Hreidmar's stiffening finger and pushed it onto his own. 'What a fine piece of jewellery.' He tapped the ring against his teeth and grinned. 'Well: I'll just pack up the rest of the gold, then I'll be off.'

'Hold on,' said Regin, 'you're not taking it all. I'm entitled to half of it.'

'Why, what have you done to win it?' said Fafnir. 'If you want some of this gold, you'll have to fight for it, like I did.'

Regin fingered his sword nervously, then backed away.

'You pathetic mouse,' said Fafnir. He turned to the pile of gold. Some of it had slipped out of the otter skin, over the edge of the table and onto the floor: there seemed to be more of it now than before. He fetched a sack and quickly shovelled the whole lot into it. Then he opened the door and strode out.

Regin watched him go.

Fafnir walked briskly along the road, then turned up onto the lonely, wind-swept slopes of a heath. He trudged on, dark against the pale dawn sky, bent under his precious load. He headed for a rocky hillside, dotted with fissures and caves. Here he stopped and tipped the gold into a hollow. Next, he turned his attention to the ring, making sure it was still wedged firmly on his finger.

Finally, muttering an eerie spell, he lay down on top of the gold – and transformed himself into a dragon.

Years went by.

All that time, Fafnir-dragon lay licking the Ring he wore on his claw, brooding on the gold. Month by month, the pile of gold around him grew ever bigger.

As for Regin, he stayed down in the valley and took up work as a blacksmith. He got commissions from kings and chieftains, so that people thought he was respectable. However, in truth he was twisted by grotesque cravings. For his nightmares were haunted by the gleaming of the Ring; and in his mind's eye, all he ever saw was Fafnir's treasure.

One day a young man called at Regin's workshop, asking for a job.

'What's your name?' demanded Regin.

'Sigurd,' replied the youth.

Regin looked him up and down. Sigurd was tall, broad shouldered as an ox, finely dressed and very handsome: judging by his appearance, he came from a wealthy family. Regin was suspicious. He said, 'You don't look as if you need to work for a living.'

'You're right,' answered Sigurd. 'My father was Sigmund of Hunland, the son of Volsung.'

'Whoa!' said Regin. 'Everyone's heard of Sigmund and Volsung. They were both exceptional warriors and truly mighty kings.'

'Unfortunately,' said Sigurd, 'I never knew either of them. My grandfather died long ago; and before I was born, my father was killed in battle. I've promised my mother I'll avenge his death. But to do this I need treasure to pay an army, and a sword to carry out the deed.'

'I understand your situation exactly,' said Regin. 'In fact, I've got a problem of outstanding vengeance myself, though it's less straightforward than yours.' He sniffed thoughtfully and narrowed his eyes. 'We might be able to help each other out. For a start, I'm a master blacksmith, so I can certainly make you the sword that you need. And if you'll use it first to kill *my* enemy, that's all the service I require from you: I guarantee to pay you really well.'

'Who do you want me to kill?' asked Sigurd.

'It isn't a man,' said Regin. 'It's a dragon.'

'That's an interesting challenge,' said Sigurd. 'What's the fee?'

Regin cleared his throat. 'This dragon's lying on a great hoard of treasure.'

'What sort of treasure?'

'Gold,' said Regin. 'Also, on his claw he wears a wonderful magic ring.'

'Magic in what way?' said Sigurd.

'The ring has power to make the gold increase,' said Regin. 'When the dragon first went to the wild heath where he lives, he only had a single bag of gold. Now the treasure is piled right up to the top of his lair. If you kill the dragon, I'll give you a generous share of it.'

'I'm badly tempted by this,' said Sigurd. 'So how about this special sword?'

'Come into my smithy,' said Regin. 'I'll make you one straightaway.'

'Wait,' said Sigurd. 'It's not as simple as you think. You see, the sword I need can't be made from raw iron: you have to use this.'

He went to his horse and pulled two objects from the

saddlebag: a long, rusted blade; and a broken hilt richly ornamented with precious stones.

'These two fragments once formed my father Sigmund's sword,' said Sigurd. 'For many years it was indestructible and brought him much victory and glory. However, when he was fighting his last battle, a one-eyed old man approached him, brandishing a spear. My father assumed he was one of the enemy, so he struck the spear with this sword. To his astonishment, his opponent's spear was undamaged – but my father's sword snapped clean in two. Soon after that, his lifetime of good luck came to an end and he was mortally wounded by the enemy. My mother believes that one-eyed spear bearer was Odin himself; and that he was summoning my father in person to take his place in Slain Hall.'

'A magnificent way to die,' said Regin. He smiled wryly. 'And it confirms that our fates must be entwined. Because I believe that my family too once had unsettling dealings with Odin.'

Sigurd continued, 'While my father lay bleeding to death, he ordered my mother to give these fragments to his unborn son – that's me – to be fashioned into a new sword. Any new weapon forged from them will surely be invincible, since the fragments are hallowed by Odin's touch.'

'I'm honoured to work with them,' said Regin, 'and I'll do my best.'

Making the new sword wasn't a task to be rushed. The sun rose and sank many times, the moon waxed and waned as Regin melted the fragments in the fire, fused them into a single piece of steel, filed it and tempered it. At long last an exceptional weapon emerged, seven spans long, with a blade so finely honed and polished that flames seemed to leap from its edge.

Sigurd said nothing, but took the sword eagerly to test it. First he smashed it down onto Regin's anvil: it split the iron clean in two. Then he went to the water's edge, dropped a tuft of wool into the river and struck it with the sword as it floated on the current: the wool was cleanly shredded.

'You've done a good job,' he said. 'Now let's test it on this dragon of yours. Show me where he's lurking.'

They saddled horses and Regin led Sigurd up to a wild heath. Clouds of stinging midges hung over its fetid swamps. The peat was almost barren, and the few plants dotting it were charred and shrivelled. Regin stopped by a broad track, formed by the regular tramping of gigantic feet, and pointed towards a distant hill.

'That's the way to the dragon's lair,' he said. 'Every day he paces down this path to that cliff at the far end, and leans over it to take a drink. To give you an idea of how big he is, the water lies thirty fathoms below the edge.'

'That's quite a size,' said Sigurd. 'Even with this sword you've made me, I'm not certain I can overcome him by fighting single handed, face to face.'

'Best not to try,' said Regin. 'It would be wiser to use some cunning. Well, I don't want to get in your way, so I'll leave you to it.'

When he was gone, Sigurd looked carefully around the desolate landscape, pondering his plans. He went to the middle of the dragon's track, cut a circle in the peat with his sword and used his bare hands to dig out a deep pit. He lowered himself into it, covered the top with branches of withered heather, and settled down to wait.

Very soon the earth began to quiver. The air thickened

with dark, putrid smoke and blood-curdling howls.

Slowly, the dragon came heaving towards him, belching out fire. His overstuffed, warty belly scraped along the ground. When he reached the pit, his foul stench grew so strong that Sigurd could hardly breathe. Yet he did not hesitate or falter. He leaped up at once and thrust his sword straight into the dragon's breast.

The dragon shrieked. Black and green venom gushed from his wound. He staggered, his claws grappling wildly at the damp air. He roared; then began to croak in a human voice: 'You! Who dares to attack me?'

Sigurd answered quickly: 'Who am I? Hah! I am the Noble Beast, the son of No One.'

'Do you really think that concealing your name will save you from your inevitable fate?' the dragon mocked him. 'You're after my treasure, aren't you? And most of all, my magic ring. Well, let me warn you, Noble Beast, they will cause you an end every bit as gruesome and shameful as my own. There is only one way to escape this evil destiny: flee now and forget your promised reward!'

Then, with a fearsome groan, the dragon keeled over and died.

The next moment, Sigurd heard a shout. He turned, and saw Regin striding towards him.

'Right,' said Regin. 'I can tell you everything now. That dragon was really a man. He'd changed his shape by magic. His name was Fafnir and he was my brother. *You killed him.*'

'Only because you begged me to,' said Sigurd. 'You even forged a sword to ensure I didn't fail.'

'Nevertheless,' said Regin, 'he's my kin and you're his killer, so you owe me reparation. And don't expect to get away with it, just because you're a king's son: if you don't pay up, I'll get you outlawed.'

Sigurd said carefully, 'I don't think much of this ruse; but now I know the truth, I'm honour bound to accept my obligation. How much do you want?'

'Here are the terms,' said Regin. 'Before we discuss what treasure you owe me, you must carry out a simple task. Roast the dragon's heart over a fire until it's tender enough for me to eat. But don't you dare steal any of it for yourself, or even taste it.'

'That's bizarre,' said Sigurd. 'But I'm obliged to do it.'

Regin sloped off. Sigurd cut the dragon's heart from the corpse. Then he lit a fire and set the heart on top of the flames. He waited for it to cook, squatting between the gnarled roots of a tree. In accordance with Regin's prohibition, he carefully used twigs to withdraw the monstrous flesh and test if it was tender. However, as he did so, some of the juices ran free and badly scalded him. He gave a yelp of pain and jerked his hand unwittingly to his mouth to soothe it.

As soon as the dragon juice touched his lips, a curious thing happened. He found that he could understand the birds twittering in the branches above him, as if they too were using human speech.

There sits a great hero, said one. *What a pity he's not as wise as he is valiant.*

Exactly, said another bird. *Then he wouldn't so naively obey the swindler who deceived him.*

Why doesn't he eat the whole dragon heart himself? said a third. *Doesn't he want to double his strength and dazzle the world with his power?*

Sigurd did not wait to hear any more. He snatched the whole roasted heart from the ground where it had fallen and gobbled it greedily down.

At once, an eerie vigour rushed recklessly through his veins. He felt strong enough to uproot a mountain, so fearless he would gladly wrestle a whole troop of giants.

As he savoured it, Regin came slinking back. His eyes shifted over the scene, and saw that his repulsive prize was lost.

The two men faced each other. Sigurd, fortified beyond human strength by his meal, snatched up his sword with the dragon's blood still dripping from its blade. He whipped it through the air – and struck the blacksmith dead.

Then he turned his back on the scene and ran towards Fafnir's den to seize the treasure hoard. However, to reach it, he had to step past the carcass of the dragon. As he did so, for the first time his eyes fell upon Andvari's Ring. Bright as a star it flashed up at him, blindingly bewitching.

'So,' he thought, 'here's the ring that both Regin and the dragon mentioned. What a prize! I'd be a fool to heed the dragon's warning: I'm bound to die some time, but so long as I live, I vow to enjoy all the riches I can lay my hands on!'

In a frenzy of desire, he snatched at the ring – found it stuck fast – slashed at the dragon's claw until the ring came free – and at once rammed it firmly onto his own finger.

It was a perfect fit.

He fetched his horse from the edge of the heath and galloped on to the dragon's lair. This was built into a desolate, windswept hillside and defended by heavy iron gates; but his sword easily smashed them down. Inside Sigurd found all the golden nuggets which Loki had once paid to Hreidmar – multiplied a thousand times over by the power of Andvari's Ring. Hastily, he crammed as many as he could into his saddlebags, then mounted his horse and triumphantly rode away.

And there, for now, we must leave this hero, exultant with victory and the taste of dragon-flesh, proud possessor of both boundless treasure and the ominous curse of Andvari's Ring. Many perils and adventures still lay ahead of him: forests and lonely peaks, castles and kingdoms, lust and betrayal, shape-shifting, avarice and the cunning of queens.

But that is another story.

For note on this story, see page 327

CRUEL AND SWEET IS A WOMAN'S REVENGE

This is the story of two noblewomen who were not afraid of the sword. They lived long ago in the age of the mightiest warriors, in the lands that lie far south of here and east of the River Rhine.

One was Brynhild, daughter of King Budli of Hunland. Her brother was the infamous tyrant Atli: he comes into the story later.

The other was Gudrun, princess of a neighbouring kingdom where even the winters were warm. Her parents were King Gjuki and Queen Grimhild; and she had three brothers called Gunnar, Hogni and Gutthorm. We'll hear more about these three too.

Brynhild was like her brother – restless and stout-hearted – and she despised the decorum expected of her at court. So as soon as she was full grown, she borrowed weapons and armour and disguised herself as a man. She even went off to join a war. She fought so bravely that no one guessed her deception.

However, Odin on high watches over everyone and sees through all concealments. He came down into our world, masked as a bent, old, one-eyed greybeard. While Brynhild was in the thick of battle, he brushed past her like a shadow and left her with this whisper:

You impress me, shield-maiden, so I grant you the honour of working for me. Your task shall be to strike down those warriors whom I choose to die. Then you must lead them across the Shimmering Bridge to drink mead with me in Slain Hall.

In this way, Brynhild became one of Odin's valkyries. But her glory did not last long, for one day, in a battle between two kings, she struck dead the wrong man – a grave mistake! Odin showed no mercy. He cast her out and imprisoned her on the mountain of Hindafjall, in a lonely hall guarded by a rampart of shields and an unquenchable circle of flames. He ordered Brynhild to lie upon a great bed that stood within, still fully clad in armour.

'Wait for the man who knows no fear,' he said. Then he stabbed her hand with a sleeping-thorn and Brynhild sank into oblivion.

Time went by.

Suddenly a sword blade broke into Brynhild's dreams, slashing through her armour. She opened her eyes and saw a stranger standing over her: a strong, handsome man with a penetrating gaze.

'Intruder!' she cried. 'How did you break through my master's fire?'

'Easily,' he answered.

'What is your name?'

131

For a moment he seemed to hesitate. Then he said, 'You may know me as Gunnar, the son of King Gjuki.'

'Why have you come?'

'To make you my bride.'

'You reckless fool!' she cried. 'I don't want a husband. I won't be a submissive lover. Doesn't that unnerve you?'

'No,' he answered. 'I have no fear of anything.'

Brynhild sighed. 'Odin has surely fated our meeting, so I dare not refuse you.'

'Then let me further prove that I am worthy of you,' he said.

He lay down beside her, and gently cut away her corselet with his sword. Brynhild accepted his embrace willingly, for she had been lonely for too long. There was much passion between them; and by the end of the night he had satisfied her so well that she willingly pledged herself to him. They agreed to marry as soon as Brynhild was released by Odin. Then her lover rose, dressed and prepared to leave.

'Wait,' said Brynhild. 'Where's my morning gift, to seal your promise?'

'As soon as you come to my father's hall,' he said, 'I'll give you half my treasure.'

'That's generous,' she said. 'Even so, I want a small token from you now.' Her eyes narrowed. 'Give me that golden ring you wear on your finger.'

'No,' he said.

Now she became insistent: 'But it's my right to have a gift. And it would look so much finer on my hand than on yours.'

'I can't give you this, Brynhild,' he said. 'It isn't an ordinary piece of jewellery, but Andvari's Ring, the work of mountain dwarfs. It's dangerous. All who wore it before me have suffered from its curse.'

'Pah!' she said. 'This supposed curse has obviously done *you* no harm, so what evil could it bring to me? Let me have it, Gunnar.'

He shook his head. She implored him to change his mind, over and over. Finally, he was so inflamed by her and so maddened by her nagging, that he pulled the ring from his finger and slipped it onto hers.

Then Brynhild let him go.

It has already been told that Gunnar was the eldest brother of the other heroine of this story, Gudrun. Up until then, Gudrun had enjoyed a tranquil life and a lucky one – for she was married to none other than the illustrious hero Sigurd, killer of a fierce dragon and owner of that dragon's treasure.

Gunnar and Sigurd were very friendly and had sworn an oath of allegiance to each other by mingling their blood. They were so close that Sigurd had accompanied Gunnar on his quest to win Brynhild from her fiery fortress on Hindafjall.

Gudrun had been uneasy about this and she was greatly relieved when Sigurd returned safely. However, she soon noticed that the expedition had caused an unsettling change in her husband. His desire for her seemed less urgent, and his eyes were glazed like one who constantly relives a dream. In despair, she asked her mother, Queen Grimhild, for help.

Grimhild said nothing to Sigurd. Instead she took her son Gunnar aside and questioned him closely about what had happened on Hindafjall. Very soon Gunnar made the most extraordinary confession.

'I did not really break into Brynhild's fortress myself,' he said. 'Sigurd did it for me. For my horse refused to cross the supernatural fire that surrounded it; but Sigurd's horse had no fear of the flames so long as he was its rider. So Sigurd conjured up an enchantment that enabled us to exchange shapes. He looked exactly like me in every way; and in this form he entered Brynhild's fortress, bedded her and won her promise on my behalf. As you see me, now we are back in our true forms. I am the happiest man alive that soon Brynhild will be my wife, and she will never know what happened. But I am sorry the adventure has unsettled Sigurd and made him neglect my sister.'

Queen Grimhild was intrigued but not too concerned. For she too was skilled in the magic arts and knew a quick cure for Sigurd's unfaithfulness. She went to her store of medicinal herbs and mixed some carefully chosen ones into a drinking-horn full of strong wine. This she proffered to Sigurd, saying, 'Here's a drink to honour your undying gallantry, son-in-law!'

Sigurd accepted the compliment and emptied the horn in a single draught. However, unbeknown to him, it was really a potion of forgetfulness. Thus, as soon as he had swallowed it, his mind began to drift. He still knew himself, and his valour was undiminished; but the memory of his night with Brynhild was washed swift and clean away.

In due course, Brynhild came to King Gjuki's hall, where her wedding to Gunnar was celebrated with a magnificent feast.

In this way, Brynhild and Gudrun were now thrown together as sisters-in-law.

Unfortunately, they had nothing in common, for Brynhild was a war-like valkyrie, whilst Gudrun was a demure and conventional princess. Relations between them were very strained.

One day the two women both decided to go and bathe. They walked down to the river together but made little conversation. After a while, Brynhild waded upstream.

'Where are you going?' called Gudrun.

'I'm making sure I use the water before it reaches you,' Brynhild answered. 'It's my right to do so, for I am superior to you.'

'Whatever makes you think that?' retorted Gudrun.

'Because I have the more valiant husband,' said Brynhild.

'Nonsense!' said Gudrun. 'My Sigurd is a dragon killer. Gunnar has never achieved such a mighty deed.'

'Oh, many men kill dragons,' said Brynhild dismissively. 'But only Gunnar had the courage to ride through Odin's impenetrable fire and rescue me from Hindafjall.'

'Are you sure?' said Gudrun. 'Look at your ring, Brynhild – the one you say Gunnar gave you as your morning gift. It's the split image of a ring that *Sigurd* used to wear. Strangely enough, his own ring disappeared on the very night he helped Gunnar rescue you. I've asked him many times to explain how he lost it, but never had a satisfactory answer. I'm starting to suspect it was really Sigurd – *my* husband, not yours – who breached Odin's flames to seduce you, and thus gave you that ring.'

'You liar!' cried Brynhild.

She rose haughtily from the river and hastened home,

where she took to her bed and would not speak to anyone. When Gunnar came to placate her, she refused to lie with him, and confronted him with Gudrun's accusation:

'I was lured here to marry you by a cruel conspiracy. Your caresses have never given me any pleasure since our wedding, and no wonder, for it was Sigurd – not you – who once made love to me so sweetly on Hindafjall. I can't bear the torment of looking at him, knowing that it's your sister who now enjoys him every night. Gunnar, I want you to kill Sigurd!'

Gunnar did not deny anything. All he said was, 'I can't kill Sigurd, I can't even fight him, because we're sworn blood brothers. We're bound together by a sacred oath made in Odin's name.'

Brynhild swept out with a snarl of contempt and went prowling round the hall and its outbuildings. Eventually she cornered Gunnar's younger brothers, Hogni and Gutthorm.

'Listen,' she hissed. 'Sigurd is a rapist and a pimp. He disguised himself to ravish me, then sold me on to Gunnar. And in doing this he betrayed Gudrun. He's brought shame upon your family!'

Hogni and Gutthorm shook their heads incredulously and shrank back. Brynhild circled them, tossing her hair.

'It's true,' she said. 'Gunnar admits it, but because of an oath, he can't kill Sigurd, so you two must do it instead.'

'Not me,' said Hogni quickly. 'I'm Sigurd's blood brother too.'

Brynhild turned to Gutthorm. He was still only a youth, too young to swear on Odin's name. At first he just flushed and said nothing. But when Hogni turned away, he met Brynhild's eye and nodded.

That night, Gutthorm went to Brynhild. In the darkness she fed him snake-meat and wolf-flesh until he was slavering with bloodlust. Then she led him to Sigurd's bed.

Sigurd was sleeping quietly beside Gudrun. His unsheathed sword lay across his feet – the same weapon with which once he had killed a dragon. Brynhild gazed at him wretchedly for a long moment. Then she seized the sword and pressed it into Gutthorm's hand.

Gutthorm raised it and struck Sigurd – so hard that the blade went right through him, pinning him to the bed. Sigurd cried out and jerked awake as blood spilled from his wound. He heaved the sword from his mutilated body and at once hurled it back at Gutthorm, slicing the youth in half. For an agonised moment, Sigurd looked with sudden remembrance at Brynhild. Then he drew his last breath and died.

Now Gudrun awoke, screaming, in a pool of her husband's blood. Gunnar and Hogni, her two surviving brothers, came running. Hogni ran to comfort her, but Gunnar turned to Brynhild.

'What have you done?' he cried. 'A curse upon you!'

'I'm cursed already,' she answered coldly.

She ran to her storage chest, drew from it her old suit of armour and pulled it on. The corselet still dangled open from where Sigurd's sword had teasingly slashed it on Hindafjall. Now she snatched up that same sword and stabbed herself with it.

'Where are my maids?' she shrieked. 'Where are my slave girls? Come to me, hurry!'

They rushed to her.

'Don't try to heal my wound,' she told them, 'for I long

to die. But you, inoffensive women, you shall inherit everything I have. You take my furs; you have my fine linen; and you my silks. Golden cups for you – and to you I leave my jewellery. Take it all from me, then go!'

They accepted her gifts and fled.

Brynhild was staggering crazily, her face white as sea-bleached bone, her dress sopping with blood. 'Don't pretend you're upset,' she hissed at Gunnar. 'We both regret our marriage. Even so, here's a parting gift.'

She wrenched off Andvari's Ring, stumbled up to Gunnar, seized his hand and forced it onto his finger. 'Here, it's yours now. May the suffering it brings you be even worse than mine!'

And with those bitter words, Brynhild died.

At the funeral that followed, Sigurd and Brynhild were laid on separate pyres. But the flames consumed them side by side.

Soon after this, King Gjuki died. Gunnar and Hogni became joint rulers of the kingdom. Their wealth was beyond compare, for being Sigurd's blood brothers, they inherited all the treasure he once won from the dragon.

Andvari's Ring had once been possessed by the dragon too. It was a fine trophy but Gunnar wore it uneasily.

As for Gudrun, her heart was broken. She slipped out quietly and travelled north for many days, through forest and wilderness, to the realm of Denmark. There she found sanctuary with another noblewoman who gave her comfort in the time-honoured way of women, stitching sorrow and bitterness into exquisite golden embroideries.

Seven seasons passed. Then Gudrun's mother, Queen Grimhild, tracked her down.

'It's time to stop grieving and take a new husband,' said she. 'I've had an offer of marriage for you.'

Gudrun asked who it was.

'Atli Budlisson,' said Grimhild.

'But he's the brother of Brynhild!' said Gudrun. 'If I married him, I'd be sanctioning Sigurd's murder.'

'Pah! Don't let emotion get the better of common sense,' said Queen Grimhild. 'Of course you miss Sigurd, for he was once the greatest champion alive; but everyone says that Atli has superseded him, and he'll keep you in the manner you're accustomed to, or even better. He's become king of the Huns and he's conquering people all over the world. No army can withstand him – which makes a problem for us, because he's declared a feud against our family. He blames us for Brynhild's death. However, he's willing to make peace if you'll marry him.'

Gudrun refused. But Queen Grimhild, anticipating this, had come armed with another secret potion, a murky brew blended from earth, sea and a child's blood. Once Gudrun had been persuaded to drink it, she sighed and agreed to accept Atli the Hun's proposal.

'It seems I can't avoid this,' she said. 'But I predict that Atli will bring even more trouble to our family than his sister did.'

The wedding of Gudrun to Atli was not a happy one. Gudrun made it clear that she had no affection for her second husband. Nevertheless, Atli claimed he had made peace with her family. To prove it, he sent a messenger to Gunnar and Hogni, inviting them to a feast.

Gudrun did not trust him. So she pulled the wedding band from her finger, bound it with wolf hair as a sign of danger and cut it with these ominous runes:

TREACHERY: DO NOT COME

Then she waylaid the messenger as he was leaving on his errand, and ordered him to present this gift to her brothers.

Unfortunately, during the journey the messenger examined the band. When he read the runes, he was outraged to realise Gudrun's disloyalty to his master. So he scratched out her message and cut over it these new runes of his own:

ATLI GIVES WARM WELCOME.

Eventually, the messenger arrived at Gunnar and Hogni's hall. At first they were wary of Atli's invitation, but when they saw the fraudulent message carved into Gudrun's wedding band, they changed their minds. However, Gunnar's new wife and Hogni's wife were less persuaded. They saw that the runes had been altered, and their dreams turned dark with foreboding.

'It's a trap,' they warned. 'Don't go.'

As is often the case in such matters, the men ignored their wives' good advice. They were, however, persuaded to take two precautions. Firstly, they called up an army of warriors to support them; and secondly, they cast Sigurd's treasure into the deepest waters of the River Rhine – and with it, Andvari's Ring.

Despite this, Gunnar did not escape the ring's curse.

For as soon as he and Hogni arrived at Atli's hall, they were ambushed. Their army fought back fiercely, but nearly all of them were killed. Finally both Gunnar and Hogni were captured, bound in chains and dragged before King Atli and Queen Gudrun.

It was Gudrun who spoke first: 'My brothers, why did you ignore my warning? Surely you knew it was impossible to overcome Atli's might?'

Gunnar and Hogni were shamed and had no answer. They demanded of Atli: 'What are the terms of this latest quarrel against us?'

'Oh, just another aspect of the same old score,' said Atli. 'My late sister Brynhild was deceitfully seduced by Sigurd, and he owned a magnificent treasure. If he had married her as was his duty – instead of palming her off on a worm like you – half that treasure would have been hers and passed into my family. Give it to me.'

'It's not ours to give,' said Gunnar. 'The waters have it now.'

'A devious trick,' said Atli. 'Tell me where it's concealed and I shall let you live.'

'Never,' said Gunnar. 'And don't think you'll gain it by killing us, for my brother and I are the only ones in the world who know its location.'

'Indeed?' said Atli. 'Well, at least your deaths will punish you – and your sister too, for her coldness to me in our marital bed. You first, Hogni. I'll have my men cut out your heart while you're still alive.'

'Enjoy the spectacle,' answered Hogni. 'I won't add to your fun by begging you to spare me.'

So Atli had his men slowly cut a deep incision into

Hogni's chest, then pull out his heart even while it was still beating. Hogni did not flinch or cry out, but died laughing.

This enraged Atli even more. He had Gunnar strung up on a gallows, above a pit filled with a knot of thrashing, hissing vipers. Atli jeered at him for a few moments then strode away to relieve himself.

At once, Gudrun seized her chance: she ran to the snake-pit and tossed Gunnar a harp. Though his hands were bound to the gallows, he caught the harp deftly between his feet and began to pluck it with his toes. He played such an exquisite melody that the courtiers watching his ordeal ceased their mockery and began to weep. The vipers were affected too, and grew drowsy...

Until suddenly, one of the snakes roused itself and reared up. It bit Gunnar below the breastbone and sank its fangs relentlessly into his liver. In this way, slowly and painfully, he died.

Now Gudrun understood that her erstwhile enemy, Brynhild, had been wiser than she realised. There was no advantage in a woman displaying meekness, but everything to be gained by taking up arms. Revenge was both urgent and irresistible.

So when Atli taunted her about her brothers' deaths, she gave him no reaction. Instead she feigned loyalty and organised a feast as if she wished to celebrate Atli's victory over them. At the feast, she made a great show of attending to Atli, endlessly topping up his drinking horn until he was helplessly drunk. Then, before the assembled court, she hauled him onto a bench, disrobed him and ostentatiously caressed him. When he was helpless with desire, she snatched up his sword and stabbed him.

'What a pity you'll miss your own funeral,' she hissed. 'It's going to be magnificent.'

Gudrun was as good as her word. She drove the hounds outside, slammed the door shut behind her and flung a firebrand into the thatch. At once the hall exploded into a dazzling blaze of flames.

By morning Gudrun had vanished into the sea. And the once unassailable might of Atli the Hun was nothing but a pile of ashes.

For notes on this story, see page 331.

RIDDLES

Who is the great one that glides over the earth,
swallowing sun, wood and water?
He fears no one but the wind.
Solve my riddle!
>   *Your riddle's good but I've guessed the answer.*
>   *It's the fog.*
>   *None but the wind can chase him away.*

What bloody-backed beast shelters brave men,
laying its body against its lord's left hand?
>   *Your riddle's good but I've guessed the answer.*
>   *It's a shield.*

Who are those two tall women on the wild fells?
One has borne a child by the other
yet no man has ever touched them.

> *Your riddle's good but I've guessed the answer.*
> *They are two angelica stalks standing side by side*
> *with a shoot coming up between them.*

Who lives on the high mountains?
What falls in the deep dales?
Who lives without air?
What is never silent?

> *Your riddles are good but I've guessed them all.*
> *It is the raven,*
> *the dew,*
> *the fish*
> *and the roaring waterfall*

Who are the two
who run on ten feet?
They have three eyes
but only one tail.
Solve my riddle!

> *Your riddle's good, but I've guessed the answer.*
> *It's Odin riding on Sleipnir.*

For notes, see page 334.

NOBLES
FARMERS
SLAVES
&
VILLAINS

'The behaviour of young men today
is not what it was when I was young.
In those days men hankered after deeds of daring,
either by going raiding
or by winning wealth and honour through exploits
in which there was some element of danger.
But nowadays, young men want to be stay-at-homes,
and sit by the fire
and stuff their stomachs with mead and ale;
and so it is that manliness and bravery are on the wane.'

– Ketil the Large,
son of Orm Broken-Shell, a 9th Century Norwegian
quoted in *Vatnsdaela Saga*

IN PRAISE OF SLAVES, PEASANTS AND NOBLES

Let's hear it for the slaves!

Stand up, Dumpy, Frumpy and Stumpy. Show us your muscles, Sluggard and Big Mouth; and you, Horse-Fly, Fatso and Brawny. Don't be shy, Chatterbox, Crane Legs and Crooked Nose. Give us a wave, Tatty Coat, Screamer, Shagger and Stink.

Where would we be without you? You come from the great-grandparents of all workers. Yes, you, with your bent backs and your fat fingers, your ugly faces, sunburned arms and clomping feet. What do we care if you're spattered in mud? You're so strong. You're so willing.

There you go all day, dragging home firewood, cleaning pig-styes, digging peat and smothering the fields with dung. Guzzle down your bone soup, stuff yourselves with coarse bread. Gobble up so you can work more, more, more.

Praise the wise god who made you. Spend all your spare time rolling in the hay – we need you to keep breeding!

Come, friends, let's have a top-up, and drink a hearty toast to our slaves!

Now let's hear it for the peasants!

Welcome to the feast, good people! Yes, you: Broad Shoulders, Smith and Farmer; Short Beard, Householder, Owner and Thane. You're the salt of the earth, the backbone of our country. Make yourselves at home, Lass and Bride, Missy and Damsel, Bashful, Lively, Daughter-in-Law and Dame. You all keep house so splendidly.

You're bred from the grandparents of diligence and respectability. You're always so well groomed and neatly dressed, always so practical and busy. You keep sworn promises with true honour.

Farmers, freeholders, how patiently you tame your oxen; you set them to pull the plough that your own hands crafted. Your carts roll over the ground as smoothly as water. Though your cottages are simple, they're filled with easy cheer.

Farmwives, the sound of your jingling keys reminds us that all is well. The scent of fresh bread and simmering meat drifts from your homes, making us weak with desire. We're dazzled by the speed of your spinning and weaving.

Praise the wise god who made you, solid, dependable people. Linger under coverlets embroidered by your own hands, produce large families and raise them well.

Peasants, we raise a hearty toast to you all!

There, our duty's done. Now, above all, let us praise our noble lady and her earl!

My lady Capable: we all admire your snow-white neck, your wisdom and your wit. Your trailing linen dress is dyed the colour of summer skies. Your headdress is magnificent.

The brooches pinned to your bosom are shimmering silver. All the furnishings in this great hall bear the mark of your slim, dainty fingers.

My lord, my leader: your fair hair and glowing cheeks testify fine breeding. Men do not hesitate to kneel before you, for your eyes flare grim and fierce as a dragon's. Your father raised you with restrained and courtly manners; your mother nourished you on rich meats, white loaves and pitchers of southern wine, served upon crisp ironed linen. Your playthings were bows, javelins, shields and spears; at a tender age your sword became an extension of your powerful right arm. Your eye is true, your aim certain. Your knowledge of runes is equal to All-Father's. As soon as you came of age, you rode boldly through mountains, forests and dales to claim the twice-nine estates which now bow before your rule.

Your children are all males: Well Born and Heir, Kindred, Boy, Offspring, Kinsman, Kin and Son. They are the fastest swimmers, the craftiest at table games. Under your calm guidance they tame horses, carve shields, quench fires, calm seas and even learn the speech of birds.

Generously, you hand out treasure and horses, and wisely too. Ah, soother of sorrows, most generous giver of rings! Your influence has spread so far that enemies throughout the world tremble at the very mention of your name.

My earl, my lady, your honoured family: the whole world raises a hearty toast to you all!

For notes, see page 335.

KING GEIRROD
THE MAGNIFICENT

There was a king called Hraudning, who had two young sons. The elder was called Agnar, and he was everything a father could ask for: confident, audacious and above all courteous. The younger boy, Geirrod, on the other hand was given to objectionable silence and hostile moods.

One day, Agnar took his brother fishing out on the open sea. Just as they lowered their nets, a terrible gale blew up, so sudden that it seemed like bewitchment, with gigantic waves that tossed their small boat about like a feather. Geirrod cursed his brother for leading him into such danger. However, they both managed to cling on through the tempest until at last the tide drew them in to land and smashed the boat against a cliff, wrecking it completely.

They survived without serious injury, and scrambled from the wreckage and over the rocks to a lonely beach. It was littered with shells and seaweed, and overlooked by a single tumbledown cottage. Shivering with cold and exhaustion, they made their way towards it and knocked upon the door.

It was opened at once by a bent old peasant woman. 'Ah, so you've arrived,' said she with a smile. 'We were expecting you. Come in, my lads, and stay with us until the winter storms are over.'

Being princes raised in luxury, they hesitated to enter such a humble dwelling. However, they had no idea where they were or what else they could do, so they stepped inside. In a thick gloom softened only by a single lamp, they made out an old greybeard warming his feet beside a hearty fire. He too welcomed them warmly, and told them to sit opposite him on the plain, uncushioned wall-benches. The old woman busied herself, cooking a meal of bone-soup and coarse bread, while the old man talked to them softly. When they had eaten their fill, the exhausted boys wrapped themselves in the moth-eaten furs they were offered, then slept on the benches beside their hosts.

The storm continued day after day, endlessly raining and snowing amidst a driving wind. It raged so strongly that the old woman forbade Agnar and Geirrod even to think of trying to find their way home. Besides, their hosts had no boat of their own that they could borrow; and though the old man promised to build them a new one, he was a slow worker. Thus they were compelled to stay in the austere cottage as month after month went by.

The old woman treated Agnar with particular kindness, saying she had always longed to be blessed with a stout-hearted son like him. She said to the old man, 'When Agnar comes to inherit his father's kingdom, I'm sure he'll rule it wisely.'

'What do you say to that?' the old man asked Geirrod. 'No doubt you are proud of your elder brother, and look forward to serving under him.'

'I'm not and I don't,' he replied with a scowl. 'Just

because I was born after him, doesn't mean that I'll grow up to be any less powerful.'

The old man laughed. 'Ambition is admirable,' he said. 'But take care to achieve it wisely, lest your deeds come back to haunt you.'

When spring came, the sea calmed. One morning, the old man said to the princes, 'I've finished building your new boat.' He led them down to the beach.

'Run ahead, Agnar, and untie the ropes that hold the boat to its mooring,' he said. 'Not you, Geirrod: walk beside me right to the shore, for I have some advice to give you.'

The old man spoke earnestly and at length to Geirrod. From afar, Agnar saw his brother nodding, then mouthing some words as if making a vow, while the old man listened intently. At last, Geirrod came running down the beach and climbed into the boat beside him. Soon they were making good headway over the waves.

'What did the old man say to you on the beach?' said Agnar.

Geirrod guffawed and said, 'I'm not allowed to tell you; but you'll find out soon enough.'

'It's not wise to keep secrets from your own brother,' said Agnar; but he did not press him.

They rowed on steadily. Soon a familiar coastline came into sight, and they drew into the jetty below their father's hall.

'Home!' cried Agnar. 'How good it is to be back in our own kingdom.'

'And I shall be the first to step ashore in it,' said Geirrod.

He seized the rope, hurled it over a post to moor the boat, and jumped out.

Ah, if only Agnar had been less gallant, if only he had stopped his younger brother from pushing ahead of him. For as soon as Geirrod's feet touched dry land, he leaned over, punched Agnar to the floor of the boat, seized the oars and tossed them into the deep. Then he drew his knife, sliced through the mooring rope, and shoved the boat out onto the ebbing tide, back towards the open sea.

'What are you doing, fool?' Agnar shouted. 'How am I supposed to come ashore? Throw me a rope, brother – haul me in!'

'Never,' Geirrod called back. 'I'm getting rid of you. Now I can reveal what the old man told me. He said that *I* am superior to you, and *I* should be our father's heir. As for you – go and live with the troll-wives!'

At that moment the sea began to swell and a strong current caught hold of the boat, tossing it around and sweeping Agnar away. Nobody else was near to see what happened, nobody heard his cries as he was carried to the horizon and vanished beyond its edge. He was never seen in that realm again, and it is not told where he washed up or what became of him.

Geirrod, meanwhile, turned his back and walked proudly up to King Hraudning's hall. Courtiers came running out to meet him, shouting with amazement and joy to see that he was still alive.

'Where is my father, King Hraudning?' Geirrod asked.

'Dead,' they answered. 'Where is your elder brother, Agnar?'

'Dead too,' he lied.

'Then you are the new king,' the courtiers said.

They hurried him into the hall, enthroned him on the high-seat and invited him to give them orders. Thus began the terrible reign of King Geirrod the Magnificent.

Geirrod ruled his kingdom ungenerously and with an iron hand. He kept all but his most senior followers on short rations and behaved abusively to any unfortunate passing travellers who sought lodging with him. He arranged his court in such a way that it was impossible for any to oppose him.

He married and had a son. In a malicious twist, he named this boy Agnar the Younger, admitting that was the name of his long-lost uncle, but never revealing the truth of how he went missing.

One day, a strange woman in a ragged cloak arrived at the door of Geirrod's hall, asking for the king.

'Go away,' the guards snarled at her. 'Outsiders aren't welcome here.'

'Don't worry,' the woman answered, 'I'm not seeking a bed or even a meal. I'm a soothsayer and I've come to give King Geirrod a warning. You can just as well pass it on to him yourselves. Tell him to beware a sorcerer who has newly arrived in his realm.'

'How should this scoundrel be recognised?' they asked her.

'Easily,' said the soothsayer. 'For your dogs will be too afraid to attack him.' Then she turned and went on her way.

The guards hurried into the hall and gave the message to King Geirrod. Like many of his kind, he lived in constant

155

fear of treachery, so he took the prophesy very seriously. He gave orders that if the sorcerer was ever spotted, he must be immediately seized.

Some time later, a stranger in a hooded cloak as dark as midnight came knocking at the door.

'Who goes there?' the guards challenged him.

'Grimnir,' he answered.

'What's your business?'

The stranger did not deign to reply, but elbowed his way past the guards and entered the hall unbidden.

As soon as King Geirrod saw him, he leaped to his feet. 'Impostor!' he roared. 'Set the dogs on him!'

But the dogs cowered and whined and slunk away. The king cracked his whip at them; he kicked them, seized them by the ears one by one and shook them hard. Still they refused to obey.

'This is surely the sign that soothsayer warned of,' roared Geirrod. 'This man must be the sorcerer. Seize him!'

His guards snatched Grimnir and dragged him to the centre of the hall.

'Shackle him between the fire-pits,' Geirrod ordered.

The guards bound Grimnir to a bench with heavy chains. On either side of him, slaves stoked the fires until each flared up to a furious blaze. The air turned stiflingly hot. Rivers of sweat began to run down Grimnir's face, and his skin turned red as coals. But he sat motionless and calm.

'So you've come to destroy me with your spells, eh?' King Geirrod hissed at him. 'Well, know this, stranger, my power is stronger than anything you can conjure up. I won't free you from this blaze until you confess who you are and swear on Odin's name never to harm me.'

In the shadow of his hood, Grimnir smiled but said nothing.

Nights passed and and days passed. All this time Grimnir sat in fetters smothered in heat from the fires. No one brought him any food, nor even any drink, for King Geirrod had forbidden it. Grimnir's scorched skin began to thicken and peel away, like bark from a lightening-blackened tree.

By the ninth day, Grimnir's cloak was smouldering. Prince Agnar the Younger sat watching him, his face clouded with growing horror. Finally he stood up, fetched a drinking horn, filled it to the brim with ale, pushed past the guards and carried it to Grimnir.

'Get back, disobedient wretch!' King Geirrod bellowed.

'But this man hasn't done you a whit of harm, Father,' the boy retorted. 'He hasn't even threatened you. You're torturing him solely on the hearsay of that weird soothsayer – who you didn't even bother to examine yourself. How can that be honourable? You can punish me however you want to, but I'm not sitting here any longer watching this innocent guest suffer.'

He held the full horn to Grimnir's lips saying, 'Comfort yourself with this, sir.'

Grimnir drank from it, long and deep. He sighed and smacked his lips. Then, in a single quick movement, he strained at his fetters so that his arms and legs burst free.

'Flames,' he cried, 'be quenched!'

At once, the fires both died down as if invisible barrels of water had been poured on them.

'See, Agnar,' King Geirrod hissed, 'the soothsayer spoke the truth. This man has proven that he's a sorcerer.' He clapped his hands. 'Guards, decapitate him!'

His men drew their swords and crept forward.

'I'd advise you not to try using weapons against me,' said Grimnir softly. 'As for you, Geirrod, you don't have long left to live. Your son shall inherit your kingdom and rule it wisely – as his uncle would have done, if long ago you had not caved in to temptation.'

The guards froze. Agnar stared up at Grimnir with wide eyes.

'You lie,' King Geirrod spat at him. 'I have my kingdom set up so that it's totally impossible for anyone to oppose me. I have only to give the signal, and even your uncanny powers will be extinguished.'

'I think not,' said Grimnir. 'For I am not what I seem. You have met me before, Geirrod, when you were just a young lad. I was the old man who gave you sanctuary from the storm I called up. I was the tempter who exposed your weakness by persuading you to do evil; and I am the master who will punish you.'

'Everyone knows that sorcerers try to gain power by spinning outrageous stories,' King Geirrod spat at him. 'I will not succumb to you.'

'Indeed, there are mortal men strong enough to withstand common magic,' said Grimnir. 'But my mastery over you is of a different order. Grimnir is only one of my countless names. I am also called Battle-Mast, Wanderer, War-Lord, Knowing and High; Truth-Getter, Masked One, Shield-Shaker, Corpse-Father and Much-Wise. Do you not yet know me? Then come here, Agnar, young hero. No need to be diffident, for despite your youth, you are already a hundred times nobler than your father. Speak, friend, reveal to him exactly who I am.'

Agnar stepped forward with a straight back and said in a clear voice, 'Are you...? Sir, I believe you must be Odin All-Father.'

Geirrod had turned as white as bones. '*Odin,*' he whispered. 'Had I known... but how could I? My lord, forgive my ignorance. It was not my fault! It was fuelled by a stranger's slander...'

'How could you allow malicious gossip to defy the ancient laws of hospitality?' said Odin. 'Only an evil man attacks the stranger who comes to his door.'

Geirrod's hand trembled as he began to rise from his high-seat. 'Let me kneel before you, All-Father,' he whimpered, 'let me beg forgiveness...'

In his panic, he forgot that his own drawn sword lay balanced across his knee. As he stood up, it slipped, landing with the hilt balanced upon the floor and the blade pointing upwards. He stumbled against it and tripped.

The sword impaled him on its point and was driven into his heart.

'All-Father!' cried his son, Agnar. 'What should I do?'

But it was too late. For King Geirrod was already dead; and Odin had vanished.

For notes on this story, see page 338.

AMLETH

Some men keep badgers or bears in cages and entertain their friends by baiting them for a gamble. However, King Fengi of Jutland had a more unusual captive creature, guaranteed to provoke uproarious hilarity whenever it was goaded. It wasn't an animal, but a simpleton – his own stepson, Amleth.

Amleth was a tall, strapping youth with broad shoulders and bulging muscles; but his brawn was in no way matched by his brain. He spent most of his time stretched out on the floor next to the fire-pit, tracing patterns in the ashes with his uncut fingernails which resembled filthy claws. He talked garrulously, his words spilling out in torrents of drool, and consisting entirely of nonsense. His face was always streaked with mud, his hair uncombed and his clothes torn. He spent most of his time hidden away in a small, unfurnished hut behind King Fengi's hall.

However, each time Fengi held a feast, as soon as the tables were cleared away, at least one of his guests was sure to shout, 'My lord, let's have some fun. Bring out the fool!' Then Fengi's wife, the tremulous Queen Gerutha, would be sent to fetch her son, and no amount of tears or pleading on her behalf could get her out of it. Amleth would be made to stand on a bench, while the guests poked and prodded him until he started to dance like a berserker in full frenzy, collapsing in a heap of idiotic giggles. Fengi would drag him back onto his feet, while people took turns to fire questions at him, trying to provoke ever more ridiculous answers.

Once a guest said, 'How do you know he's not faking it, Fengi?'

'Because I've given him an infallible test,' said Fengi. 'I got another lad to take him into the forest, abandon him in a glade and spy on him. I'd set up a slave girl to lie in wait for him there, totally naked. Instead of pouncing on her and taking his pleasure like any normal youth, my spy saw him take the girl's hand like a chaste mother with her suckling, and trip around the glade with her, picking wild flowers. Can you believe it? Flowers! When he'd tired of this, he still didn't take the slut, but got on his horse back-to-front, re-fastened the bridle over the beast's tail, and somehow managed to ride home in reverse, scattering petals all the way.'

The hall erupted in laughter.

Fengi was shaking with mirth too. 'He never even guessed he was being watched,' he gasped. 'It's all entirely genuine.'

Amleth would have continued as the star turn of King Fengi's feasts for ever, if only Queen Gerutha hadn't implored Fengi, night after night, to leave her son alone.

'It's better than being ashamed of him,' said Fengi. 'I'm turning his madness to good use.'

'Amleth wouldn't be mad if it wasn't for you,' Gerutha retorted. 'He was so young when you murdered my first

161

husband – your own brother, Fengi – Amleth's father! It was *you* who unhinged him. Seeing a crime like that at such an impressionable age, no wonder he lost his mind.'

'Amleth was born idiotic,' said Fengi. 'Don't deny it.'

'But I will,' said Gerutha. 'When I nursed him at my breast, he was bright and full of promise.'

'Really?' said Fengi incredulously. 'How sad that he never progressed beyond that infantile state. By the way, murder is rather a strong word, don't you think? A king has to live by his sword or he'll be a laughing stock; and a weak king like Amleth's father was best swatted out of the way. So what if he was my brother? The general opinion is that it was a good job I got rid of him, that I'm a far better ruler than he ever was – and a kinder husband to you too.'

'Opinion would soon change,' said Gerutha, 'if people knew how you forced yourself on me when I was still in mourning – and continue to force yourself on me night after night.'

Fengi smirked. 'Oh, things could be much worse for you, wife. At least you can't complain of neglect. And you should be glad I allow your imbecile son to live with us.'

'I'd be far gladder,' said Gerutha, 'if he didn't – and if *I* didn't either. Fengi, set us free! Send us both away.'

Fengi regarded her scornfully for a long moment. Then he said, 'Don't you dare accuse me of being heartless, for I shall heed your request at once. I'll send Amleth abroad.'

Gerutha's eyes lit up. 'Oh, thank you, my lord! I shall hasten away to pack for us both.'

'You need to listen more carefully,' said Fengi. 'I said Amleth shall go – but not you, Gerutha. I forbid you to leave me.'

'You can't send him travelling alone,' cried Gerutha. 'You know full well, he's totally incapable.'

'Calm down, you pathetic woman,' said Fengi coldly. 'I'll send two of my most trusted aides to look after him.'

'But...where will they take him?'

'Across the sea to Britain.'

'So far away!'

'My men will escort him to the palace of a British king who's an ally of mine,' said Fengi. 'They'll be carrying a rune-stick stating that Amleth is my stepson, and asking the British king to treat him according to my wishes.'

'What *are* your wishes?' said Gerutha. 'Let me see this rune-stick.'

Fengi shook his head. 'Dealings between kings aren't for a woman's eyes.'

He summoned Amleth. Before the youth had time to grasp what was happening, Fengi ordered his servants to bundle him down to the harbour and onto one of his ships. The tide was rising at that very time, so the ship set sail at once.

A year passed. Amleth did not return and there was no news of him.

'I fear he's dead,' said Gerutha.

Fengi didn't deny it.

Gerutha went into mourning.

Fengi, on the other hand, was greatly relieved; for he had irrationally feared that the half-wit might one day pose a threat to him. So he said, 'Although we don't have a body to bury, we'll throw a funeral feast to mark Amleth's passing.

After that's over, woman, there's to be no more crying and moaning; I forbid you ever to mention him again.'

Fengi decorated his hall with magnificent tapestries. He ordered astonishing quantities of food and wine. He sent invitations to all the nobles in his realm. No one dared to refuse him. Crowds of people came to the feast, adorned in fine clothes, laden with golden jewellery.

As they sat at the long tables, gossiping and drinking, suddenly the cheer was interrupted by a resounding knock. Before the guards could respond to it, the door burst open and a man walked in –

Amleth!

A stunned hush fell over the hall.

'Ach!' cried Fengi. 'A ghost, risen from the dead!'

The apparition looked exactly as Amleth had done on the day he was taken away. He still staggered and drooled, his tongue stumbling over streams of nonsense. He scratched himself and screeched; his arms and legs jerked about randomly; his face was daubed in mud.

He giggled: 'A ghost? If you say so, Uncle, I mustn't argue with you. Can I join in your feast?

'Go back to your grave, spectre,' hissed Fengi.

Amleth stamped his foot. Some of the guests laughed nervously. He turned a cartwheel, danced up close to Fengi and gurned in his face.

'Let me stay, Uncle. Watch, I'll make myself useful.'

An attendant was standing nearby, holding a clutch of overflowing drinking horns. Amleth grabbed them all, danced his way to the nearest table and handed them around to the astonished guests.

'I'll play at being your slave, Uncle,' he simpered.

He spun round and gambolled to the wine barrels. There, he grabbed more horns and cups, filled them to their brims and began rapidly distributing them. Fengi yelled orders for his retainers to seize Amleth; but he slithered away from them like a fish. He topped up another cup, pounced on his uncle and poured its contents straight down his throat. Fengi was thrown off balance: he coughed and spluttered. Amleth forced more wine on him, and called the servants to do likewise to all the guests. Fearing to offend a ghost, they hurriedly obeyed.

Only one person missed Amleth's attentions – and that was Gerutha. When the entire gathering was rolling around in a daze of drunken mirth, Amleth ceased his tomfoolery, took his mother's arm, and led her outside.

There, close to his mother, at last he grew still and quiet.

In the darkness, Gerutha fell into his arms and began to sob. 'My son,' she wept. 'My dear, poor, sweet fool. So warm, so solid – I can't believe you have risen from the dead. Isn't it really you, still living? But how ever did you find the wits to make your way back across the sea and return here?'

'I didn't need to *find* any wits,' said Amleth, 'because I always had them. Did you never suspect, Mother, that I was not really mad? All through those long years, it was merely a guise to fool my uncle.'

'I hear your voice so steady,' said Gerutha. 'And now your touch is as firm as a seasoned warrior's. Yes, I believe you. But...where have you been all this time? What has happened? Why did you take so long to return?'

'I went to the palace of a king in Britain, just as my uncle intended,' said Amleth. 'However, on the way there, when the stooges Fengi had sent to guard me dropped off to sleep, I stole the rune-stick they were carrying to the king and read it. I'm sure you won't be surprised to learn that it bore a malicious message. Fengi sent his warmest greetings – and instructed the British king to kill me.'

'I always feared such treachery,' Gerutha said. 'So you destroyed it?'

'I did not,' said Amleth. 'Instead I turned Fengi's trick to my own advantage. I scratched out his runes and replaced them with new ones. I left Fengi's greetings untouched, but underneath I instructed the king to give me his daughter in marriage – and to kill the two who had carried the message to him. Then I returned the rune-stick to my escorts. The British king carried out both my instructions exactly and very willingly. It's unsettling how eagerly monarchs go around murdering people, don't you think? No matter: this gave me a second advantage. For after my wedding to his daughter, I accused my new father-in-law of killing my companions without just cause. This placed him in such a difficult position, that he immediately agreed to pay me blood money for their lives – so now I am rich!'

'My son, you have done well,' said Gerutha.

'As yet,' said Amleth, 'I have done nothing. But tonight, at last, I will appease my dead father's spirit.'

He pressed some gold into Gerutha's hand, urging her to take a horse and flee with all speed. Then he hurried back into the hall.

The whole place was silent, for all the guests had now fallen into a drunken stupor. Amleth walked stealthily amongst them, peering into every man's face, seeking out his uncle, Fengi. There was no sign of him.

Amleth hauled down all the tapestries from the wall and spread them over the slumbering guests to prevent them from rising. Then he snatched some smouldering brands from the fire and flung them across the tables. The wood caught light at once and sent flames licking at the tapestries. The inferno spread rapidly across the hall.

Amleth hurried out, slammed the door shut behind him and prowled around the courtyard, searching the outhouses. At last he came to a small booth, set up some distance from the hall, and softly opened the entrance flap.

Inside he saw a bed; and on it lay Fengi, flushed with wine, his sword slung on a hook beside him. Silently, Amleth crept in, removed the sword, then drew his own. He stood facing his uncle, brandishing a blade in either hand.

'Awake, Fengi!' he roared.

Fengi stirred, belched, opened his eyes – and saw Amleth. He threw off his torpor, leaped to his feet and reached for his weapon – only to find his hand grappling with empty air.

'You despised me as a fool, Fengi,' said Amleth, 'but the real fool was *you*. Did you seriously think I would fail to avenge the murder of my father and the whoring of my mother?'

And with those words, he struck his uncle dead.

For notes on this story, see page 339.

A SLAVE WOMAN'S STORY

There was a princess of Ireland called Melkorka, the daughter of King Myrkjartan. She was a very beautiful and spirited girl. When she was just fifteen, pirate raiders attacked her father's hall. As well as stealing much treasure, they also abducted Melkorka and carried her off to Norway.

She didn't fear for her life, but was terrified she would lose her chastity. However, the pirates knew that an untouched young woman of royal blood was a most valuable commodity, so they left her alone. Later, because she was a liability to carry around, they sold her to a slave trader. He too saw the sense in maintaining her condition, and sold her on yet again, at a good profit. Eventually she fell into the hands of a Russian dealer who went by the name of Gilli.

Of course, all this time, Melkorka had longed to escape. But what chance does a young girl have against bands of callous ruffians? Besides, now she was so far from home, where could she flee to, and who could she trust? In the end, she took up the only defence she could think of to maintain her dignity: she refused to speak to her captors. Because of this, they assumed she had been born dumb.

Soon after Gilli the Russian acquired her, King Hakon of Norway organised a great royal assembly in the islands. All the Norse kings were invited to it, as were numerous other prominent men and their followers. There were sporting contests, poets, musicians and other entertainers and an endless supply of drink. There was also a great market. Gilli took Melkorka there to sell, alongside eleven other young slave women.

When Gilli arrived at the assembly, he put up a splendidly adorned booth and curtained off the back section. His lackeys forced all the slaves to sit there while Gilli waited for customers. The young women were allowed to chat quietly to pass the time. Melkorka, however, maintained her usual silence.

Suddenly the curtain was pulled aside and Gilli walked in with a strange man. He stared at the slaves one by one, then pointed at Melkorka.

'She looks a good lay,' he said with an Icelandic accent. 'How much do you want for her?'

Melkorka scowled disdainfully.

'This one isn't cheap,' Gilli said. 'Her price is three marks of silver.'

'Three!' said the Icelander incredulously. 'That's triple the going rate.'

'True,' said Gilli, 'but she's triple the quality. This lot are all good lookers, as you can see, but the one you're after is of royal blood…'

'Nice.'

'…And she's guaranteed a virgin.'

'I'm very tempted,' said the Icelander.

'You can have any of the others for one mark,' said Gilli. 'But if you want the best, three is what you'll have to pay.'

The Icelander stared Melkorka up and down. When he

finally met her eyes, she gave him a look that would have made most men quake. He grinned and opened his purse.

'Before I take payment, I ought to warn you that she can't speak,' said Gilli. 'There's still time to change your mind.'

'I appreciate your honesty – but that doesn't matter for my purposes,' said the Icelander leeringly.

He handed over some silver nuggets, Gilli weighed out the correct amount on his scales, and they shook hands on it. Gilli unbound Melkorka's fetters. The Icelander seized her hand and dragged her out into the market place.

'I'm Hoskuld,' he introduced himself. 'I'm going to take you back to Iceland, where I'm a powerful chieftain. Do everything I tell you, sweetheart, and I'll make you as happy as you're about to make me, ha, ha! I tell you what, let's start by getting you some decent clothes.'

He took her around the market, showing her this stall and that, asking what she would like to wear. Melkorka held her silence. In the end, Hoskuld bought her a fine dress and apron, some handsome new brooches and a set of gleaming glass necklaces. Then he hauled her back to his tent and unceremoniously raped her.

Melkorka considered her options. Even though she was surrounded by royalty at this assembly, she had no way of proving she was a princess herself. And there was no point in trying to flee if it resulted in her being recaptured and sold into bondage again; or, indeed, if she ended up working long hours as a free but lowly servant. At least this Hoskuld seemed to have some status in his home country. If she towed the line with him for a while, and satisfied his lust, maybe he would keep her in style.

So she put up with his nightly sexual demands without resistance; playing dumb made it easier. When the assembly was over, she rode compliantly by his side to his ship, and travelled across the sea with him in her new finery. She began to come to terms with her situation.

But when they arrived in Iceland, she got a shock. Hoskuld hadn't given any indication that he was already married, with four children. His wife, Jorunn, was a similar age to him – nearly old enough to be Melkorka's mother – and the sort of woman who didn't stand for nonsense. When she saw Hoskuld had brought home a beautiful young concubine, she almost exploded.

'Ugh! What's that? You haven't taken this slut into your bed, have you? Oh, the thought of it…! I'd never have let you go to Norway, Hoskuld, if I'd suspected… Get rid of her!'

'But I paid good money for her,' Hoskuld protested. 'She's a royal…'

'That might impress them out in Norway,' said Jorunn, 'but no one cares about royalty here, as well you know.'

'I thought she could be company for you,' said Hoskuld. 'You can set her to do all those chores that you hate. She's no threat to you, honestly: she can't even talk.'

'What? You've wasted silver on a useless dumb dolly? I can't believe this.'

'Be kind to her,' Hoskuld pleaded.

'I will, if you take her right out of my sight for ever, and swear you'll never touch her again,' said Jorunn.

So Hoskuld was obliged to take Melkorka away. He installed her in a small hut on the far edge of his estate and set her up there with firewood, food and everything else she needed. Then he left her to her own devices and went shamefacedly back to his wife.

The best thing for Melkorka was that she never had to suffer his intimate attentions again.

News of Melkorka's arrival quickly spread. Some of Hoskuld's serving women came to her hut and tried to befriend her. She accepted their attentions with a grateful smile, but maintained her pretence of being dumb.

After a few months, Melkorka's belly began visibly to swell. For although Hoskuld was no longer harassing her, she was already carrying his child. The other women rallied round to help, and she gave birth to a strapping baby boy. Hoskuld visited her surreptitiously. He was delighted with their son, whom she called Olaf.

Now that Melkorka had a child to care for, she broke her silence in private. She worked diligently to raise Olaf as a knowledgeable and well-mannered child, and immersed him in tales of their lost royal heritage. He quickly mastered speech in both the Norse and Irish tongues.

One day, when they were busy chattering away together, Hoskuld unexpectedly appeared. As Olaf rushed to greet his father, Melkorka glared at Hoskuld angrily.

'So,' she said, 'my secret's out.'

'You kept it well for a long time,' said Hoskuld. 'Will you talk to me now?'

She agreed to, for the child's sake. She revealed her name and royal background, and told how she had been captured and taken into slavery.

Hoskuld said, 'If you'd told me all this at the outset, I might have treated you differently.'

'Why should it make any difference?' Melkorka answered coldly. 'Whether a woman's a princess or a pauper, she doesn't deserve to be bought and sold like goods, and raped.'

'I'll make amends to you,' said Hoskuld humbly.

He gave her unconditional freedom with immediate effect. Then he moved Melkorka and Olaf out of the hut, and installed them in a proper farm with a full tally of servants.

When Jorunn heard about this, she was not pleased. She accused Olaf of favouring his bastard child over the four that she had legitimately borne him. There were rumours that once the two women had happened to pass along the road, and attacked each other viciously.

Hoskuld, being in thrall to his wife, reduced his visits to Melkorka and Olaf. Soon he was totally neglecting them.

Olaf grew up to be a splendid youth. Everyone who knew his mother's story said that he was a fitting heir to a king. But still, they called him a 'bastard' and a 'slave woman's son'.

'I know how to stop all this nasty talk,' said Melkorka. 'You need to be recognised by your grandfather, the king in Ireland.'

'I'm eager to visit him,' said Olaf.

'The problem is,' said Melkorka, 'I don't have any money to buy you a passage on a ship.'

Round about this time, a neighbouring farmer known as Thorbjorn the Feeble was courting Melkorka. He knew her story and had often helped on her farm. When she mentioned her aspiration for Olaf to visit Ireland, Thorbjorn gave his full encouragement and promised to fund the voyage if she married him. Because of this, Melkorka readily accepted his proposal.

When Olaf was ready to sail, he said, 'Mother, there's just one thing that worries me. When I arrive at King Myrkjartan's hall, I'll have no way of proving that I'm really his grandson.'

Melkorka pulled a golden ring from her finger and gave it to him. 'My father gave me this teething gift when I was a small baby,' she said. 'Show it to him and he'll instantly know that you really are who you say.'

Then she went into the house and returned with a knife and a belt. 'If, by good luck, my dear old nurse is still alive,' she said, 'give these to her.'

They embraced and said goodbye.

Olaf was gone for a year. When he returned the following spring, dressed in a very fine set of brightly coloured clothes, he was not a mere passenger but captaining a ship of his own. He rode straight to his mother's farm, bearing armfuls of precious treasures. She was overjoyed to see him.

'My grandfather gave me a rapturous welcome when I showed him your teething ring,' said Olaf. 'And I seem to have made a good impression on him, because he offered me his kingdom when he dies.'

'My son, the future king!' cried Melkorka. 'Everything has come out right after all.'

'But I declined,' said Olaf. 'Remember, Mother, your eldest brother is King Myrkjartan's rightful heir: there would be endless trouble if I usurped him. Besides, your father's realm is constantly at war, and suffering raids from pirates like those who captured you. I prefer life here in Iceland.'

'That's a mature and wise decision,' said Melkorka. 'And is my old nurse still alive? Did you see her?'

'She is and I did,' said Olaf. 'She was bedridden when I first arrived. Apparently, when you were abducted, she was so overcome by grief that she became a recluse; and of course now she is very old. But on hearing that her beloved Melkorka's son had come to visit, she jumped out of bed, tossed aside her walking sticks and literally ran to greet me. I gave her your gifts and she wept such tears of joy that no one could quieten her until the next day. All during my stay there, she was as fit and well as a woman half her age.'

At these words Melkorka was truly happy for the first time since she was fifteen.

She and her husband had a son of their own called Lambi. He too grew up as a fitting heir to his royal ancestry, with as noble a bearing as his half-brother. He and Olaf got on very well.

When Melkorka's days finally ended, it was said that she drew her last breath with a smile on her face, and went to her grave in contentment and peace.

For notes on this story, see page 340.

AUD THE DEEP-MINDED

Did you hear? That old lady who lived over the mountains at Hvamm has died – the one they called Queen Aud the Deep-Minded. There's been a huge funeral. They built a great mound to bury her in, and carried her into it laid out in a real ship, surrounded by heaps of treasure.

The whole area's in mourning. She lived an extraordinary life, and she was such a wonderful person.

Of course, she wasn't born here in Iceland; she came from Norway originally, back in the time when Harald Finehair was forcing all his rivals to accept him as high king. Her father, Ketil Flatnose, was too bloody-minded to submit to Harald; so he uprooted his family and moved them all across the sea to Scotland…

A lucky move for Aud! For no sooner had they reached their new home, than she fell in love.

The object of her passion was Olaf the White, a powerful young warrior. Olaf was waging a war of his own, out in Ireland. Spurred on by Aud's championing, he quickly became victorious and installed himself there as king. Aud became his queen, with all the grand life that went with it: ensconced in a splendid hall, adorned with jewellery and fine silks, fawned over by courtiers…

But the good times didn't last long. You know how it is

with kings: no matter how much power and land and treasure they have, they're always lusting for more; and they have enemies crowding in on every side. So Olaf never stopped fighting battles. He only ruled for a few short years, and then he was slain.

Poor Aud. One moment she was a glorious queen, and the next she was left defenceless, with the enemy circling her like crows, threatening atrocities. Her father was long dead. Her brothers were far away overseas and out of touch. Who could she could turn to for help?

No one but herself.

Somehow, Aud found an inner strength. She gathered up her infant son, Thorstein, hired a boat and implored the skipper to take them to some outlying place beyond the reach of Olaf's foes.

So they headed north to the wild islands of the Hebrides. There Aud established her household above a lonely bay, and single-handedly brought up her boy in the true manner of a king's son.

She raised him so well that he grew up to become a king himself. Surely you must have heard of him – Thorstein the Red who, from Caithness, ruled half of Scotland and all its islands? According to the poets, with his rust-coloured beard and endless tally of valiant deeds, he was even mightier than his father. He honoured his mother with a place beside him on the high-seat, and listened daily to her wise advice.

But Thorstein too was killed before his time. Once again, Aud was kicked out of her realm, again she lost everything.

She was well past her prime. And this time, she was not only homeless, but also left in charge of Thorstein's seven children.

Did she despair? No, not her. Instead, she came up with an astonishing solution.

'If we want to survive, we'll have to turn our backs on our old lives,' she told her grandchildren. 'Stop thinking of yourselves as royals, give up lording it over other people. As for me, from now on, I'm no longer a queen.'

As her family digested this, Aud had quiet words with her eldest granddaughter, Thorgerd. Then she took the girl to meet a young nobleman called Koll. He'd been a right-hand man of Thorstein the Red and a regular at the family fireside, so they knew him well.

'I need a steward to manage my affairs,' Aud told him. 'You'll be ideal.'

'I'm greatly honoured,' Koll answered, 'but – forgive me for asking, my lady – how will you pay me? It's common knowledge that you've lost all your treasure.'

Aud nudged Thorgerd. The girl stepped forward with a toss of her hair, and spoke up brazenly. 'Not quite *all* of it,' she said. 'Grandmother managed to hide away a sizeable hoard. She intends to divide it up between me and my siblings. If you'd like to marry me, I'll gladly share my portion with you.'

What a proposal! Naturally, Koll didn't turn it down; and he agreed to become Aud's steward too.

Then Aud threw him another thunderbolt: 'Since you're marrying my granddaughter, you'll have to sail abroad with us.'

'Where to?' asked Koll.

'Right away from war and death,' said Aud. 'To a country which doesn't have either an army or a king.'

Koll said, 'No doubt you're talking of Iceland.'

He got to work at once, organising their journey. He had a splendid ship built for Aud at a secret place deep in the forest; and once it was finished, he set about finding a crew.

'King Thorstein had plenty of followers who lost their estates when was slain,' he said. 'They'll be ideal.'

But Aud said firmly, 'I'm not having fighting men on board my ship.'

'Then who will you take instead?' asked Koll.

Aud said, 'Plain speaking peasants and slaves.'

'They're not suitable companions for a queen,' said Koll.

'Maybe not,' said Aud. 'But remember, I'm not a queen any more.'

Despite that, she still had her air of authority, and Koll didn't dare disagree.

It was an unlikely group of people, indeed, who joined Aud's ship. The voyage itself was even stranger. For once they were out on the open sea, Aud stood at the helm and made an announcement:

'Listen, all you slaves. I'm liberating every one of you, immediately and unconditionally.' She looked around at the rest of the crew. 'From now on, everyone on board this ship is not only free, but also equal.'

A shrewd move! It bonded all her company into a tight fellowship; and that, in turn, helped them survive a terrible journey. For it's a long way from Scotland to Iceland, especially with winter fast approaching. The sea was endlessly rough and they constantly ran into storms. When they finally reached the coast of Iceland, a freak wave dashed their vessel onto some rocks, leaving them shipwrecked.

How did they make it to safety? They all said it was

entirely due to Aud's encouragement and courage. And then it was the good lady herself who went walking from farm to farm through the sleet and the wind, knocking at doors and begging, refusing to give up until she found a household willing to shelter the whole group through the winter.

When spring came and the weather improved, Aud bought horses for everyone in her band. Then she led them on a long ride westward. They ended up on the far side of these very mountains, where there was still a large tract of land waiting to be taken.

Aud went to the local chieftain to lay claim to it. But her commanding manner got the chieftain's back up, especially when he discovered her royal background. He looked down his nose at her and addressed all his remarks to Koll – even though the steward had only gone along to be Aud's witness.

'It's me you should be speaking to,' Aud interrupted him.

The chieftain snorted contemptuously. He turned his back on her and searched through the dusty corners of his memory, until he rooted out a ridiculous old edict.

'I don't care what the rules are where you come from, ' he sneered, 'but here in Iceland a woman's only allowed as much land as she can walk around between dawn and sunset with a two-year-old heifer in tow. Which for someone of your age probably isn't very much. On the other hand, a man is entitled to all the land that he and his followers can carry fire over in a single day – a far larger area. So I advise you to keep your mouth shut, lady, and leave the claim to him.'

Insult any man like that and he'll certainly lose his temper and start a fight; even most women wouldn't take it lying down. Aud, however, merely shook her head at the chieftain and gently but insistently began to argue. She kept it up right through the day; she nagged him deep into the night. In the end, the chieftain couldn't stand it any more. He caved in and ratified her ownership of all the land that she wanted.

But that wasn't the end of it. For as soon as the land was officially Aud's – she astonished everyone by giving most of it away. No matter whether they were free-born or former slaves; every single one of her followers got an equally generous plot.

They all queued up to shower her with thanks.

'No need for that,' said Aud. 'It's my pleasure to help you all, because I'm a Christian.'

That got people worried: they'd heard about Christians in other countries forcing people to convert to their religion.

But Aud reassured them. 'Don't worry, you can all carry on worshipping however you want. For my own use, I'm going to have a little church built; but beside it, I'll be raising a fine temple to *your* gods. Then, while I celebrate mass, the rest of you can go next door and make sacrifice to Frey and Thor.'

Now you understand why people were so impressed by her; now you understand why they called her 'Deep-Minded'. She did so much for them. She guaranteed their security. She offered them a chance to prosper by giving them land. She was open minded, magnanimous and tolerant.

Everyone loved her.

But as Aud herself already knew, love can't make someone live beyond their allotted time.

The years crept by, on and on – until this year. Just as she'd always done, to mark the end of summer, Aud threw a grand feast for all her kin, neighbours and friends. With the excellent harvest just gathered in, the food and drink were literally overflowing. The guests couldn't help noticing that Aud had grown very old and bent and slow. But that didn't stop her entertaining with her usual gusto. She even handed out splendid gifts to everyone – just like the queen she once was. She also made a point of talking to every single one of her guests in private. No one's revealed what Aud said to them; but it was clearly very inspiring because many were moved to tears.

At the end of the evening, Aud stood by the door, as was her habit, waving her guests goodbye. Then she bid her household a cheery goodnight and shuffled off to her bed-closet...

Which is where they found her next morning. True to form, without any fuss or bother, she passed quietly away in her sleep.

For notes on this story, see page 342.

NJAL THE PEACEMAKER AND HIS ANGRY SONS

Njal Thorgeirsson reckoned he was invincible.

Don't get it wrong: he wasn't a warrior. In fact, he never carried a weapon, and he'd never taken part in any fight. To tell the truth, although he'd fathered seven children, physically he was rather puny: he couldn't even grow a beard.

However, what he lacked in brawn was more than compensated by his phenomenal knowledge and intellect. Njal was a fixer. He knew the entire law code inside out and back to front. Even better, he understood how to twist the laws to suit whatever purpose he wanted. People from all over Iceland used to come to him for help with their legal tangles.

Njal worked on the basis that a clever argument laced with silver was far more powerful than a sword. He willingly dealt with trivial disputes over land ownership or marriage dowries; but what he especially relished was sorting out killings and revenge. Whatever the problem, Njal always ensured that all parties ended up satisfied, without spilling any blood.

Njal's talents were unique. They won him a great

reputation, and made him extremely rich

However, every family has its flaw.

One day, Njal's three sons came to him, saying, 'Father, we've got ourselves into a spot of bother.'

'How so?' said Njal.

The eldest son, Skarp-Hedin, said, 'I've just killed a man.'

Njal sighed deeply and shook his head. 'You fools! Why have you ignored my advice? I've told you many times, lads, the hand that strikes soon regrets it. Who did you kill?'

'There's no regrets in *my* hand,' said Skarp-Hedin. 'It was Thrain Sigfusson.'

'That's even worse news,' said Njal. 'Thrain was twice-over a kinsman to my best friend, Gunnar.'

'So what?' said Skarp-Hedin. 'Gunnar's been dead for years. And we've never forgotten that Thrain once helped to kill our foster-father.'

'But that was years ago too,' said Njal. 'And I negotiated really good reparations for your foster-father's death.'

Now his second son, Grim, spoke up. 'You think money solves everything, Father, but it can't cure resentment. Thrain paid up all right, but that didn't cure his malice – in fact, it made him even worse. Don't you remember? When we were all abroad last year, travelling in Norway, he got us into serious trouble with Earl Hakon.'

Njal shook his head disapprovingly. 'Ach, that silly misunderstanding…'

Njal's third son, Helgi, said, 'It wasn't *you*, Father, who was humiliated by being falsely accused and put in chains.'

'That's no justification for killing him,' said Njal.

Skarp-Hedin said, 'Yes it is. What Thrain did to us in Norway scratched the unhealed scab off our old wound. It reminded us that we never got the revenge we deserved for the death of our foster-father – who was also *your* friend, Father. You should applaud us.'

'I'll do no such thing,' said Njal. 'I've spent my whole life trying to steer everyone away from killings. There'll be terrible repercussions.'

'Of course,' said Skarp-Hedin. 'But you'll handle them in your usual brilliant way. You'll search your memory for the perfect law to get us off the hook from being outlawed – or even indicted of any crime. And you'll pay Thrain's kin generous reparations from your treasure store. We all know it's overflowing with fees paid by all those other grateful offenders whose cases you've fixed in the past.'

True to form, Njal swung into action straightaway. To prevent his sons' foolhardiness from escalating into further revenge killings, he volunteered to pay extraordinarily generous compensation to Thrain's brother.

Over and above this, to guard against hard feelings from developing in the future, Njal took Thrain's young son, Hoskuld, into his home and fostered him. Njal gave Hoskuld all the privileges that his own sons enjoyed, and publicly ordered them to treat Hoskuld like a true brother.

Njal's resolution of his sons' crime, and his skill in turning a tricky situation to many people's advantage, won him even more acclaim and turned out very well for his legal business. For now more people than ever travelled from far and wide to consult him.

However, it is truly said that many a man has lost his life through overconfidence. As Njal basked in this latest glory, malicious rumours began to spread. At the same time, a long forgotten enemy of his was busy sowing the seeds of trouble.

The rumours claimed that Njal favoured his foster-son, Hoskuld, over his own children. These grew stronger and more toxic when the lad grew up, because Njal contrived to have Hoskuld made a chieftain – even though he'd never organised any similar honour for his natural sons.

The old enemy of Njal's was a man called Valgard the Grey. His resentment was so petty that Njal had let it slip right out of his mind: long ago, Njal had strongly advised a woman not to marry Valgard because of his venomous nature. She'd ignored Njal and gone ahead with the wedding anyway, but Valgard had never forgiven the insult. Over the years his bitterness festered. Now he was an old man; but he charged his son, Mord, to redress this wrong. Like father, like son: Njal's sanctimoniousness and wealth infuriated Mord in equal measure. He was more than eager to destroy the great lawyer.

Being a coward, Mord didn't launch a physical assault on Njal. Instead, he devised a plan to dupe Njal's own family into doing the dirty work for him.

He travelled to Njal's farm for a social visit, pretending to be full of good cheer. Njal made him welcome, and agreed that Mord could have lodgings there for a few nights. While he was their guest, Mord persuaded Njal's sons into the habit of going for an evening walk with him after their work was done. At first the talk was totally innocuous. However, one evening when Njal himself was well out of earshot, Mord brought up the subject of their foster-brother, Hoskuld.

'He's done exceptionally well for himself, hasn't he,' said Mord. 'And it's all thanks to your father getting him made a chieftain. You know, I've never understood why he never did the same for any of *you.*'

None of the Njalssons offered any explanation.

'I saw Hoskuld recently,' Mord went on, 'and the subject came up in conversation. He's very smug about it.' He lowered his voice. 'He told me this in confidence, but I feel it's right to repeat it to you, so you know exactly where you stand. He said that your father often runs you three down, criticising you for going abroad in your youth instead of staying at home to learn the law from him.'

The Njalssons made no comment.

'Also,' said Mord, 'Hoskuld's never forgiven you for killing his father, Thrain. He wants proper revenge for it. He's going to organise a hit squad to get rid of you all.'

The next morning Mord went on his way. But his words were like thorns in the flesh of the Njalssons, constantly irritating them. They discussed Mord's devastating revelations over and over; and each time the thorns seemed to grow bigger and more painful.

In the end, they decided they had better kill Hoskuld Thrainsson before *he* struck against them. They didn't mention their intention to Njal, because they knew he'd be against it. Besides, all three agreed it was high time they freed themselves from their ageing patriarch's control.

So a few days later, the three Njalssons ambushed Hoskuld. Each of them carried a sword and each struck a potentially fatal blow; for they had agreed to share responsibility for his death.

Hoskuld's widow was distraught. Her uncle, a chieftain called Flosi, promised to organise a revenge killing.

Not surprisingly, Njal was appalled at his sons' latest crime, and especially at the implications for the family.

It so happened that it was time for everyone to assemble at the Althing. Njal's usual sanguine demeanour had vanished: he rode there in a state of high panic. He spent the first few days visiting everyone whom he had helped during his long legal career, begging them for support.

Soon the three Njalssons were summonsed to stand before the law rock and charged with Hoskuld's murder. But before any of them had a chance to defend himself, Njal himself leaped to his feet.

'Law lords,' he cried, 'jurymen. You know that all my life I have always bowed humbly before the edicts of the law.'

Some people snorted and nudged each other; remembering how Njal was, in fact, always twisting those very edicts to suit his own ingenious purposes.

Njal went on, 'My sons' crime was not just committed against Hoskuld's widow and kinsmen, but also against *me*. For Hoskuld was my foster-son and they know I loved him as if he too were my flesh and blood. You might say that *I* should also seek revenge against them, alongside Hoskuld's kinsmen. Yet that is impossible for they are my own family.'

He turned to Chieftain Flosi, who was representing Hoskuld's widow. 'I stand alongside you and your kin in your grief. On behalf of my sons, the killers, I volunteer to pay such generous reparations that you will not be able to refuse them.'

'How much?' asked Flosi coldly.

And Njal answered, 'Six hundred ounces of silver.'

An astonished murmur ran around the crowd. Six hundred! This was totally unprecedented.

'I doubt that you can raise such a sum,' said Flosi. 'Show it to me, Njal.'

A weigher was called over to set up his balance. Njal carried a large bag of silver bars to him and tipped them into the scale pan.

'One hundred ounces here,' called out the weigher.

Njal turned imploringly to his sons. 'You are the cause of this trouble,' he hissed. 'Contribute!'

Skarp-Hedin, Grim and Helgi stepped out, blank faced, and added more silver.

'That brings the total to two hundred ounces,' announced the weigher.

'My friends!' cried Njal to the assembly. 'Those who are still in debt to me, and those whose lives and kin I have saved in the past. Will you help me in my own time of need?'

A murmur rippled through the crowd. One by one, men and women began to walk towards the law rock, each holding out an offering. The weigher added them to the scales, calling out the tally, while a group of chieftains recorded it on a rune-stick.

When at last a truly enormous pile of silver was

glimmering in the watery summer sunlight, the Law Speaker called out, 'Six hundred ounces of silver has now been paid in full. Flosi, do you accept it?'

Chieftain Flosi stared at the pile of silver. He circled round it, chewing the ends of his moustache. At last he turned to Njal and said, 'Well, well, Old Beardless, you've excelled yourself, managing to raise this extraordinary sum. It's a pity I don't know how to congratulate you formally – because with that smooth chin of yours, I can't tell whether you're a man or a woman.'

Skarp-Hedin flushed angrily. 'How dare you insult my father!' he snarled.

'Hush, son,' Njal implored him.

But Skarp-Hedin hissed back at him, 'Shut up, old man. We've had enough of heeding your coward's counsel. Why shouldn't I defend you against this piece of filth for the sake of our family name?' He turned back to Flosi. 'Njal is far more of a man than you are, Flosi, for he's fathered seven children – whereas you have none. And everyone knows that's because every nine nights you go out dancing on the high fells – and shape-shift into a simpering woman to lie with the trolls who lurk up there.'

Chieftain Flosi stared at Skarp-Hedin for a long moment. He spat at Njal contemptuously. Then he lashed out at the pile of silver with his sword, scattering it across the ground.

'I refuse compensation from this family of rogues,' he said quietly. 'I hereby give notice that before the year is over, I will be taking full blood revenge.'

Not even the greatest man can withstand what is fated.

Njal and his family returned home. For the next few months they went quietly about their business. Old scores and quarrels were laid aside. No one spoke of what had happened, or of what lay ahead.

Two months before Winter Nights, Flosi led a hundred armed men to Njal's farm and surrounded the house. They were carrying firebrands.

The Njalssons came out to face them with their own band of thirty men – kinsmen and male servants – brandishing swords, axes and cudgels. There was a short battle. The Njalssons had the hollow satisfaction of wounding quite a few of Flosi's cronies.

Suddenly Flosi roared, 'Fire!'

His men hurled their brands at the roof. The thatch caught light at once.

'Open the door, Njal,' Flosi shouted. 'Send out your women and your children. For tonight, anyone who stays inside your house will be burned alive!'

Behind the door, women began screaming. The Njalssons' wives ran out with their offspring in tow, followed by a stream of maids.

Flosi went to the open doorway and called in, 'Hurry up, old woman – Njal's wife, Bergthora. This is your last chance to escape.'

A quavering voice drifted out in answer, 'Go away, leave me be. Njal's the love of my life. I want to die beside him.'

Flosi shrugged. He turned back to his men. 'Faster,' he urged them, 'throw in more brands!'

His men responded with a shower of smouldering sticks. The roof caved in, a mass of dazzling, crackling flames. Over the top of the exposed turf walls, the blaze leaped onto the wooden rafters and pillars...

Until the whole house collapsed in a single, blinding fireball.

For notes on this story, see page 344.

A TALE OF GRETTIR THE STRONG

Grettir the Strong could wrestle a bear to death, and lift enormous boulders with his bare hands. His sword came from a death-mound, snatched brazenly from a ghost.

Grettir the Strong was a villain. At the tender age of fourteen, he got himself exiled as an outlaw because of a killing; and he collected enemies like flies around a cow's backside. His tongue was spitting with slanderous poems, but no man dared return his insults for fear of losing his life.

However, Grettir the Strong was also a hero. He once climbed twenty fathoms down a sheer gorge to slaughter a rampaging troll. Another time, he destroyed a monstrous spook that had been haunting a farm, then fearlessly shouldered its curse.

Grettir the Strong was well-bred but angry. Grettir the Strong was indomitable; yet he died of sorcery and nightmares.

This is one of his stories.

After Grettir was first outlawed, he went on the run in

Norway. He came to an island and knocked on the door of the local chieftain – Thorfinn Karsson was his name.

'I want to stay with you for a while,' Grettir demanded.

Chieftain Thorfinn didn't like the look of him. But he guessed there would be trouble if he refused, so he let Grettir sleep in his barn. He didn't tell his wife.

It was winter and almost time for the Yule Feast. Thorfinn was planning to spend it with some kinsfolk who lived far away on the mainland. Unfortunately, just as his household was all packed up and ready to go, the daughter – an attractive young woman – fell sick and took to her bed.

'She's much too poorly to travel,' said Thorfinn's wife. 'We'll have to stay at home.'

'You stay here and look after her,' said Thorfinn. 'I'm not missing the festivities. I'll go without you.'

The wife was a nervous woman and she wasn't happy about that. 'Suppose there's a break-in while you're away?' she said.

'I'll leave some servants behind to look after you,' said Thorfinn curtly. 'And just in case there's any serious trouble, you can get help from an Icelandic traveller who's sleeping in one of the barns.'

'You never told me about him,' said the wife. 'What's his name? Is he trustworthy? Why would he be of any use?'

'He calls himself Grettir the Strong,' said Thorfinn, 'and the nickname isn't a joke. He's a big, fearless fellow, the kind that other men don't mess around with. I've given him free hospitality for the last couple of months, so in return, he's honour bound to protect you.'

He knew that if he mentioned his suspicion that Grettir had caused trouble in his home country, she would beg him not to go. So he kept his mouth shut, wished his daughter a speedy recovery, then hastened away on his journey.

Shortly after he'd gone, the girl felt better. She got up from her bed and sat by the fireside with her mother.

Unbeknown to them as they warmed their hands at the flames, a small warship was hauling up on the beach below their hall. Twelve men climbed out of it, all heavily armed, and strode arrogantly up onto the island. At that very moment, Grettir the Strong happened to come to the doorway of the barn where he was lodging. He watched the new arrivals carefully, observing that they outnumbered him, and that none of them were weaklings. He noticed that they were all clad in mangy bearskins, of the kind favoured by berserkers. He drew himself up to his full height, then strode down to meet them, holding out his hand.

'Welcome,' he said. 'What's your business here?'

Two men stepped to the front, obviously the leaders. Both were nearly as tall as Grettir.

One lurched behind the weight of a huge beer-gut. He spat at Grettir and said, 'They call me Thorir Paunch.'

The other's face was scarred and pitted. 'And I'm Ogmund the Evil. No doubt, you've heard of us?'

Grettir shook his head.

'Well, you have now,' said Ogmund. 'If you're master of this farm, your safest bet is to hand over everything we ask for. If you're not, either help us seize it or stand aside. We're mainly after the women.'

'Wa-hoa! You couldn't have come at a better time,' said Grettir. 'The chieftain who owns this place has gone away for the whole Yule Feast – and he's left his wife and daughter behind for your pickings. The wife's not bad for her age, and I can promise you, the daughter's sweet as ripe cloudberries. Wouldn't mind a taste of her myself. There's some pretty luscious maidservants hanging around here too. So you'll all be able to pleasure yourselves right through the festive period, without even needing to fight anyone off. You'll be exhausted by the end of it.'

Grinning broadly, he led the berserkers straight into the hall, where the chieftain's wife and daughter were sitting unwittingly by the fire. Around them, maidservants were hanging tapestries and setting up the table for a modest Yuletide meal. When they saw thirteen strange, hefty men stride in, they all jumped up in alarm.

Thorir Paunch and Ogmund the Evil sized up the women and grinned lasciviously. Grettir winked and signalled at them to wait. Then he went up to the chieftain's wife.

'Greetings, mistress,' he said, 'we've not met before, but your husband's left you in my protection. They call me Grettir the Strong.'

'So I hear,' the wife said. She was shaking and her face had turned ghostly white. 'But... who are these others?'

Thorir and Ogmund stepped forward, leering eagerly at the daughter.

'Oh!' screamed the wife. 'Ugh! Thor and Jesus save me! You're berserkers – filthy ruffians! Get out! Don't you dare touch my daughter... Grettir, if you're protecting us, why ever did you let these horrible men in? Send them away, quickly! Keep them off us!'

The maids all squealed. The manservants backed away.

'There's no need to get all worked up like that, mistress,' said Grettir. 'These fellows have come to cheer you up. They heard how annoyed you were when your husband abandoned you so heartlessly just before Yule, so they've come to make up for it. They'll give you some jolly male company for the festive meal; and when you go to bed at the end of it, you won't feel lonely, because they're going to snuggle up beside you in your husband's place.'

The berserkers all cheered lewdly and started to crowd round the wife and the girl, who were trembling and crying.

'Whoa, there, friends,' Grettir teased them. 'There's plenty of time to feast on the ladies – ha ha! But first you look as if you could all do with a drink.'

'You're right,' said Thorir Paunch, patting his belly. 'We're parched.'

'Well, sit down,' said Grettir. 'Make yourselves at home, lads. I'll get these flunkies to bring you something strong.'

The berserkers seated themselves on the wall-benches, guffawing and stretching out their legs. The wife and her daughter got up and surreptitiously started to sidle out.

Grettir was acting as if he owned the place. 'Bring out all the booze you can find,' he ordered the servants. 'Ale, wine, especially mead. Fill these men's cups to the brim and keep them topped up.'

The servants jumped to it. Grettir turned back to the berserkers. 'Make yourselves more comfortable, lads. Take off your sword-belts, lay your weapons aside – you won't need them during your stay: I'm the only real man left on the premises and I won't be fighting you.'

The berserkers cheered again. They all unbuckled themselves and hurled their axes and swords into the corner.

'You don't need meat knives either,' said Grettir. 'The mistress here is well stocked with all the tools you need to enjoy the meal that's coming. And – ha ha! – you don't want them getting in the way when you lie with the ladies afterwards, do you? Now, where's that booze? Hurry up, girls, bring round the flagons. Friends, hold out your cups.'

Soon the men were all drinking. The chieftain's wife and her daughter managed to slip right out of the hall. They ran into the grain store and barricaded themselves in.

'Drink up,' Grettir urged the berserkers. 'And while you do, I'll entertain you.'

He started reciting some poems. They were all ludicrous but very clever, outrageously titillating his audience about the night's expected pleasures. Between his declamations, he kept signalling the servants to refill the berserkers' cups.

Soon all the men but him were lolling about, gibbering nonsense or falling asleep where they sat.

'Wake up, lads!' Grettir roared at them. 'You don't want to be too tired to give the ladies what they're waiting for, eh? And look at you, all pissing yourselves and dribbling. Come outside for some fresh air. Then I'll help you borrow some of Chieftain Thorfinn's clothes to smarten yourselves up. And while you're about it, you might as well grab some of his treasure.'

The berserkers staggered out after him, grumbling and laughing.

Inside the grain store, the wife and her daughter heard them go past and clutched each other in fear.

Grettir wrenched open the door of another large storehouse nearby and led the berserkers inside. It was filled with big, heavily carved chests. Grettir burst their locks then started tossing their contents about. Richly dyed breeches, embroidered tunics and cloaks trimmed with expensive fur came flying out, alongside women's silk dresses, aprons and linen shifts. There was also a load of jewellery: arm-rings, neck-bands, finger-rings, brooches and strings of glass beads. The berserkers pounced on them as they fell and snatched them up. They kissed the women's shifts and made obscene gestures at them. They festooned cloaks and dresses comically over their heads and decked themselves in the glittering jewellery.

None of them noticed Grettir dodge outside. They didn't hear him slam the door and fasten it with a heavy padlock.

Grettir dashed back to the hall, elbowed the jittering servants out of the way and broke into Chieftain Thorfinn's bed-closet. An array of armour and weapons was hanging above the bed. Hastily Grettir pulled on a mail shirt and helmet, seized a sword and a barbed spear, hurried out and bounded back to the storehouse.

Just as he arrived, there was a great crash. The berserkers had finally realised they were trapped inside; so they massed together, pressed their shoulders to the padlocked door, busted it open and came swarming down the steps. Thorir and Ogmund led the way, making an awesome display of their talents, howling like wolves, foaming at the mouth, tearing off their clothes and flinging neck-bands and other heavy objects around.

All this made them ridiculously easy prey. Grettir hurled the spear. It struck Thorir – went right through him – and straight onwards into Ogmund – joining them at the waist by the shaft. They staggered briefly, as if in a crazy dance – then both slumped to the ground, stone dead.

Now the other berserkers rushed forward. Weaponless and drunk out of their minds, they were like newborn lambs to an eagle. Grettir gripped the chieftain's sword and fought them all off single-handed, striking them down one by one. Within no time, the yard was littered with blood and corpses.

By now it was snowing. With new-found authority in his voice, Grettir strode to the hall and ordered the servants back to their normal work. While they stoked up the fire and finished preparing the meal, he went and knocked on the door of the barricaded grain store. At first the chieftain's wife and daughter were too terrified to emerge. But Grettir coaxed them with news of his triumph and gentle words; he even made them laugh with some witty verses about the battle he had just won. Eventually they believed his assurances that all the intruders were dead, and that he himself was harmless. They crept out and followed Grettir back into their home.

The wife's gratitude for what Grettir had done knew no bounds. She swore that if Grettir wished to marry her daughter, she would do everything in her power to persuade Thorfinn to agree to this as soon as he returned. Grettir eyed the girl up and down for a long while, then said ruefully that he just wasn't the marrying kind. Instead, he accepted her invitation to move out of the barn and sit in the high-seat before the fire for the remaining days of the chieftain's absence.

Thorfinn finally came home at the end of Yule festivities. When his wife told him what had happened, he was astonished, and swore to spread news of Grettir's heroic deed far and wide.

So for a while Grettir became acclaimed as a truly valiant hero.

For notes on this story, see page 348.

GISLI THE OUTLAW'S LAST STAND

There was a man called Gisli Sursson who murdered his sister's husband.

You don't need to know why: it was the usual chain of resentment and revenge.

His sister was called Thordis. Some years earlier, she'd already lost a lover to Gisli's sword, so this was the final straw. After the funeral, she shared her grief with her dead husband's brother, Bork the Stout, and they got married. They went to the local assembly together to complain about Gisli's crime. The law chiefs there agreed they had a strong case, and condemned Gisli to be a full outlaw.

You know the implications: Gisli lost everything for the rest of his life. His wife, Aud, was forced to kick him off their farm against her will. Everyone was ordered to shun him; no one was allowed to offer him food or shelter, no one could protect him, no one could help him. He had fewer rights than a slave. He could be killed with impunity: his life was worth nothing.

Gisli accepted his sentence phlegmatically. He roamed like a fox through wild weather, summer and winter. He slept rough in lava deserts and below gale-swept mountains.

He survived by stealing and foraging. His brother disowned him; yet an old widow regularly risked her life by hiding him in her underground store. As for Aud, her loyalty to him was undiminished, but she was powerless.

Bork the Stout promised sixty pieces of silver to anyone who could track down Gisli the Outlaw, and kill him. Nobody won it – for after six bitter winters on the run, Gisli feigned his own death by drowning.

Three more years went by, then rumours started up:

'Have you heard? Gisli the Outlaw's still alive after all. *She's* been hiding him all this time – Aud, his wife.'

Bork the Stout sent spies to Aud's farm. They broke in one night and searched it from top to bottom, from one end to the other. But they didn't find Gisli, because Aud had caught wind of their coming and she'd already moved him on.

Thordis was scathing. 'Spies are no use,' she said to Bork. 'You'd do better to heed the farmwives' gossip. Everyone's saying that it's Gisli's cousin, Ingjald, who's sheltering him now – that fellow who lives like a recluse on an island because his son's a simpleton. Now you know where he is, stop wasting time and send a hitman out there to get rid of him.'

Bork hired a bruiser called Eyjolf the Grey, who came with a band of fourteen prizefighting thugs, and sent them out to Ingjald's island.

But it's impossible to conceal a boat on the open sea. Ingjald saw them coming and hurried to warn Gisli – who was hiding in a dugout on his land. Bork disguised Gisli as his simpleton son and smuggled him into a boat with a slave to row it. They went straight past Eyjolf the Grey and his gang, right under their noses. As they drew close, Gisli started yelling nonsense and waving his arms around, in keeping with his disguise. Eyjolf and his thugs looked away in embarrassment and quickly rowed on. They never suspected a thing...until they arrived at Eyjolf's place and found Bork's real son loitering there.

By that time, Gisli was safely back on the mainland, lying low in a cave. As soon as darkness fell, he raced along the seashore to a place called Haug, because he'd heard that the fellow who farmed there, Ref, was scornful of authority. True enough, when he realised Gisli was the infamous outlaw and he was being chased, Ref eagerly offered help and ushered him in.

'We're old hands at this game,' he said. 'I know exactly what to do. Quickly – get into bed.'

Gisli didn't argue. As soon as he'd slipped into the bed-closet and under the covers, the farmwife – a jolly and curvaceous woman – got in beside him.

'Don't mind me,' she said. 'We'll show 'em!'

Eyjolf the Grey and his band soon picked up Gisli's trail. They announced their arrival at Ref's farm by unceremoniously breaking down his door.

'Are you the master here?' they asked Ref.

'Not me,' he gabbled. 'I'm just a servant. The master's already abed with his wife.'

Meanwhile, the farmwife whispered to Gisli, 'Keep still and hold your tongue.' She heaved herself right on top of him, covering him completely. Then she started loudly smacking her lips and giving shrieks of pleasure.

The next moment, the closet was wrenched open. Eyjolf and his men crowded in the doorway, staring in goggle-eyed.

'Aagh!' the farmwife shrieked. 'Voyeurs! You smutty creeps! Fancy spying on a hard-working woman enjoying some innocent fun with her own husband. Get out! I've got the *dark knowledge* and if you dare lay a hand on us, I'll curse the very balls off you…'

'Whoops!'

'Sorry ma'am!'

They slammed the door shut and made a hasty retreat. Gisli had escaped yet again.

'If there's one person who knows where Gisli's hiding,' said Thordis, 'it'll be Aud.'

So Bork despatched Eyjolf the Grey to Aud's farm. Aud knew who he was and guessed his business. But she didn't want her house turned upside down again, so she listened to what he had to say.

'I'm bringing you a proposal,' said Eyjolf the Grey. 'Bork's authorised an exceptional payment if you'll co-operate and tell me where Gisli is.'

'How much?' said Aud.

'Three hundred pieces of silver.'

'That's five times the amount I heard was on offer before,' said Aud.

'Yes, well…Bork realises that a woman expects to be paid well in return for betraying her husband,' said Eyjolf.

'He's right,' said Aud. 'And to tell the truth, after what I've been through, the thought of so much money…'

'All women are weak,' said Eyjolf encouragingly. 'It's nothing to be ashamed of.'

'I'm very tempted... But I'm worried about...'

'You're no doubt terrified of violence,' said Eyjolf. 'Don't worry, you won't have to watch us kill him.'

'And can I do whatever I want with Bork's payment?'

'Obviously,' said Eyjolf. 'Once it's paid, what you do with it is up to you.'

'Then I'll take it,' said Aud.

Eyjolf the Grey fetched his saddlebag and tipped a heap of silver into her lap. Aud didn't stop to count it, but tossed it quickly into a wooden chest, locked the lid and clipped the key back onto her brooch.

'Since you said it's up to me what I do with it,' she said, 'I'm keeping the payment and not telling you a thing.'

'That's not what I meant!' cried Eyjolf. 'You can't do that, you can't have the silver for nothing...'

'Can't I?' said Aud. 'All right, then in exchange I'll give you *this*...' She clenched her fist and slammed it hard against his nose. Blood ran. '...the unforgettable memory of being struck by a woman. Weak? Terrified of violence, eh? You've chosen the wrong quarry today, you base and loathsome scoundrel. Shame on you for thinking I'd betray the man I love. Our deal's done, so go. You know now that I mean what I say: if you don't leave at once, I'll physically boot you out.'

The truth was that Gisli had been easily within Eyjolf's reach. He was hiding in a network of passages dug beneath Aud's house and below her fields. He stayed there all through the summer.

Bork had his suspicions and Thordis' hearsay fed these. On the night of the autumn equinox, he sent Eyjolf the Grey and his gang to surround Aud's farm. Once again, Aud had warning of their approach.

There was a full moon; it was icy cold. Eyjolf's scouts found two sets of footprints in the frost, a woman's and a man's, starting from a foxhole in the middle of Aud's fields. These led through pasture and scrub, to a towering cliff.

On a ledge near the top Gisli the Outlaw was awaiting them, brandishing a sword and an axe. Beside him stood Aud, armed with a massive club.

Eyjolf's fighters drew their weapons, then set off up the rock face towards them.

Gisli and Aud stayed motionless. Neither of them flinched.

The first fighter came up level with them and swung back his spear to attack. In one quick movement of Gisli's sword, he was disarmed, stabbed, sliced clean in two and sent tumbling from the cliff.

More men clambered up after him, like ants. One by one, with astonishing dexterity and strength, Gisli dodged their weapons and calmly slaughtered them.

Meanwhile, Eyjolf the Grey slipped off round the cliff, onto a sheep track. He ran up it to a hillock, jumped down onto the ledge and sidled along it, closer, closer…

Aud heard his footsteps. She swung round, red-faced like an enraged giantess, and swiped her club at him with unnatural force. Eyjolf reeled back, stumbling and groaning.

His men came swarming over the ledge, besieging Gisli on all sides. Gisli and Aud pelted them with heavy rocks.

Several fell instantly to their death, but others dodged the missiles and ran at their prey, hurling spears. Many met their target: Gisli was quickly bespattered with bloody wounds. That didn't stop him smashing some of his assailants off the cliff with his axe, and beheading others with his sword, until the ground below was littered with a gruesome pile of bodies.

As Gisli struck the penultimate man, he teetered momentarily off balance. Eyjolf the Grey, seeing his chance, rammed him from behind; and at that moment, the last of his aides leaped up, seized Gisli's arms, hurled him to the ground and rained sword blows all over him.

Gisli's abdomen split open in an enormous gash so that his very guts spilled out. He used his free hand to shove them back inside, securing them in place with the cord of his shirt. Then he resumed his fight as if nothing was amiss – until finally, with the frenzy of impending death, he drove his sword into the last thug's head, split him down to the waist – and collapsed into his wife's arms.

For notes on this story, see page 351.

WORDS OF WISDOM

THE IMPORTANCE OF GOOD REPUTATION

Cattle die and kin die.
You'll die just the same.
But words of praise never die
for the one who earns a good name.

Few people are spoken of
in the way they would choose.

It takes time to test a man's worth

No one is so good that he has no faults –
nor so bad that he's good for nothing.

An over-praised man will always let you down.

HOW TO HANDLE WEALTH

Wealth can vanish in the blink of an eye;
gold is a treacherous friend.

The brave and generous live the best lives
and seldom feel worry or sorrow.

COMMON SENSE

A fool lies awake all night
Brooding on everything.
When morning comes, he's exhausted –
Yet everything's just as bad as before.

In so many cases where tempers are provoked,
there are two sides to the issue.

No one ever had a more decent friend
Or a better burden to carry
Than a good store of common sense.

For notes, see page 353.

TALES OF
LOVE
&
HATE

Ancient stories tell that Borgny, King Heidrek's daughter,
came to Mornaland in terrible pain.
Oddrun, Atli's sister, heard of her plight.
She saddled a black horse
and let it run over smooth earth tracks
until she came to a high-standing hall.
She entered it and walked its length calling,
'What is happening here in Hunland?'
'I am lying here, overcome with pain,' said Borgny.
'Dear friend, help me if you can!'
'But which warrior has brought you to this disgrace?'
'My lover's name is Vilmund,' said Borgny.
'He kept me warm in his bed for five years,
without my father ever finding out.'

— *Oddrunargratr,* **Poetic Edda**

OF LOVE AND GODDESSES

What makes women and men fall in love?

Ask not 'what?' but 'who?' Love is the handiwork of goddess Sjofn. It is she who steals people's composures, and teases their hearts with affection and desire.

Where should a girl turn, if she wishes to guard her chastity?

She should seek protection from Gefjun and Fulla, the immortal virgins. Like them she should let her long hair flow free and wear her untouched womanhood with pride.

Is it worse never to know love; or to find love and then lose it?

Who can say which pain is worse, which rewards the greater? Some claim that women who never love shrivel up like dry leaves; yet in death they are destined to become honoured attendants of the goddess Gefjun. As for those who love and lose, they may justly rank themselves alongside the goddess Freyja. For she lost her husband, Od, when he left her behind to go travelling, never to return. In her sorrow, she wandered all the worlds endlessly in search of him, weeping tears of red-gold, but she never found him again. However, though her man abandoned her, he left her a priceless treasure: Hnoss, the beautiful, precious daughter whom he sired on her.

Supposing I am in danger of compromising my honour: which goddess should I pray to?

Frigg will hear your entreaties, and surely send her helper, Hlin, to protect and save you.

And what if some malicious love rival taints my reputation by accusing me of dishonourable deeds that I did not commit?

Do not despair, but call on Syn. She places barriers before those who make false allegations, and will ensure that your denials are justly heard.

What can a woman do if a man breaks the promises he made to her?

She needs do nothing. For justice will come through the goddess Var, who listens to all oaths and secret promises made between women and men. Rest assured: she punishes those who break them.

And what can a woman do if her father or kinsmen refuse a marriage proposal that she herself longs to accept?

She should not weep but pray to the goddess Lofn, whose heart is truly generous. She may be moved to obtain permission for the marriage from the highest ones, Frigg and Odin All-Father, thus overriding the refusals of men.

For notes, see page 353.

THE LOVE TRIANGLE

There was a man called Osvif who had a daughter called Gudrun. She was a very beautiful girl: in fact, everyone said she was the loveliest in all the local valleys. She was also exceptionally clever and self assured.

Unfortunately, Osvif didn't appreciate her outstanding qualities, and the old fool gave her away at a tender age to the very first suitor who asked for her, a fellow called Thorvald Halldorsson. Although Thorvald was stinking rich, that didn't in the least make up for the fact that he was tiresome and moth-eaten, with less courage than a mouse.

All the local families came to the wedding, and there was plenty of gossip, for everyone thought it a very strange match. The other girls couldn't stop giggling and shuddering at the thought of going to bed with such a repulsive namby-pamby. They couldn't understand why Gudrun hadn't stood up for herself and refused to marry him.

They found out soon after the wedding. Apparently, at first Gudrun had indeed strongly resisted. But Thorvald was totally infatuated with her. The more she said 'No', the more he tempted her with extraordinary promises, and he kept nagging Osvif too. In the end, Osvif convinced Gudrun she'd be naive to turn him down. For Thorvald had offered to let her take charge of all *his* wealth as well as her own. He swore to buy her all the jewellery she wanted, no expense spared or questions asked. And what finally clinched it was the escape clause: if they got divorced – even if the marriage hardly lasted any time – she would get a full half share of Thorvald's estate as well as keeping her own dowry.

Anyway, Gudrun managed to put up with Thorvald for quite a while, which must have been an ordeal for her.

Then a man called Thord Ingunnarson moved into the farm next to theirs. He was very capable and dashing – everything that Thorvald wasn't. Thord Ingunnarson was also stuck in an unhappy marriage. He and Gudrun found each other very attractive.

Thord Ingunnarson made himself friendly with Thorvald, which gave him the perfect excuse to visit whenever he knew that Gudrun was at home. The servants soon noticed that most of the conversation on these occasions wasn't between the two men, but between Thord Ingunnarson and Gudrun. Eyebrows were raised and knowing looks exchanged.

One summer's evening, Thord Ingunnarson called by when Thorvald was up at their shieling, far away on the fell tops. That didn't stop Gudrun eagerly inviting her neighbour inside. Soon she was confiding to Thord in a very familiar way.

'Just look at this bruise on my cheek,' she said. 'It's Thorvald's fault. He promised before witnesses at our wedding always to buy me whatever I want. But when I asked for a necklace from that merchant ship down in the fjord, he refused, called me a greedy bitch – and *slapped* me really hard.'

216

'That's disgraceful,' said Thord Ingunnarson. 'A man who hits a woman is lower than a beast.'

'I can't stomach him any longer,' she said. 'You understand the law, Thord, don't you? Can I divorce him for this violence?'

'Well,' said Thord Ingunnarson, 'some chieftains would oppose it on principle: they'd say you must have provoked Thorvald to hit you. I've got a better idea. You must sew Thorvald a new shirt, with a really wide neck opening, and make it much longer than usual – so that it could be mistaken for a woman's dress. As soon as he tries it on, scream loudly and accuse him of being a transvestite. Make a really huge fuss so that the servants all rush over to see what's up – they're your witnesses. Thorvald's so meek, he'll never convince them that you tricked him to wear it. A husband dressing like a woman is incontestable grounds for divorce.'

Gudrun didn't need telling twice. Thord Ingunnarson's plan worked perfectly. Thorvald was compelled to give Gudrun her freedom, plus the full half of his estate which he had pledged to her. She was only seventeen years old – but already on the way to becoming a very wealthy woman.

Shortly afterwards, Thord Ingunnarson divorced his own obnoxious wife, and Gudrun married him. They got on splendidly and it seemed that her life was working out well, despite that unlucky start.

But then the sorcerers moved in.

Yes, that's right, *sorcerers*: a whole unsavoury family of them from the wild islands of the Hebrides. They built a house right next to the farm that belonged to Thord Ingunnarson's mother, and within days they were blighting her sheep and crops with evil spells.

Thord Ingunnarson was compelled to take action to save his mother. Gudrun begged him to be careful, pointing out the dangers of opposing supernatural powers. However, Thord reckoned that the law was mightier than any magic.

He gathered nine supporters and sailed round the coast to the sorcerers' house. There he charged the sorcerers with witchcraft, and summonsed them to appear before the Law Chiefs at the next Althing. The sorcerers just guffawed and spat at him.

However, as soon as Thord and his men set sail for home, the sorcerers climbed onto a ricketty driftwood platform and started chanting incantations and making ear-splitting screeches. Almost at once, the sky darkened, a wind blew up and hailstones bucketed down.

Thord Ingunnarson's ship thrust against the tempest, lurching and teetering. Suddenly a freak wave rose alongside it, dark and huge as a whale, a solid wall of water. It spun the ship round – then smashed it hard against a ridge of rocks.

They didn't have a chance. The entire crew was drowned, including Thord Ingunnarson.

Gudrun's dreams and hopes were all smashed too, for now she was a widow.

Gudrun returned to live with her parents. Time went by and she gradually got over her tragic loss. Her beauty blossomed more than ever. Her broken spirit healed.

She was at her most radiant when she met Kjartan Olafsson.

Before the story goes on, you need to know some things about Kjartan's background, because they had a direct bearing on Gudrun's fate.

Firstly, Kjartan had a cousin and foster-brother to whom he was very close, called Bolli. They'd grown up together in the house of Kjartan's father, a rich and well-respected farmer called Olaf the Peacock. The foster-brothers were of similar age, both strong, handsome and very accomplished; and they were virtually inseparable. But Kjartan always had a slight edge over Bolli; some people reckoned that Bolli lived in Kjartan's shadow.

Secondly, there was a curse hanging over the family.

This came about through Kjartan's older sister, Thurid, who was given in marriage to a rather nasty fellow called Geirmund the Noisy. Thurid wasn't at all sorry when he deserted her. But she was so furious that he didn't provide any means to raise their child, that she snatched away Geirmund's most precious family heirloom, a sword known as 'Leg-Biter'. In revenge, Geirmund made this ominous curse: *'May Leg-Biter cause the death of the best man in your family – and in the most atrocious way.'* Thurid just laughed at him, took Leg-Biter home and gave it to her foster-brother, Bolli. For a long time, the curse on it was forgotten.

Now, back to Gudrun.

Near her father's farm, there were some hot springs – a

popular place for young people to meet, bathe, chatter and flirt. Being unattached again, Gudrun became a regular there – just like Kjartan and Bolli. Whenever the two young men went to the hot springs Gudrun was there; and whenever she went, they were there. The three became very good friends.

After they had been meeting up regularly for a while, Kjartan got in the habit of nudging Bolli when Gudrun arrived. Then, with a sigh, Bolli would tactfully slip away to chat with some other people. Left alone together, Kjartan and Gudrun couldn't stop talking to each other. Sometimes they would wander off into the hills together – where, no doubt, they couldn't keep their hands off each other either.

'Don't you think Kjartan and Gudrun make an ideal couple?' everyone said to Bolli. He didn't deny it, but then he didn't agree with them either.

On the other hand, Olaf the Peacock had misgivings, and he was frank about them. 'Gudrun won't bring you any luck,' he said to Kjartan grimly. And he started looking around for a way to distract his son from the affair.

Despite his father's warning, Kjartan blithely continued to lead Gudrun on... Until one day, totally out of the blue, he announced that he and Bolli were going abroad.

'One of my uncles is a merchant,' he explained. 'He's asked us to sail across to Norway and deliver a valuable cargo to King Olaf Tryggvason in Trondheim.'

Of course, it's not unusual for young men to go travelling before they settle down. So at first Gudrun just nodded and asked, 'When will you be back?'

'Well, while we're out there, we want to take a good look around,' said Kjartan. 'And we hope to spend some time in the king's court, like my father did when he was young – try to get ourselves noticed there, perhaps even win some treasure.'

'For how long?' she pressed him.

Kjartan said, 'Long enough to make my mark with the king. Hopefully I'll be back this time next year.'

'A whole year!' said Gudrun. 'I'll miss you.' Then she suggested something that really threw him. 'You know, I've always wanted to see the world too. You mentioned that Bolli's going with you. Let *me* come as well.'

'Don't be ridiculous,' he said. 'I can't have a *woman* tagging along!'

'Why ever not? Lots of women go on voyages.'

'The time will soon pass,' said Kjartan quickly.

'I'm sure it will for you,' said Gudrun. 'But for me it will seem like for ever.'

'I'll soon be back,' he said. 'I swear I'll be true to you.'

'What, with all those exotic ladies in the king's court?' she said. 'I don't believe you.'

'I have to do this to prove myself worthy of you,' he said. 'Please, just be patient and wait for me. As soon as I come back, we can…'

'You've made me a worthless promise,' she said. 'I'll be more honest, and promise you nothing.'

And so the couple parted on very bad terms.

Despite refusing to commit herself, Gudrun still nursed a hope that Kjartan would return to her. She kept away from the hot springs and spent the whole year working quietly at the weaving loom on Osvif's farm. At long last she had a visitor, newly returned from Norway. However, it wasn't Kjartan – but his foster-brother and dearest friend, Bolli.

'Where's Kjartan?' were Gudrun's first words. 'Is he all right?'

'He's still at the royal court in Trondheim,' said Bolli. 'The king's holding him prisoner!'

Then Bolli told her in detail about their exploits. 'Norway's in uproar,' he said. 'King Olaf is introducing sweeping changes, trying to convert the whole country to Christianity – and Iceland too. Well, one night we were in a drinking hall talking to some fellows who were grumbling about all this, and Kjartan said, "If you don't like it, you should set fire to the royal palace." He didn't realise that the whole place is crawling with spies. The next day he was hauled up before the king, charged with treason. As you know, Kjartan's no coward, so he immediately admitted his guilt and invited the king to kill him in whatever way he fancied…'

Gudrun gasped.

'But King Olaf's reaction was extraordinary,' said Bolli. 'He said, "I can see you believe in honesty, Kjartan. Well, as a Christian, *I* believe in *forgiveness*. So I'm going to pardon you." Kjartan couldn't believe his ears. "You're crazy!" he said. "No I'm not," said King Olaf, acting all self-righteously. "I intend my good example will inspire you to change your beliefs." And then he revealed the catch. "In return for sparing your life, you've got to stay in my court until you've become a baptised Christian."'

'What ever did Kjartan say?' asked Gudrun.

'He decided that it was in his best interests to go along with it.'

Gudrun was astonished. 'So Kjartan has forsaken Thor, Frey and Odin?'

'It was the most realistic solution,' said Bolli. 'He assumed that once he had converted, the king would let him go. But you know how persuasive Kjartan is? Well, king Olaf noticed that too, and he decided to put it to good use. He said that he still wouldn't let Kjartan return to Iceland unless he agreed to convert everyone *here* to Christianity too.'

'And what did Kjartan say to *that*?'

'Naturally, he refused,' said Bolli. 'He pointed out that we Icelanders don't let kings order us about. King Olaf was furious, and now he's holding Kjartan hostage until the whole of Iceland has taken up the new religion. He's sending out missionaries to achieve this very soon, but who knows how long that will take – or even if it will ever happen? So there's no knowing how long Kjartan will be kept in Trondheim.'

'Did he send me any message?' said Gudrun.

'Oh yes,' said Bolli. 'He sends his greetings.'

'His *greetings*?' said Gudrun. 'Is that all? Anyway, why doesn't Kjartan escape? He's so clever, surely he could if he wanted to? Or is he happy to stay there? No men were ever closer friends than you two, Bolli. Tell me!'

'Well,' said Bolli evasively, 'there's a lot of very pleasant company in King Olaf's court.'

'What sort of company?' said Gudrun.

'Oh, the usual: warriors, noblemen...and of course lots of Christian priests.'

'And...does King Olaf also socialise with ladies?' said Gudrun.

'Only his own kinswomen,' said Bolli.

'I think you're hiding something from me,' said Gudrun, 'and that's unkind.'

'Right then, I'll tell you the truth,' said Bolli. 'King Olaf has a sister, the lady Ingibjorg. She's very fond of Kjartan.'

'And what are Kjartan's feelings?'

At last Bolli looked Gudrun directly in the eye. 'He certainly spends a lot of time with her.'

Gudrun became very withdrawn.

Bolli, meanwhile, moved back onto Olaf the Peacock's farm and started visiting Gudrun regularly. At first he pretended this was just to cheer her up – and himself too, for he also missed Kjartan. But soon his visits became more frequent. Then he brazenly asked Gudrun to marry him.

Gudrun politely declined.

Shortly after this, a band of missionaries arrived in the area, just as Bolli had predicted. They preached clever sermons and argued strongly in favour of the new religion. Gudrun, for obvious reasons, converted straight away. Quite a few other people went over eagerly too, naively hoping that Christian 'forgiveness' would bring an end to blood feuds. Other people weren't so enthusiastic, so the missionaries used violent threats and even carried out some brutal killings to make them change their minds. In the end, the lingering doubters capitulated just to be left in peace. It was the same all over the country. Finally, the Law Chiefs sent word to King Olaf Tryggvason that Iceland was now officially Christian.

Once the dust had settled, Bolli proposed to Gudrun again.

'But surely Kjartan's on his way home now?' she said. 'King Olaf promised to set him free once Iceland was fully converted.'

'Well, there's no sign of him, is there?' said Bolli. 'He's probably decided to stay in Trondheim after all. You can't wait for him for ever, Gudrun. Kjartan's a great fellow, but he can be very fickle and he often forgets his promises. Most likely, he's put you right out of his mind and leaped at the chance to marry King Olaf's sister, Ingibjorg. I know you always used to prefer him, but remember it was *me*, not him who rushed home as soon as I could. Marry me and you can be sure of a steady and faithful husband.'

While Gudrun was wringing her hands over this disappointment, Bolli hurried to her father, Osvif. Unfortunately Osvif hadn't learned from his mistake in forcing Gudrun into her first, ill-fated marriage. So he got his five sons to help him exert pressure on Gudrun to make a sensible choice and settle down. Eventually she caved in and accepted Bolli's proposal.

The wedding feast was marred by Gudrun making it obvious that she wasn't at all in love with Bolli, and was marrying him against her better judgement.

Even so, she might have made the best of it if Kjartan hadn't suddenly come swaggering home. Unsettling gossip soon reached Gudrun's ears. Apparently, Kjartan looked more handsome than ever, and he went about in a set of stunning bright red clothes gifted him by King Olaf. He had also brought home some marvellous treasures, including a magnificent sword that protected its user from wounds, and a fine linen headdress richly embroidered with gold thread, intended for his future bride.

'Let's go to my foster-father's farm at once,' said Bolli. 'I can't wait to see Kjartan again and tell him our exciting news!'

'The thought of seeing Kjartan makes me feel distinctly ill,' said Gudrun. 'Besides, we don't have any "exciting news". Our wedding was a dreary occasion, and life since then has been excessively tedious.'

So Bolli went by himself to welcome Kjartan. When he came home, he didn't look exactly cheerful, and he wouldn't tell Gudrun what had happened between them.

Kjartan never came to visit them, not once, and the two men never met up again voluntarily. The once devoted foster-brothers were now completely estranged.

Gudrun's beauty paled and her habitual expression grew bitter.

Some months later, they heard that Kjartan had made love to another woman and they were getting married. She was called Hrefna and she was the niece of the sea captain whose ship had brought Kjartan back from Norway. Olaf the Peacock was delighted. Obviously Bolli, being Kjartan's foster-brother, was invited to the wedding with Gudrun.

Kjartan and Hrefna seemed very happy. Kjartan publicly presented Hrefna with the exquisite royal headdress – a gift ten times more wonderful than anything Bolli had ever given to Gudrun. All the guests were very impressed. But Gudrun was heard muttering that the sight of Hrefna wearing it was like a stab wound in her heart.

The following winter, Olaf the Peacock held a week-long feast. Obviously, he invited his son Kjartan with Hrefna, and his foster-son Bolli with Gudrun. The atmosphere between the two couples was so cold that it was a relief for all the guests when the merriment was over and it was time to set off for home.

Kjartan and Hrefna were the last to say goodbye. Before mounting his horse, Kjartan checked his bags to make sure he hadn't left anything behind – and let out an angry shout: 'Hey, someone's taken my sword!' He was very agitated. 'The one that King Olaf gave me. It's priceless!'

Olaf the Peacock tutted, double-checked Kjartan's luggage and helped him search right through the house and outbuildings. They didn't find the missing sword. Kjartan was fuming.

'I bet Bolli's got one of his flunkeys to steal it,' said Kjartan. 'The creep! Not only did he snatch Gudrun from me…'

'Shut up!' said Olaf the Peacock. 'Don't you realise how lucky you are that Bolli *did* take Gudrun before she could sink her scheming claws into you? You can be sure it's her who set this up, not Bolli. Don't diminish yourself. The best thing you can do is ignore it.'

However, there was more to come. Before winter's end, it was Osvif's turn to hold a long feast. Naturally, Gudrun and Bolli were there. And so were Olaf the Peacock and Kjartan with Hrefna, since they were Bolli's foster-kin.

As they arrived, all the ladies handed their belongings to the servants to take care of. Later on, they changed into their best dresses and jewellery, ready for the meal. Hrefna had brought the gold embroidered headdress that Kjartan had given her; but mysteriously mislaid it. She was very upset all through the festivities.

At the end, as everyone was leaving, Kjartan stormed up to Bolli.

'I don't know what I've ever done to offend you,' he said quietly. 'If anyone should bear a grudge, it's me. We won't talk about what you did behind my back while I was held prisoner in Norway. But I've had enough of our things going missing. First my sword, then Hrefna's headdress. Where are they?'

'How should I know?' said Bolli.

Olaf the Peacock looked at Gudrun, raising his eyebrows accusingly. She threw him an angry look. Then she turned to Kjartan and hissed at him pointedly, 'You've always been so careless of your belongings. And you've never expressed regret about your *greatest* loss.'

Then to Hrefna she sneered: 'What a pity that headdress is missing: you looked so much better when you wore it.'

Kjartan's sword was eventually found, thrust into a bog, covered in rust and slime. The headdress was never seen again.

Some time later, Kjartan took his revenge. Gudrun and Bolli were staying with Osvif for a while, when a servant came rushing inside, in a panic.

'Sir,' he said to Osvif, 'there's a band of men setting up camp just outside the house! We're besieged by tents!'

'What men?' cried Osvif. 'How many?'

'I counted about sixty, sir. And you won't believe who's leading the siege: it's Bolli's foster-brother, Kjartan Olafsson!'

'Are they carrying weapons?'

'Yes, but they don't look as if they're going to attack unless we challenge them. The thing is, though... They're camped between the house here and the privies, completely blocking access to them.'

'That's disgusting,' said Gudrun. 'Go back outside, speak to them courteously and request that they at least let the ladies through when necessary.'

The servant came back a few moments later, looking more grim-faced than ever.

'Kjartan Olafsson says *no one* can use the privies so long as they're camped here.'

'To think that the man I once loved could stoop so low!' said Gudrun. 'Bolli, surely you can persuade him to see sense?'

'All my life, I've never managed to persuade Kjartan to do anything,' said Bolli. 'Least of all since he returned from Norway.'

'Then overpower him,' said Gudrun. 'Send him on his way.'

'I haven't brought my sword,' said Bolli. 'I didn't expect to need it. Besides, even with your father and brothers fighting beside me, we wouldn't have a hope against Kjartan's sixty men.'

The siege lasted for three days. All through it, Gudrun was in a furious temper. Finally, under cover of darkness, Kjartan and his men slunk away. Osvif's house now stank, and took days to clean out. It was an outrageous humiliation.

They'd scarcely got over that, when Kjartan made trouble again. Bolli and Gudrun were in the process of buying a new farm nearby. However, before it was finalised, Kjartan heard about it, went galloping over to the seller, and persuaded him to renege on the deal and sell the farm to him instead.

'Tit for tat,' said Bolli wryly. 'Kjartan's getting his own back twice over, in return for those two things of his that disappeared. Just like when we were lads. He always did get the better of me.'

'I'm ashamed of you laughing off such deep insults like that,' scolded Gudrun. 'My father and brothers keep asking what plans you've made for vengeance, and all I can say is, "I don't know".'

'Don't you realise? Times have changed,' said Bolli. 'This new Christian creed says we should love our enemies and forgive bad deeds, not fight over them.'

'Forgive? Don't be ridiculous!' said Gudrun. 'We're laughing stocks! You've got to redeem our honour.'

'You seem to forget that Kjartan is my cousin and foster-brother,' said Bolli.

'I don't care! You can't let him get away with this.'

Osvif and his sons suggested numerous plans for vengeance; but they never came to fruition, for Bolli always had an excuse for not organising the deed.

It was an old woman who finally pushed him over the edge. Thorhalla the Gossip lived at Osvif's farm, where her sons worked as labourers. One day she happened to meet Kjartan along the road and coaxed him to have a chat with her. When she came home that night, she looked very smug.

'You know this new Christian Easter festival?' she told Bolli. 'Well, the day after it's over, Kjartan Olafsson is going on a long journey. He'll only have one companion, and I know exactly the route they're going to take.'

'The perfect chance,' said Osvif. 'Bolli, my sons will help you ambush him along the road. At last! It will be easy to get rid of him once and for all.'

'No matter how good the opportunity,' said Bolli, 'it doesn't make it any easier for me to kill the man I grew up with.'

'Ugh, you feeble milksop!' cried Gudrun. 'You'd better do what's needed this time. Otherwise, I'm divorcing you.'

Gudrun and her brothers mobilised several kinsmen and friends to support them. This gave Bolli a great advantage: he was to lead nine men against Kjartan's two. Having no choice now, he stopped making excuses. He armed himself with Leg-Biter, the sword that Kjartan's sister had once given him. Maybe he'd forgotten its ominous curse; or maybe he thought that it couldn't make things any worse than they already were.

The nine lay in wait by a lonely ravine along the road specified by Thorhalla the Gossip. Sure enough, Kjartan and his companion appeared at the expected time. Kjartan spotted the ambush ahead but didn't try to avoid it. He rode right up, then jumped boldly to the ground, sword drawn, and faced his assailants.

His attackers fell on him at once – all except Bolli who just stood aside, hovering and gawping. Kjartan gave battle fearlessly. Even when his companion staggered away with a mortal wound, Kjartan fought on single-handedly against all his opponents – and in no time at all killed two and sent the others sprawling helplessly to the ground.

'Come on Bolli!' he yelled. 'Don't just stand there. You used to love beating me up when we were lads – what's happened to you? I see you've brought Leg-Biter: let's fight hand to hand, and find out what it can do.'

Bolli wavered, his fingers trembling over the hilt of his sword, still uselessly enclosed in its scabbard.

'You timid virgin!' Gudrun's brothers roared at him. 'Shame on you!'

At last, very reluctantly, Bolli drew out Leg-Biter and walked slowly towards Kjartan.

'You're caught between me and Gudrun, aren't you?' said Kjartan softly. 'You know that if I kill you, she might persuade me to free myself to marry her – and you can't bear to think of it. But if *you* kill *me*, you'll never forgive yourself – and nor will she. Either way, you're a loser. And yet... Once each of us would have done anything for the other. So let me at least make it easy for you, brother.'

He tossed his own sword to the ground.

'There. I'm defenceless now. Just do it. Go on, kill me. By Thor and Jesus, how I pity you!'

So Bolli raised Leg-Biter and dealt Kjartan Olafsson his death blow.

But he caught Kjartan as he fell. They sank to the ground together, and Kjartan drew his last breath, cradled in his foster-brother's arms.

Every deed has its consequences; and the worse the deed, the more serious they are.

Bolli was tortured by agonising remorse.

Kjartan's mother – who had raised Bolli tenderly alongside her own children – was now filled with pure, utter hatred for him. Within a year she had successfully goaded her other sons to kill him. Her husband, Olaf the Peacock – bereaved father, betrayed foster-father – died of a broken heart.

As for Gudrun, she didn't shed a single tear for Bolli. But she grieved long and silently for Kjartan.

She did have one more attempt at marriage and found a few brief years of happiness. But her fourth husband met an untimely death too, drowned in a storm at sea.

After that, Gudrun – so beautiful, so passionate, yet so many times disenchanted – simply couldn't take any more. She retreated totally from the world, wrapped herself in dark sackcloth and spent the rest of her life as a recluse.

For notes to this story, see page 354.

VOLUND THE SMITH

There was a king of Sweden called Nidud. He had two sons, but his eldest child was a daughter called Bodvild. When she came of age, King Nidud asked Bodvild if she would like to choose the man that she should marry.

'Yes indeed,' she answered. 'I have long set my heart on Volund, the youngest son of the King of the Finns.'

'Then think again, my daughter,' said King Nidud. 'For the Finns are fey people: it is often said that they have dealings with Dark Elves.'

'That doesn't deter me,' said Bodvild, 'Volund is the man that I want. For I have heard that he is not only strong and valiant, but also a great smith, and that he makes the most wondrous golden rings. If only I had a husband who could adorn me with such jewels, I would be a happy woman indeed.'

So King Nidud sent envoys far northwards to Wolf Dales in the Finns' kingdom, where Prince Volund lived on the shores of a remote lake. They found him there alone, working at a forge behind his hall. Just as Bodvild had said, he was busy hammering red gold into rings. The envoys presented their credentials and said that King Nidud was offering his only daughter to become Volund's wife.

'Tell your king that I do not accept his offer,' said Volund.

'That's a fool's answer,' the envoys said. 'Bodvild is a beautiful maiden and she comes with a generous dowry.'

'That's nothing to me,' said Volund. 'For I am already married.'

The envoys looked around. Volund's hall, like two others dotted around the lakeside, was falling into ruin. Through its open door they saw that the fire-pit was cold. The building was empty but for a rotting wall-bench draped with a tangle of mangy furs.

'It doesn't look as if a woman is in charge of your household,' they said. 'Where is your wife?'

Volund sighed, stood up and went to the door, gazing at the snow-capped mountains.

'It's a sad story,' he said. 'Many winters ago my two brothers and I left our father's court. We travelled on snowshoes and let fate lead us where it would. In time we came to this valley, and we liked it so much that we settled here and each built ourselves a hall.

'One morning we went down to the lake together to fetch water, and were astonished to find that some strangers had also found this lonely place. They were three women, sitting on the shore, spinning flax. On the ground beside them, tossed carelessly to one side, were their cloaks, made of pure white swans' feathers.

'They told us they were valkyries, and also kings' daughters. Their names were Swan-White, Ale-Rune and Strange-Creature, and they had come into this realm by flying over the vast shadows of Mirkwood. They assessed us carefully, then each chose one to be her husband. My own bride was Strange-Creature: I fell in love with her as soon as she wrapped her white arms around my neck to claim me.

And so we married them and all lived here in great happiness.

'However, after seven years our valkyrie brides became restless. By the time eight years had passed, they were talking ceaselessly of their old lives on the battlefields in Odin's service. We tried over and over to dispel their discontent. But nine years after our joint wedding, our beloved wives all donned their swan-feather cloaks and flew away. Nothing any of us could say or do was sufficient to prevent them.

'For many months we hoped that they might regret their flight and return to us. But they never did. My brothers decided to desert their homes, and even now they are travelling southwards and eastwards, ever seeking their lost wives. But for me such a quest would be pointless. When my beloved Strange-Creature left me, with many tears and deep declarations of affection, I promised to wait here for her return – for the rest of my life if necessary. And so you find me compelled never to leave this spot, with my heart already taken. Even if the princess you are offering me is the finest in the world, you understand why I can never marry her.'

The envoys returned to King Nidud and gave him Volund's answer. To Nidud this refusal was like a spear in the flank of an angry bull. He roared with sarcastic laughter at the tale of Volund's valkyrie wife, and swore that he would use any means to ensure that Bodvild got the husband that she wanted.

So hard on the heels of his envoys, now he sent a band of

warriors to Wolf Dales to snatch away Volund the Smith.

However, when they arrived, Volund was away in the mountains hunting: both his forge and his hall were deserted. The warriors did not dare return to their lord empty handed, so they broke into the hall to see what treasure they might seize from there. They were greeted by the sight of seven-hundred gleaming golden rings, all hanging on ropes that dangled from the rafters. They did not attempt to snatch them all, but chose only the most precious, a perfect specimen engraved with patterns so fine and graceful that they resembled swan's down. This they cut free and carried back to Nidud.

Volund was gone on his hunt for many days. At last he returned wearily to his hall, dragging the corpse of a great she-bear behind him. He skinned it, butchered it and set a steak to roast on his fire. While it was cooking, he paced around his hall, inspecting the ropes on which his handiwork was slung, counting his rings.

It did not take him long to notice that the finest ring was missing. He had forged it only the previous month, working it so exquisitely as a gift to his long-lost wife, in the hope that she might yet return. 'Strange-Creature must have come home while I was out in the mountains,' he thought. 'She must have guessed it was for her and taken it. She will surely be back here soon.'

With this sweet thought he feasted alone on his meal of bear meat. Then he fell into a happy reverie, and from that into a long, exhausted slumber.

He did not hear hooves outside, or the clanking of weapons. He did not feel hands seizing and binding him. He was not conscious of being thrown across a horse's back with the indignity of a stuck boar. He was not aware of a long journey in that humiliating state, southward through forest and mountain.

When at last he awoke, he found himself sprawled on a stone floor, his arms and legs trussed up in iron bonds. On a high-seat above him sat King Nidud of Sweden wearing Volund's own sword in his belt. A grim-faced queen sat beside him; and on the queen's other side was a young woman with handsome features and a haughty expression, their only daughter, Bodvild. He struggled upright.

'Welcome, Volund,' said the queen. 'As you can see, we have managed to tame you and drag you away from your wild home. Prepare to celebrate your wedding! Feast your eyes on Bodvild here, for she is soon to be your bride.'

'I am already married,' said Volund coldly, 'and my wife is the only woman I will ever look at.'

The queen snorted disdainfully. 'You yourself told our envoys that it is many years since you held that unknown woman – if she even exists – in your arms. You know you will never see her again. You will soon forget her, Volund, when you have the lovely Bodvild in your bed.'

'No,' said Volund.

King Nidud rose and came to stand before him, with his hand clasped in a fist. He opened it to reveal the golden ring that his warriors had stolen from Volund's hall. He displayed it tauntingly before Volund's face, then turned to Bodvild, took her hand and slipped it on her finger.

'See,' he said, 'the deed is already half done.'

'Yet it shall always remain unfinished,' said Volund.

Nidud spat at him and had him dragged away. He ordered Volund's legs to be lamed by hamstringing so he could not escape, then had him ferried across the sea to an island. There he was freed from his bonds and given a forge to work in.

Thus Volund returned to his old occupation, smithing gold in solitude and silence. Apart from an occasional supply boat, no one ever came to visit him. By day he was compelled to fashion jewels at King Nidud's command. But at night, unable to sleep, he worked secretly on an endeavour of his own, shaping a sheet of gold into a perfect likeness of the swan cloak that had once clad his beloved Strange-Creature.

Then one day a different boat drew up at the island. Two young men – King Nidud's sons – stepped from it, walked up the beach and entered Volund's forge.

Volund glanced up at them, then went back to work without a word.

'Volund,' said one, 'you must give us the key to the chest where you store your finished handiwork.'

'Must I?' Volund answered contemptuously.

'You are our father's prisoner,' they retorted. 'You have no power to refuse us.'

'Oh, I won't refuse you,' said Volund. 'I'll do something else for you instead.'

He seized his sword and, in two short blows, hacked off both the princes' heads. He dug a cavernous hole in the earth beneath his anvil, hauled their decapitated bodies into it and covered them in grit and dirt.

But their heads he kept for his own use. He cleaned the flesh from the skulls, removed the eyes from their sockets and pulled out the teeth. When he had washed the blood from his hands, he sliced the tops off each skull and plated them with molten silver so that they looked like ceremonial drinking vessels. Then he boiled the eyes, hardened them and polished them until they gleamed like gems. Finally, he dipped their teeth in gold then fashioned them into a magnificent pair of brooches.

Some days later, the supply boat arrived with his meagre ration of food. In exchange for this, Volund handed the boatman the silver skulls, the jewelled eyes and the golden tooth brooches.

'Present these from me to the king, the queen and their daughter,' said he; but he gave no hint of how he had made them.

King Nidud and his queen believed that their two sons were away hunting in some distant forest, so they never guessed the origins of these gruesome treasures. As for Bodvild, she took Volund's gift of golden brooches to be a sign that his feelings towards her had altered.

So now she too visited him on his island. Travelling alone and in secret, she presented herself in her finest gown at the door of Volund's forge.

He did not bid her welcome and kept his vow not to look at her. 'What do you want here?' he demanded.

'Two things,' said Bodvild shamelessly. 'Firstly, I wish to thank you for the gift you sent me,'

'You ignorant simpleton,' Volund mocked her. 'And what is the second reason you have come?'

Bodvild pulled a ring from her finger. It was the golden ring engraved with a pattern of swan's down, the one that Volund had made for his beloved lost wife. She held it out to him.

'See, Volund, a crack has formed down the middle of

this,' she simpered. 'I have brought it for you to mend.'

Volund guessed she had broken this priceless jewel as a cunning ploy. He let her soft, white fingers drop the broken ring into his own rough hand, then drew her into his forge. He brought her a cup of ale and, as soon as she had drained it, gave her another and another, until at last she was helpless and totally under his power. Then he laid Bodvild onto a bench and ravished her, brutally fulfilling her desire.

When she had sunk at last into shameful sleep, Volund drew his golden swan cloak from its hiding place, draped it over his shoulders, raised his arms beneath it and rose aloft, finally making his escape.

Bodvild was found at last by her fearful family. She bore the bastard child she had conceived by Volund and lived the rest of her life in disgrace.

But Volund the Smith vanished and was never seen again.

For notes on this story, see page 356.

HELGI & SIGRUN

A queen woke in the darkest reaches of the night. Eagles were screaming; water rained down as if the very rivers of Asgard were in flood. As she stepped from her hall, a wind rose; and on it came a rush of eerie women's voices.

'Who is passing?' the queen called.

They answered, 'We are norns.'

'Where have you come from? What news do you bring?'

'We are fresh from watching the birth of a boy-child,' they answered. 'It is written in the runes of this child's future that he is destined for greatness. He will slay his father's bitter enemy, a mighty king. Many ravens will feast on the blood spilt by his sword. None shall vanquish him. For a thousand years, poets will sing his praises.'

'What is he called? Whose son is he?'

'Helgi is his name. His father is King Sigmund the Volsung.'

'Then he springs from a matchless lineage. Who will be good enough to marry him?'

'Either a fool or an exceptional woman. For Helgi will never grow old, and the woman who goes to him will not find comfort for long unless she is willing to follow him beyond death. Now listen, lady. Soon you will be with child, and will give birth to a daughter. Heed our warning. If you wish her to find happiness, keep her away from this hero.'

Then the norns hastened away. The queen went back to the bed where her husband, King Hogni, was waiting to pleasure her. Before the year was out, just as the norns had told, a daughter was born to them. They called her Sigrun. Naturally, they were anxious to avert the norns' prophesy, so they betrothed her at an early date to a man who was already old, a neighbouring king called Hodbrodd.

The boy born on that night, Helgi Sigmundsson, was proud and fearsome. As he grew up, he never tired of listening to talk of glorious battles. Often he would hear his father scorning a despicable enemy called King Hunding, ruler of the realm of Hunland and a rapacious raider. By the time he had lived through fifteen winters, Helgi was resolved to prove his mettle by ridding the world of this foe.

Helgi was a deep thinker. He perceived that cunning was a useful accessory to strength, and that surveillance could be a powerful weapon. So before embarking on his campaign, he shamelessly shaved his beard, donned a dress and apron to disguise himself as a maidservant, and thus found work in King Hunding's household. In this way, he rooted out the secrets of his enemy's weakness.

Then he gathered a host of his father's most valiant warriors and led them out to war in Hunland. The battle was fierce but short lived: Helgi easily slaughtered Hunding and all his troops.

The air echoed with the grief of the slain king's sons – yet they were too feeble to vow revenge. Instead they demanded recompense, rings and other treasure, like affronted old maids. Helgi blithely cut down these cowards too and threw them to the wolves alongside their father.

Helgi's men celebrated his first magnificent victory by sacrificing cattle on a beach. They devoured the meat raw and bloody, and anointed their leader with his hero's name: Helgi Hunding's-Bane.

Suddenly a shadow darkened the sky. From its midst, in a radiance of dazzling weapons, nine valkyries sank to the ground. They cast aside their helmets, slipped from their winged cloaks and stepped lightly amongst the corpses of Hunding's defeated men.

'Welcome, spear maidens,' Helgi greeted them. 'What is your business this evening?'

One answered, 'On Odin's orders, we come to fetch the dead warriors he has chosen to feast and fight forever under the golden thatch of Slain Hall.'

'When your work is done,' said Helgi, 'come back and join our celebrations. There is enough mead and wine for you all, and we will gladly entertain you through the night.'

But the valkyries shook their heads.

Another stepped forward saying, 'There is no time for merrymaking, for before our work today is even finished, we wish you to undertake a task, Helgi.'

'Name it,' said he.

And she answered, 'You must fight a new war – for me.'

Helgi looked at her closely. He saw that she had great beauty; and that her eyes were defiant and wild.

'Who are you?' he asked her. 'And why do you choose me to defend you?'

'I am Sigrun, King Hogni's daughter,' she told him. 'I choose you because all through my childhood I have heard tales of your coming, and my heart has constantly yearned to find you. But my father forbids me even to think of you; for he has promised me in marriage to a decrepit old man. In order to avoid this terrible fate, I fled my father's house and beseeched the priests of Odin to make endless sacrifices on my behalf. As a result, these women who ride at evening have accepted me as a sister; but I will never be truly free until my betrothed is dead.'

'Tell me the name of this wretch,' said Helgi.

'It is King Hodbrodd,' she said. 'Seek him out and kill him, Helgi. Then protect me from my father's anger.'

'What will be my reward for doing this?' he asked.

Sigrun smiled at him. 'My love, Helgi. Win this war for me, and I promise I shall always be yours.'

Helgi did not refuse her. Nor did he waste any time. He travelled far and wide through his father's realm, summoning up even more fearless warriors until his band stood twelve-hundred strong. Together they boarded a fleet of great ships, then sailed in all haste to the hateful King Hodbrodd's realm.

As they neared the enemy coast, a violent tempest struck. A gale whipped up, the clouds burst and lightening set the masts aflame like a row of blazing suns. The ships were certain to capsize, drowning all the men.

However Sigrun and her spear-sisters were watching over them. Just as it seemed that all was lost, they came galloping through the sky into the very eye of the storm. Within moments they had quelled it: the wind calmed, the downpour ceased and Helgi's army sailed safely in to land.

Hodbrodd had news of their coming and was awaiting them. Alongside his own massed warriors, there stood another king: Sigrun's own father. Behind him were all her brothers. They were outraged at her rebellion, and determined to defend their honour by giving her to Hodbrodd.

Helgi landed. The two armies stood face to face.

Hodbrodd opened the hostilities with mocking laughter and a torrent of shameful insults: 'What do you want, you cur, you little wound-sucker? Run along! Go skulk under a haystack with the slave girls. No one's scared of you – not since the troll-wives cut off your balls!'

Helgi Hunding's-Bane answered coldly, 'Iron speaks louder than a coward's jibes.'

Then he ordered his army to brandish arms and charge at Hodbrodd's troops without delay.

It was a ferocious battle but by the end, Hodbrodd and all his followers were slain. Alongside them lay Sigrun's fallen kinsmen.

As Helgi claimed the victory, the nine valkyries descended from the clouds. Sigrun ran joyously to embrace him.

'You have earned your reward well, Helgi,' she cried. 'Go and reap red-gold rings from the vanquished one's coffers. Then come to claim your promised reward: Sigrun Hognisdaughter as your bride!'

'My love,' Helgi answered, 'not everything has worked out as you might have wished it. Though I felt your presence guiding my hand in battle, ill fate was at work elsewhere. For your father and most of your kin are now wolves' pickings. Only one of your brothers still lives, and he will not ignore what I have done.'

Despite this foreboding, Sigrun and Helgi were joyously married. However, their first passion had scarcely cooled before the war came back to haunt them.

For as Helgi had told, one of Sigrun's brothers, a man called Dag, had survived his wounds. At the end of the battle, he feigned a truce with Helgi's forces, using false oaths to buy him time for vengeance.

Dag went to Odin's temple and sacrificed generously to the War-Father, petitioning him for help. Soon after, a spear came into his hands, tempered so sharply that not even the greatest champion would be mighty enough to withstand it. Then he tricked Helgi to come alone to a deserted place and ruthlessly struck him dead.

Sigrun's tears were boundless. She spurned her brother's excuses and drove him away, wearing her widowhood like a shroud. A magnificent burial mound was raised in honour of her husband; but Sigrun was too heartbroken even to approach it.

A year passed after the funeral of Helgi Hunding's-Bane. Then one evening Sigrun's maid came hurrying to her, white faced and trembling.

'My lady,' she cried, 'I was walking through the dusk this

247

evening, past your husband's mound, when I saw a host of warriors on horseback coming towards me. Your own lord, Helgi, was amongst them.'

'Can this really be true?' whispered Sigrun. 'Tell me, what was he doing? Did he ask for me?'

'At first I was too terrified to speak,' the maid answered. 'But at last I plucked up courage and asked him if what I saw was really him, or only a dream. He answered me at once, saying, "What your eyes behold is true." I marvelled at his coming and asked if it meant that the world was ending and Ragnarok coming to pass. He assured me it was not, then added: "Give my wife a message. Tell her that her prince awaits her gentle fingers to staunch his dripping wounds." '

'I will go to him at once,' said Sigrun.

The maid's terror could not dissuade her. As the moon rose, Sigrun discarded her mourning dress for a silk gown, and hastened to the burial mound.

'Open the entrance stone!' she cried. 'Stand back and let me pass!'

The guards were astonished and dismayed, but yielded to her authority. They hauled aside the great boulder that formed the door of the tomb. Sigrun crept past them into the deathly gloom.

What did she find there? Helgi ice-cold, drenched in hail and blood.

What did she do? She slipped out to fetch linen sheets, carried them into the tomb and spread them over the chill stone as if this were their marital bed. Then she beckoned her lover's vaporous ghost to lie with her. But though he looked at her with longing, at last he only shook his head, for his men were calling him to ride on; and even as she tried to enclasp him, he faded away and vanished.

After that, Sigrun waited for him night after night. But he had been received now into the glory of Odin's hall; and from there no warrior ever returns.

For notes on this story, see page 358.

VERSES FROM
THE COURT POETS

IN PRAISE OF A SHIP

Fair lady! A fine ship
Slips forth into the sea,
A shimmering dragon
That outshines the sun's own
Gold fire, gliding proud and
Glorious to battle.

A CALL TO WARRIORS

The cock flutters his
feathers: a fresh day breaks.
Already the slaves
have set out
To toil in the fields –
So troops, tumble from your beds!
Awake and rise,
My fearless friends –
Not for wine or women
but to heed the valkyries' call to war.

A POET DECLARES HIS LOYALTY TO HIS KING

Greetings, great war king!
Your loyal servant is home.
May all men take heed
of my song.
My lord, please show me
my seat amongst your warriors.
I am overwhelmed with joy
To see your hall once more.

No doubt you heard tell
how King Knut the ring giver
asked me to work for him
instead of you.
But I said, 'I prefer to serve
My present lord for all time.'
This is the truth
as every man there witnessed.

A GREAT KING'S LAST BATTLE

The Norse lord's brutal blows
raining down in battle,
split open warriors' skulls
and severed countless shields.
Blood from dead kings bubbled
across the soil. Abandoned
weapons gleamed: a gory
glow stained the island red.

For notes, see page 359.

TALES
OF
EXPLORATION

So wise men say, that from Norway, out of Stad,
there are seven half-days sailing to Horn in eastern Iceland;
and from Snowfells Ness, where the cut is shortest,
there are four days main west to Greenland.
But it is said, that if one sails from Bergen
straight west to Warf in Greenland,
then one must keep about twelve sea miles south of Iceland.
But from Reekness, in southern Iceland,
there are five days' main to Jolduhlaup
in Ireland, going south;
and from Longness, in northern Iceland, it is four days.

— *Landnamabok*

WINELAND

'It was Karlsefni himself who told more
fully than anyone else the story of all these voyages,
which to some extent has been recorded here.'
– *Graenlendinga Saga*

There was an Icelandic sea captain called Thorfinn Karlsefni. One summer he arrived in Trondheim with a cargo of luxurious furs and casks of fine wine. This was a very unusual combination; for as everyone knows, the best furs come from the far north – whereas grapes to make wine grow only in the south. Naturally his customers were curious to know where he had acquired this ill-sorted mixture of goods. His answer was quite extraordinary. He claimed that they came from an idyllic country that no one had ever heard of before, lying right on the edge of the world.

'Wild grapes grow everywhere there,' he said, 'bigger and juicier than you can imagine. Because of that, it's called Wineland.'

Wineland? His customers found it hard to believe that such a place really existed. They demanded to know whether he had actually been there.

'I certainly have,' he said. Then he launched into a detailed explanation:

A few years ago (said Karlsefni) I sailed out west to do some trading in Greenland. You might have heard that a number of Icelandic families recently emigrated there. It's a wild place and quite remote, and the interior is uninhabitable because it's permanently covered in ice; but there's good grazing land in some areas up the west coast.

Other merchants had been out there before me, selling the Greenlanders everyday supplies that they can't produce themselves because of the harsh climate. They'd bartered these for the local people's hunting produce – furs, walrus-ivory and so on – all very high quality. It sounded like an excellent opportunity to get hold of some valuable goods to sell on.

There's only a month or two each summer when it's safe for ships to make the journey to Greenland. I was stupid enough to set out quite close to the end of this period, and by the time I arrived at the nearest settlement, the sea was already full of icebergs. So I was stranded there for the winter.

I managed to find hospitality at Brattahlid Farm on Eiriksfjord. It belongs to a man known as Leif the Lucky, son of Eirik the Red. I expect you've heard of this Eirik? He was the fellow who discovered Greenland and led the first settlers out there. In his youth he was a violent troublemaker, twice outlawed for murder, but he made good in the end. Leif himself is completely different from his father; he's very generous and likeable, and he offers open house to anyone who needs lodgings.

When I arrived, one of his permanent guests was his sister-in-law, Gudrid. Unfortunately, she'd been widowed twice, but she was still young and pretty, a wonderfully optimistic woman with a taste for adventure. I was still a single man. Right from our first meeting, we got on very well. So straight after the Christmas feast, we got married.

At that time there was a lot of excited talk going round Eiriksfjord about a mysterious country that lay even further west over the sea from Greenland. Naturally, I wanted to know all about it.

'It was discovered by Bjarni Herjolfsson,' Gudrid told me, 'an Icelandic merchant like you. He was on his way to visit his parents here in Greenland when a storm blew him off course, and then he was becalmed by fog. By the time the weather finally cleared and settled, he found himself drifting down a strange coast of lush hills and trees. He didn't stop to explore it because he was desperate to reach Greenland before winter set in. When he finally arrived here and talked about what he'd seen, no one believed him; people reckoned that the bad weather had made his entire crew hallucinate. But Bjarni insisted it was true. So the following summer Leif here led an expedition to check it out.'

Then Leif took up the story.

'The land most definitely exists,' he said, 'and it seems to be huge. Our first sighting wasn't very promising: barren cliffs, slabs of rock and glaciers, just like the wilderness north of here. But we sailed on roughly southwards, following the coast a long way down. Gradually the landscape turned green and from then on it got better and better: rich pastures, forests and great rushing rivers. We landed, took a good look around and helped ourselves to loads of timber. Then we noticed there were wild vines growing everywhere, literally smothered with grapes. Because of that, I've named the country Wineland. It's a wonderful place: even the dew on the grass is as sweet as honey.'

'It sounds almost too good to be true,' I said. 'Aren't there any snags? Is it a suitable country for settling?'

'That's what we wondered,' said Leif. 'So we decided to give it a try. The rivers and sea were teeming with fish, there were loads of edible berries just ripe for picking, and there was plenty of game, including lots of animals we'd never seen before. We built some huts and spent the winter there. The climate's much milder than here, so it went really well – no problems at all.

'When we got home, my brother Thorvald couldn't get over our fantastic cargo. So the following summer, I gave him my ship and *he* sailed to Wineland with a crew of thirty men. They found the huts we'd built, refurbished and enlarged them, and spent two-and-a-half years there.'

'And is Thorvald still out there?' I asked

Leif looked rather upset. 'He and his men had started to discuss bringing out their wives and establishing a proper colony there,' he said. 'But there was one thing they'd never taken into consideration; and since you appear to be seriously interested in Wineland, I ought to warn you about it. You see, everyone assumed that the place was uninhabited until our people arrived – but it wasn't.'

'So who was already living there?' I said.

Leif said, 'People similar to the hunters of the far north

here. We call them Skraelings. They're rather weird and their equipment's very crude. Here in Greenland they keep to themselves and don't cause any trouble, but the Wineland Skraelings seem to be aggressive. Well, to be honest, it was Thorvald's own fault. He'd been out there nearly three years without ever encountering them. Then he and some companions went off exploring round the coast and spotted some Skraelings for the first time. They were just minding their own business on a beach, but Thorvald didn't like the look of them; so he sent his men to kill them and smash up their boats. One Skraeling got away and raised the alarm. That night when Thorvald and his men were camping by the shore, a swarm of skin boats appeared and the Skraelings started attacking them. To cut a long story short, my brother was killed by one of their arrows. His men buried him out there, then beat a hasty retreat and came home.'

Obviously I was sorry to hear that.

'That's only one of the Wineland-related tragedies that afflicted my family,' said Leif. 'The second one concerned my other brother, Thorstein – that's Gudrid's late second husband. He decided to go out there and have a look round, before bringing back Thorvald's body.'

'And I was going with him,' said Gudrid. 'But we'd hardly sailed any distance when our ship ran into a storm. Instead of heading to Wineland, we were just blown up the Greenland coast to the other big settlement further north. Unfortunately, the whole community there was struck by a raging disease – and Thorstein died of it.'

'What bad luck,' I said. 'But good luck for *me*, because it enabled me to marry you! Would you still like to go to Wineland, Gudrid?'

She said that she would. So we agreed to recruit some people to join us, and sail there as soon as the ice melted.

'If we like what we see and those Skraelings don't cause any more trouble,' I said, 'let's stay there for a few years and try to make a go of it.'

Gudrid was as enthusiastic as I was. News of our plan quickly spread around the area, and soon lots of folk were clamouring to join us. With all the reports of Wineland's rich natural resources, they saw it as an unmissable opportunity.

Gudrid and I set sail with sixty men, five women and a selection of livestock. Leif said we were very welcome to borrow the huts he'd built during his own expedition, which obviously was very helpful. We had good weather all the way, and arrived without any mishaps. We found and moved into Leif's Houses, and in no time at all we'd established a small pioneer community. Just as we'd heard, there was a prolific supply of wild fruit and game, and our first year there was very successful.

By the end of winter, Gudrid was pregnant. Shortly before her time was due, we got our first sight of the Skraelings. They came out of the forest, carrying large packs. Although we couldn't understand each others' languages, they didn't appear hostile; in fact, they clearly wanted to do some trading. They'd brought a stack of really fine furs, far better than anything I'd ever seen before in all my travels. Using sign language, they offered to exchange these for some of our weapons; but there was no way I'd risk agreeing to that.

Then Gudrid came up with a clever idea. 'Did you see how scared the Skraelings were when our bull started bellowing just now?' she said. 'And they keep staring at the cows. They clearly aren't familiar with cattle. So in exchange for the pelts, why don't we offer them some milk and cheese?'

We did; and the Skraelings loved it. It sounds ridiculous, but they ended up overloading us with valuable furs in return for every last drop of our simple dairy produce.

At that point, everything seemed fine; we honestly believed they wouldn't cause any trouble, and that Thorvald's fatal encounter with them must have been an unfortunate mistake. Just to be on the safe side, though, we built a strong wooden palisade round the houses to keep out intruders. Shortly afterwards, Gudrid gave birth to our son Snorri – the only child born in the new colony.

Unfortunately, soon after that, a Skraeling broke through the palisade and tried to steal one of our weapons. One of our men spotted him and challenged him. While they were arguing, a load more Skraelings suddenly appeared and there was a very nasty fight. The Skraelings came off worst, and several got themselves killed.

After the survivors had fled, we all discussed this new development and agreed the Skraelings were bound to mount a revenge attack. It would have been pointless to hang around waiting for it, especially now Gudrid and I had our little lad to take account of. Luckily it was summer, so we packed up straightaway, launched our ships and hastened back to Greenland.

I had a really successful time there, selling all the timber, wine and furs I'd brought back. By the time I'd offloaded it all, Gudrid and I were rich. We reckoned we could do even better if we exported goods from Wineland to Iceland and Norway. However, we didn't fancy another confrontation with the Skraelings; and nor did any of our fellows.

The only Greenlander willing to take this risk was a woman: Leif's sister, and Gudrid's former sister-in-law, Freydis. At that time, two Icelandic brothers had moored their ship in a nearby fjord. Freydis befriended them and persuaded them to sail out to Wineland with her, bring back cargo together and share the profits.

That summer two ships set out, one captained by the Icelanders, and the other commanded by Freydis herself.

Exactly a year later, Freydis's ship returned – alone – overflowing with cargo. All the timber was quickly snapped up by the Greenlanders, because no trees grow out there. But she agreed to sell the rest of the goods to me – which is how I come to be selling these furs and wine here in Trondheim.

Not surprisingly, his customers wanted to know if there was now a permanent settlement in Wineland.

That I can't tell you for certain (said Karlsefni), but there are rumours... You see, a lot of folk in Eiriksfjord don't like Freydis and they resent the fortune she made from the goods she'd brought back, even though she gave her crew a generous share. As a result, there's nasty gossip circulating about her. It's claimed that she fell out with the Icelanders, stirred up a huge quarrel and goaded her crew into killing them and all their men. None of those who sailed with her admit this; but the gossipmongers insist that's because she's bought their silence.

On the other hand, according to Freydis herself, the Icelanders simply decided to stay put in Wineland. If that's true, and they haven't been troubled by Skraelings, then the answer is yes, there is a permanent settlement out in Wineland. But I have no intention of ever going back there to find out.

The wine and furs that Karlsefni sold in Trondheim that year were famed for their exotic flavour and exceptional quality, and his account was thus widely believed.

For notes on this story, see page 361.

A JOURNEY TO THE EAST

Young men: they all seem to feel they have to go travelling before they settle down. Of course, most of them don't get any further than the court of the king in Norway…

But there was a lad called Ketil who had more exotic ambitions. He wanted to see parts of the world that most of his contemporaries had never even dreamed of. So he took the usual sea route westward from Iceland to Norway, but instead of hanging around there when he arrived, he journeyed onwards right across the mountains into Sweden. There he asked around to find out if there were any expeditions to remote places that he could join.

Before long he was introduced to a young Swedish prince called Yngvar Eymundarson. Yngvar was just the sort of fellow that Ketil admired: capable, charismatic and daring. He'd grown up in the court of his uncle, King Olaf, and before he was even twenty years old, he'd proven himself as a warrior and won hoards of treasure. Unfortunately, he had a mistress who had recently borne him an infant son, and she was putting pressure on him to stay at home – which was almost driving him crazy.

'I can find a better woman than her anywhere,' he said to Ketil. 'And here in Sweden there's never anything new to do: just the same old petty squabbles. So I'm planning to head out east, get myself some new experiences and real action, expose myself to a bit of danger.'

'Sounds good,' said Ketil.

'Then why not throw in your lot with me?' said Yngvar. 'My uncle's given me a ship, and right now I'm in the process of getting a crew together. My plan is to find the source of a great river, a spring called Lindibelti – a place that no man's ever reached before.'

This was exactly the type of opportunity that Ketil had been hoping for. And what luck that it got him in with a wealthy royal too!

They left Sweden a few months later, with a crew of thirty men. Their first port of call was the palace of a Russian king called Jarisleif, who happened to be the husband of Yngvar's aunt. More royals! Ketil was beginning to get quite used to keeping such company. They spent a bit of time there, getting to grips with the local language, and then set out on their quest.

Russia, viewed from the river, turned out to be even stranger than Ketil had imagined – totally and utterly different from Iceland. They passed through vast plains that stretched in every direction as far as the eye could see, empty of everything except for windswept swathes of grass. There were impenetrable forests, and gorges where the cliffs were so high and close together that they had to light candles to find their way. As for its inhabitants: well, some of them were really hair-raising; but you'll hear more about those later on.

The river was so long that they lost track of time. Just as

they noticed that the leaves were falling, the grass was turning brown, and each day was shorter than the last, they saw a great city above the riverbank. Crowds of finely dressed noblemen and ladies were strolling amongst its white marble mansions and gilded shrines.

Yngvar said, 'Russian winters are supposed to be really severe, so we'd better hole up for a while. This looks as good a place as any. Let's go ashore and seek out lodgings.'

They wandered around together and were soon surrounded by guards.

'Greetings, Northmen,' they called. 'Our ruler commands us to take you to the palace.'

'Well, that didn't take long to get sorted,' said Yngvar to his fellows. 'A king's hospitality is always the best.'

But when they reached the royal residence, they got a surprise. For the ruler of the city was not a king but a queen. Her name was Silkisif and she was not only clever and cultured, but also exceptionally beautiful.

Yngvar eyed her greedily, and she returned the compliment. It was obvious that they both had the same thing in mind. But then Yngvar checked himself and asked her, 'My lady, are you a Christian?'

'Certainly not,' she said. 'We worship the old gods here.'

'Then I beg you to convert,' said Yngvar.

'You can beg all you like,' said Queen Silkisif, 'but I govern this city and follow no man's orders. No matter, I've heard rumours about your impressive expedition. Despite your impertinent question, I'm honoured to meet you, and I'd like to offer you all hospitality in my palace.'

'Sorry, madam,' said Yngvar, looking directly into her clear green eyes, 'we can't accept lodgings with heathens.'

Queen Silkisif smiled. 'I won't hold it against you,' said she, 'for I admire men with principles, even if they're at odds with mine. Instead you and your followers may stay in an empty house not far from here. I shall see that you are well provided with everything you need, for as long as you wish.'

And so it was arranged. Their winter quarters turned out to be almost as splendid as the palace; and with unlimited food and wine, all the crew were happy. However, although Yngvar paid regular visits to Queen Silkisif at all hours of the day and night, he banned his fellows from finding lovers of their own.

'Why?' said Ketil, incredulously.

'Because heathen women are full of filth and disease,' said Yngvar. 'And if any of you disobey this order, you'll be dismissed from the ship, to be sure that you don't spread their dirt to the rest of us.'

'But you're visiting a heathen woman all the time,' said Ketil.

'Visiting isn't the same as lying with her,' said Yngvar loftily. 'Besides, I'm working on her: I think it's only a matter of time before she converts, because she's literally burning to get me into her bed.'

Since none of the men wanted to lose his place on the expedition, they all curbed their lust and went along with Yngvar's command. Just as he had predicted, it wasn't long before Queen Silkisif announced that she had decided to adopt Christianity. She decreed that the whole city also had to take up the new religion. After that, Yngvar spent virtually all his time up at her palace. His crew benefited too, because once the conversion was officially complete, they were allowed a free hand with the local women. It's no exaggeration to say that an excellent time was enjoyed by everyone.

However, all too soon it was over.

'We've got to go,' said Yngvar. 'That Queen Silkisif's got hold of the wrong end of the stick – just like every other woman I've ever been with. I made it plain to her at the outset that I'm an explorer, that I've got constantly itchy feet and I just wanted some casual fun with her. But as soon as I'd got into her bed, what did she do? Start talking about marriage! She's even offered to hand me complete control of her realm and let me take the title of king. If I don't get out now, she'll be laying claim to me because she's pregnant, just like that silly girl I left at home. The days are getting longer and the weather's turned, so I want everything packed up tonight, lads, ready to be off at first light.'

They sailed on eastwards, further and further, all through the spring and summer, still searching for the river's source.

The forests they passed grew thicker and less penetrable; the wind that swept across the steppes grew stronger. Now, every so often, they saw small encampments of tents; and amongst them there passed people whose faces were masked by thick cloths. They encountered several giants: one lived in a house so tall that its roof was lost in the clouds; another lurked behind a massive waterfall and his footprints alone were five ells long. They were attacked by pirates in a ship disguised to look like an island amongst the reeds. After a fierce battle, Yngvar hurled a consecrated tinderbox at them so that they all went up in flames.

On and on they rowed, marvelling and sometimes shuddering at an endless stream of curious sights. They entered a landscape of rolling hills. Gradually the river narrowed and grew shallower. In the end, they had to haul the ship ashore and carry it along the bank.

'We can't be far from the river's source now,' said Yngvar.

'Maybe it's behind there?' said one of the crew, pointing.

They all turned and saw an eerie glow, as if the moon had tumbled from the sky and landed behind one of the hills. Yngvar put a finger to his lips then beckoned them to drop anchor and come ashore after him. Silently, they all trooped up to the summit to investigate.

On the far side of the hill, they saw an enormous dragon. It stretched its wings, revealing that the glowing light was emanating from its scales – for they were pure gold. Underneath the dragon, and all around it, the ground was spread with golden treasure.

'I'd like to get my hands on some of that!' whispered Yngvar. 'And I know exactly how to do it. Ketil, pop back to the ship and fetch a box of salt. We'll chuck some down into its lair. Once the dragon smells it, he'll be desperate to guzzle it down. Which will give us our chance... And while you're about it, bring up an empty sack for each of us too.'

It was a brilliant trick. Just as Yngvar had predicted, as soon as the salt was scattered, the dragon sniffed the air, then pounced on their offering, licking it up with a hideous green tongue. Yngvar and his men sneaked past it, and hurriedly scooped its gold into their sacks. By the time the dragon had satisfied its craving and realised some of its hoard was missing, the men had raced back to their ship, turned it upside-down and concealed themselves beneath it.

The sound of the dragon's fury was earth-shaking. Some of the crew couldn't resist creeping back up the hill to see what it was doing. Peering over the top, they saw it balanced on the tip of its tail, spinning round and roaring. However, no sooner had they returned and described the scene to their mates, than every one of the watchers dropped dead on the spot!

The survivors buried their comrades, then set off to explore further overland. Soon they reached another magnificent city. This one was completely deserted; and in its heart there stood a great hall with the following message carved in runes upon its door:

IF YOU WISH TO KNOW OUR STORY
SPEND THE NIGHT WITHIN

'Who's going to volunteer?' said Yngvar.

After the dragon experience, no one was keen, so they drew lots. A man called Soti was chosen.

The others waited for him outside the city walls. they didn't hear a squeak from him all night. But once dawn began to break, Soti came sprinting out through the gates, shaking from head to toe and looking pale as bones.

'What did you see?' asked Yngvar.

'Demons!' he gasped. 'As soon as night fell, the whole hall was swarming with them. They spoke to me...told me they're the servants of a long-dead princess...something to do with suicides... And that dragon we saw – that was once her sister...!'

Before they could get any more out of them, the poor man collapsed and could not be revived.

That was just about the end of their great voyage of exploration. Although, by then, they must have been quite close to Lindibelti, the fabled source of the river, they never did find it. For so many of their company had died, that Yngvar didn't have the heart to search for it any longer. Besides, he himself was sickening with a very nasty and mysterious disease.

So they relaunched the ship and rowed back downstream.

On the way, they stopped off again at Queen Silkisif's realm. She was so in love with Yngvar that she forgave him for deserting her and said he was welcome to stay with her again for as long as he wanted; this time she even promised not to try and stop him when he was ready to leave. But that didn't do her much good, for by now Yngvar was seriously ill; and while they were still in her city, he died. The crew were devastated, and so was she.

They sailed back to Sweden and broke the news to Yngvar's first mistress and son. The mistress was so disgusted by the way that he had abandoned her, that she was totally indifferent to both his great exploits and the fact that he was dead. However his son, Svein, was now a valiant lad. He vowed that, as soon as he was full-grown, he would follow in his father's footsteps and retrace his great voyage.

As for Ketil, he'd seen all he wanted of the world by now, and he'd certainly had his bellyful of giants, demons and dragons, not to mention domineering queens. So he went back over the mountains to Norway and caught the last ship of the season home to Iceland. When he arrived, he took over his father's farm, found himself a compliant wife and finally settled down.

But he never knew what boredom was, and nor did any of his friends or kin; because the astonishing tales of his great journey to the east with Yngvar kept everyone fully entertained until the very end of his days.

For notes on this story, see page 367.

PAGAN PRAYERS
AND SPELLS

Keep away, Christians!
We're busy inside,
sacrificing to elves and spirits,
keeping the old faith in
fear of Odin's fury.

Since you kept danger from me with your own hands,
May the benevolent powers help you:
Frigg, Freyja and other gods!

I must sacrifice to Thor,
I must ask for this
That he always act well towards you.

Carve runes on the horn,
then rub them with red blood
With these words I bewitch
the horn of the wild ox.

Earth works against getting drunk
and fire against disease;
oak against constipation,
an ear of corn against witchcraft,
elder against household strife
the moon must be invoked against malice
an earthworm against a bite or sting,
runes against wickedness
soil must stand against flood.

If you wish for victory,
you must know victory runes.
Cut them on the hilt of your sword
some on the sword rings, some on the sword plates.
Then twice call out Tyr's name.

If you wish to release children safely from women's wombs
You must know protection runes.
Cut them on the palm and clasp them on the limbs,
Then ask the spirits for help.

For notes, see page 369.

GHOSTS
AND
SORCERY

Then the king declared in a speech that all the men
who dealt with evil spirits, or in witchcraft,
or were sorcerers, should be banished.
He had the neighbourhood searched for such people,
and called them all before him.
Amongst them there was a man called Eyvind Kelda,
who was a sorcerer, and particularly knowing in witchcraft.
The king made a great feast for all these men,
and gave them plenty of strong drink.
When they were all very drunk,
he ordered the house be set on fire,
so that all the people within it were burned –
all except Eyvind Kelda,
who contrived to escape by the smoke-hole in the roof.
And when he had got a long way off,
he met some people on the road going to the king,
and he told them to tell the king
that Eyvind Kelda had slipped away from the fire,
and would carry on his arts of witchcraft as much as ever.

– *The Saga of Olaf Tryggvgason,* **Heimskringla**

THE KING'S AMULET

The voyage from Norway west-over-sea to Iceland takes at least four days. Even in summer it can be rough sailing, with heavy rain all the way. Many ships that set out never even arrive. So what made people emigrate there?

Everyone had their reasons. A lot left because of King Harald Finehair overrunning his rivals and beating down Norway into a single kingdom. Some were just desperate for a decent-sized plot of land, because there were too many heirs to their family farm. Others were feuding with their kin or neighbours and wanted to get away before they came to blows. Not many had stories as strange as Ingimund Thorsteinsson's.

Ingimund was a successful pirate raider with a huge store of treasure, a splendid house and a formidable reputation. He didn't need to emigrate, and he certainly didn't want to.

While Harald Finehair was expanding his power, Ingimund carefully watched which way the wind was blowing – and joined Harald's side just in time to take part in his final victory. Afterwards, in the distribution of gifts, Ingimund was generously rewarded. King Harald granted him three full-size warships, complete with crew. He also gave Ingimund a more personal gift: a small silver amulet carved with the figure of Frey.

'This came from the corpse of Asbjorn the Fleshy,' said King Harald. 'You know, that old arch-enemy of mine who you helped to kill. Keep it as a memento, my friend; and may it bring you luck.'

Ingimund stowed it in his purse and sailed home with his new ships.

Shortly afterwards, his foster-father threw a feast. It was a grand affair, with many entertainers. The star turn was a Lappish enchantress who earned her living by telling fortunes. She was an impressive-looking woman, statuesque and splendidly dressed; she installed herself on the high-seat as if it had been set up just for her. Most people didn't take much persuading to go up to her, one by one, to hear their fates – even though they were all declared in full hearing of everyone else.

Ingimund thought her predictions were nonsense and refused to join in. But the enchantress worked by her own rules. She didn't care how high-status someone was, or what success they'd achieved; she wouldn't allow anyone to rebuff her.

'My lord Ingimund,' she called. 'I'm not leaving you out. Step up, let me reveal what your future holds.'

'No, no,' he said. 'I don't go along with this sort of thing.'

'Oh, don't you?' said the enchantress. 'Well, stay right where you are if you prefer, but you're going to hear what I have to say, anyway.' Then she turned to the other guests and announced: 'I foretell that Ingimund Thorsteinsson will found a great bloodline – not here, but in Iceland.'

'Iceland?' Ingimund scoffed. 'Ha ha, lady, that proves you don't know what you're talking about. I'm one of King

277

Harald's favourites. Why would I give up my good life here for that land of volcanoes and misfits? You won't find me emigrating – not now – not ever.'

'Are you sure, Ingimund?' the enchantress said. Her voice changed: it took on a sinister tone. 'I think you are wrong, for I see things that you are blind to, I know things that you can never guess. For example: that silver amulet of Frey – the one King Harald gave you – you always keep it in your purse, don't you? But where is it now?'

Everyone began to rib him: 'Go on, Ingimund, have a look.'

With a sigh of irritation, he pulled the purse from his belt and opened it.

'It's...gone,' he said.

There was a burst of cheering and uproarious clapping.

But Ingimund flew into a rage. 'You thief!' he roared at the enchantress. 'You trickster! Foster-father, throw her out!'

The enchantress held up her hand to still the commotion. 'Hush, hush,' she said. 'Don't diminish yourself, Ingimund. I haven't got your precious amulet. It's nowhere in this hall – nowhere in Norway.' Then she paused, walked across to Ingimund and looked deeply into his eyes. 'It's in Iceland.'

Everyone started fidgeting uneasily. Ingimund's rage dried on his tongue.

'The amulet has gone,' the enchantress repeated. 'It is in Iceland, waiting for you. You may mock me, Ingimund. You may even choose to curse me. But you will have no rest until my prophecy is proved true. I swear this on my life: one day you *will* move to Iceland – and there you will find what you have lost.'

Months passed, then years. Ingimund sank even deeper roots into his home in Norway, even though his foster-brother and other relatives all emigrated westward. He spent an increasing amount of time in King Harald's court. He married a good woman called Vigdis, and they settled down to have a family.

Despite all this, the first part of the Lappish woman's prediction was definitely fulfilled. Because all through those years, Ingimund found he couldn't stop thinking about the strange disappearance of the amulet. It just didn't make sense.

Vigdis said, 'I wish you'd stop fretting about it. Perhaps you should get hold of that enchantress and ask her more about it?'

He made enquiries, but the enchantress had disappeared without trace.

'Well, find someone else to help you,' said his wife.

So Ingimund sent messengers into the far north.

One day, three Lappish wizards came to his farm. They offered to travel to Iceland on his behalf and find out if the amulet was really there. The only payment they wanted was butter and tin.

'But Iceland's a huge country,' Ingimund objected. 'Such a task could take you for ever.'

'No it won't,' said the wizards, 'for we'll not be travelling in the flesh like normal men, but making a spirit journey. That way, the amulet's magic will quickly draw us to it.'

They refused to explain anything. They even refused to reveal their names or answer any questions.

'Well,' said Vigdis, 'since you've brought them all the way here, you might as well give them a try, especially as they're not asking for much in the way of payment.'

So Ingimund followed the wizards' instructions. He locked them in an outbuilding, and left them there undisturbed for three nights and days. When they finally emerged, they looked dishevelled and exhausted.

'Master,' they said, 'Our spirit journey is complete. We successfully overcame many hazards and weird powers.

'And did you locate my amulet?'

They answered, 'Yes indeed, in the north of Iceland.'

'Where?'

'In a valley that opens into a lake,' they said. 'At the foot of a mountain, within a wood.'

Ingimund held out his hand eagerly. But the wizards shook their heads and looked grim.

'Master,' they said, 'you already know that this amulet is filled with strange sorcery. We saw it, yet could not seize it. We coveted it, yet could not control it. The amulet was drifting above the ground, floating away through trees, ahead, always ahead of us. We were severely weakened by the arduous journey out of our bodies; our spirits were draining away. To save our lives, we were compelled to return here, in haste – and empty-handed.'

Was this merely a deception? Or is Lappish magic truly stronger than reason?

Whatever the truth, it made Ingimund more disturbed than ever. He said to Vigdis, 'I'm one of King Harald's staunchest supporters. Yet by giving me that amulet, he

280

seems to have fated me to leave his kingdom to go west.'

'No one can fight against destiny,' she said sagely. 'If something seems to be inevitable, what's gained by trying to resist it?'

In the end, Ingimund was so unsettled that he put aside his old protests, packed up and transported his entire household to Iceland, just as the enchantress had foretold. He made his home in Vatnsdal – an area uncannily similar to the one described by the Lappish wizards.

Despite his misgivings, it turned out to be an excellent move. Ingimund became a great chieftain. His sons established thriving farms and admirable reputations of their own. His daughters made strong marriages.

Now, here's the final twist. Once his family had built their houses and stocked their farms, Ingimund decided to formally bless his new estate with the promise of ongoing fertility. Also, he wanted to celebrate how the king's gift had indeed led him to his true destiny. So he decided to build a temple to Frey.

As his men were digging holes deep in the ground to sink the temple pillars, their tools struck metal. This was odd, since the soil in this place had never been disturbed by any human hand before. They investigated and pulled out a small silver object.

It was the lost amulet.

For notes on this story, see page 371.

GHOSTS IN GREENLAND

There was a farmer called Thorstein the Black who lived at Lysufjord in the Western Settlement of Greenland.

Early one winter, a ship came in to the settlement. There were twenty-six men and one woman on board. Thorstein went down to find out why they were there, and if they needed any help. It turned out that the captain was another Thorstein, son of the famous Eirik the Red; and the woman was his wife, Gudrid. They lived down south in the area known as the Eastern Settlement, and they'd only been married a very short time.

'What brings you up here in such wild weather?' asked Thorstein the Black.

'It's the weather itself,' answered Thorstein Eiriksson gloomily. 'We never intended to come this way. Would you believe it, we left home months ago, heading westwards towards Vinland. But the winds have been atrocious and kept blowing us back. As you can imagine, it's been an especially difficult time for my poor wife. This is the first place we've managed to land since we set out, and now the sea's starting to freeze. Looks like you've got a good community up there. Could we stay here through the winter?'

'Of course,' said Thorstein the Black. 'I'll find

accommodation for everyone. You and Gudrid must come and stay with me and my wife Sigrid.'

Thorstein Eiriksson and Gudrid were very glad to accept his offer. However, it turned out that luck was still against them, for they hadn't been there long before a very nasty illness struck the Western Settlement and quickly spread. Thorstein Eiriksson fell seriously ill and so did their hostess, Sigrid.

Gudrid did what she could to nurse those who were laid up, but many of them wasted away and died.

One evening, Sigrid was feeling particularly poorly, shivering with fever and the winter cold. Gudrid offered to take her outside to the privy, which stood immediately opposite the main door of the farmhouse. As they stepped out into the snow, Sigrid suddenly screamed: 'Look! All our neighbours who've died – they've risen. Can you see them, Gudrid? – over there – like shadows – standing in a line. Oh, isn't it horrible!'

'I can't see anything,' said Gudrid fearfully.

'And that ill-tempered man who oversees all the labourers…'

'He passed away yesterday,' said Gudrid.

'He's there too,' insisted Sigrid, 'with a whip in his hand… Surely you can see? He's turning, he's striking it against them…'

Then she collapsed into Gudrid's arms. By the next day, she herself was dead.

After that, Gudrid's husband, Thorstein Eiriksson, also went rapidly downhill, with fever and hallucinations. He cried out that Sigrid's corpse had risen and was trying to climb into bed with him. Those who were still well, anxiously discussed what was going on. No matter whether they followed the old religion or whether they were Christians, they all tried to convince themselves that it was impossible for dead people really to walk.

A short time later, Thorstein Eiriksson also died.

It happened in the middle of the night. The faithful Gudrid had left his side for a few moments and dropped into a fitful sleep. However, Thorstein the Black was passing the bed where his namesake lay, and saw what had happened. He laid the corpse out carefully, to display his new friend in all his lost vigour, then went to fetch Gudrid. As he led her to her late husband's bedside, something very disturbing happened.

Thorstein Eiriksson's corpse moved. It twitched. It shuddered.

'That does sometimes happen when someone's only just passed away,' said Thorstein the Black, trying to hide his alarm and reassure Gudrid.

But then the corpse shifted in the bed – and wrenched itself upright into a sitting position.

Gudrid gasped and crossed herself, for she was a baptised Christian.

The corpse spoke. Its voice was a hoarse whisper, but the words were clear: 'Gudrid. My love. Stay with me a while. Forgive me all my sins.'

Thorstein the Black was trembling from head to foot. He nudged Gudrid and arched his eyebrows questioningly. She swallowed and nodded. Thorstein the Black stepped back discreetly. But he watched and listened to everything that happened as if his own life depended on it.

The corpse was still sitting up, completely drained of

colour and as stiff as wood.

Gudrid whispered back to it, 'My love, in the short time I have known you, you *never* sinned – certainly not against me. I beg you to rest in peace.'

The corpse let out a soft sigh. 'Gudrid. Don't waste your life. Don't weep for me. Fulfil your destiny. Marry again. Not another Greenlander. See the world. Have many children. Give spare money to the poor.'

Then it fell back and was quiet.

Gudrid arranged for him to be taken back home and buried in the churchyard by his father's farm. And when the period of mourning was over, all Thorstein Eiriksson's hopes for her were indeed fulfilled.

For notes on this story, see page 373

THE BIG WOMAN
FROM THE HEBRIDES

One summer a ship came in to Dogurdarness. Its passengers had sailed from Dublin and most of them had brought goods to trade.

The locals couldn't take their eyes off one of the women who stepped ashore, because her clothes were absolutely stunning. Such a beautifully embroidered dress! That deep scarlet dye of her cloak! As for her jewellery, it must have been worth a fortune. She was a tall, statuesque woman in her fifties, with chestnut-coloured hair and dark eyebrows.

The local women crowded round her eagerly, in the hope of buying some similar items from her.

But the newcomer said, 'I haven't come here to sell anything. I'm looking for work, in return for board and lodging.'

Thurid, the farmwife from Frodriver, pushed her way forward. 'What sort of work can you do?' she said.

'Oh, anything so long as it's not too heavy,' said the newcomer.

'Well, come and stay with us then,' said Thurid, eyeing her necklace enviously. 'We always need extra hands to help with the weaving. And my husband, Thorodd, might have some light outdoor jobs for you too.'

They shook hands on it. The newcomer had brought two large chests. She arranged for the crew to carry her luggage up from the ship, and followed Thurid back to Frodriver. She said her name was Thorgunna, and that she came from those wild islands west of Scotland, the Hebrides.

When they arrived at the farm, Thurid allocated Thorgunna a place to sleep on the bench at the back of the main room. Thorgunna nodded, then unlocked her chests and unpacked her bedding. Thurid gasped. The sheets were made of the finest linen she'd ever seen, whilst the quilt was thickly filled with impossibly light down and covered in silk. Thorgunna had even brought an embroidered canopy. She laid them all out carefully.

'Would you sell me those?' said Thurid. 'In return, I'd let you live here for a whole year, as a lady of leisure.'

'No,' said Thorgunna bluntly. Then she asked Thurid to show her the weaving loom and set to work on it straight away.

Thorgunna was skilled, diligent and very productive. She didn't cause any trouble. But there was something uncanny about her and nobody wanted to be her friend. Thurid's husband, Farmer Thorodd, didn't like her at all. Thorgunna couldn't care less. The only person she ever spoke to was Thurid and Thorodd's son, Kjartan, a strapping lad of fifteen.

A few days later, the weather turned really fine. First thing in the morning, Farmer Thorodd announced that it was time to get on with hay making, and everyone had to help. He gave Thorgunna the task of raking the hay to dry before it was bound into sheaves. She mucked in willingly and laboured as hard as any man.

Unfortunately, soon after midday, the sun suddenly vanished and the air turned gloomy. Heavy clouds appeared over the mountains, blowing straight towards Frodriver.

'Leave the raking,' Farmer Thorodd shouted. 'All hands – bundle and stack the hay as fast as you can – before the storm breaks!'

They set to, working in a frenzy. The wind brought the clouds ever nearer and the air grew oppressively dark.

However, Thorgunna carried on raking as if she were deaf. Farmer Thorodd tried to wrest the rake from her hand and push her towards the others; but she shook him off angrily.

The clouds burst, unleashing a torrent of rain that drummed onto the fields. The workers rushed for shelter. But Thorgunna carried on working as if nothing had changed.

The storm ended as suddenly as it had begun. The workers emerged to inspect the damage. The finished sheaves hadn't come to any serious harm. However, all the loose hay was completely sodden, and so was Thorgunna – but not from water.

For it wasn't ordinary rain that had fallen from the sky, but *blood*. The fields were dotted with thick, red puddles, and beads of red liquid dripped down from the farmhouse eaves.

'This is a bad omen,' said Farmer Thorodd. 'Really bad. I fear we're doomed.'

Thorgunna propped her rake against the wall, shrugged and went indoors. A while later, Farmer Thorodd went in to see what she was up to. He found the big Hebridean woman lying on the bare bench, sweating and moaning with fever. Blood had dried in her hair and crusted on her face: she looked grotesque, almost monstrous.

'You don't seem in a very good way,' said Thorodd.

'I'm not,' groaned Thorgunna. 'In fact, I'm pretty sure I'm dying.'

'I'm not surprised, after standing out in that unearthly storm,' said Thorodd. 'Why ever didn't you shelter from it, like everyone else?'

'Mind your own business, farmer,' Thorgunna snapped at him. 'Instead of prying, you should listen to me carefully; because once I'm gone, you need to do everything correctly. *Everything*, exactly as I tell you. If you don't, I warn you, that storm won't be the last thing to send shivers up your spine. Do you understand?'

Farmer Thorodd tried to keep his face expressionless. 'Tell me what you want,' he said. 'I'll do my best.'

'Firstly,' said Thorgunna, 'I want you to know the truth. This storm's made you all sure that I'm a witch, eh? Don't deny it, I can see it in your eyes; and I've heard plenty of folk whispering that I'm ungodly. None of you seems to realise that the Church was established back in the Hebrides long before it even came here to Iceland. I've been a baptised Christian all my life.'

'That's good to know,' said Farmer Thorodd.

'However, there are other powers at work here,' Thorgunna went on, 'which is why it's vital that you do everything correctly.'

'Of course,' said Farmer Thorodd.

'I want my body taken across to Skalholt for burial,' said Thorgunna. 'I've heard there's a strong Christian community there and I'd like them to sing mass over me. You can pay them with this gold ring I wear.'

'No problem,' said Farmer Thorodd.

'Then there's the issue of my property,' said Thorgunna. 'I'll leave out a pile of clothes and jewellery for you and Thurid to take, to cover the cost of the funeral. But you can't have any of my bed linen. That's all to be burned.'

Farmer Thorodd nodded.

'That's all,' said Thorgunna. 'Go now, please.'

Farmer Thorodd didn't need telling twice. He hurried out, but his mind was awhirl. He couldn't stop thinking, 'Thurid won't agree to burning all that lovely stuff'; and, of course, he was right.

'That's madness!' Thurid cried. 'It's a crime to let all those treasures go to waste!'

Thorgunna had died in the night. Her body was laid out in a newly made coffin, and a group of farmworkers were preparing to carry it over the mountains to Skalholt, as she'd requested. Meanwhile, Farmer Thorodd had lit a bonfire and was loading it with the dead woman's bedding.

'Please,' begged Thurid, 'don't burn it.'

'But it might be dangerous not to,' Farmer Thorodd said. 'Anyway, you wouldn't want to use the linen that she died in.'

'I agree about the pillows,' said Thurid. 'But you told me yourself, on her deathbed, she was in such a sweat that she just lay on the bare bench, with all the linen put to one side. That silk quilt must be really valuable. And I've never seen such finely woven sheets.'

She went on and on at her husband, begging him and scolding him, until in the end he gave in. He burned the pillows, but let Thurid take the rest of the bedding back indoors.

And after that, the trouble really started.

It began in a small way, en route to Skalholt – or so the corpse bearers said. When they returned to Frodriver, they told how they'd stayed at a farm overnight on the way, where the farmwife had refused to feed them, claiming she had no food to spare. Just as they were dropping off to sleep, feeling very hungry, strange noises had started up in the farm storeroom. They'd gone to investigate – and been confronted by the stark naked ghost of Thorgunna! She'd risen from her coffin and had taken it upon herself to prepare food for the bearers. The farmwife was very alarmed and apologised profusely to her guests, telling them to eat whatever they wanted. After that, the ghost vanished.

Farmer Thorodd was sceptical.

But the very next evening something eerie happened at Frodriver itself. A light in the shape of a new moon suddenly appeared on the inside wall and started circling slowly around the living room. As they all watched it nervously, there was a great crash and the shepherd burst in. He was quaking from head to foot and muttering that he'd been bewitched. Then he collapsed. Before the night was over, he was dead.

The shepherd's ghost walked.

It was seen first by a man called Thorir Wooden-Leg, a friend of Farmer Thorodd's who also lived at Frodriver. On his way back from the privy, the shepherd's ghost suddenly stepped in front of him. It barred his way then seized him and hurled him against the door.

Thorir Wooden-Leg died of fright. *His* ghost walked too.

After that, six farmhands died in similar bizarre circumstances. They also joined the hauntings.

Meanwhile, weird noises started to emanate from the store cupboard where Farmer Thorodd kept his stocks of dried fish. There were shufflings, scrapings, squeals. It was investigated several times but there was no sign of any vermin.

Everyone was really scared. No one knew what to do about it.

Then things got even worse.

It was just before the Yule Feast. Farmer Thorodd had taken five of his men out fishing. While they were away, the rest of the household was gathered round the fire at home, when suddenly there was a sharp noise.

In the corner, the floor began to crack open, like a hatching egg. Something emerged from it...a round, dark creature with huge, staring eyes.

The head of a *seal*.

It swivelled, gazing round the room, searching. Its eye fell on Thorgunna's bed linen, stacked on one of the wall-benches. The seal jerked violently and let out a long, deep grunt.

A maid leaped up, seized a distaff and boldly thwacked it over the seal's head. The seal snorted – and rose even further out of the floor.

Now its full neck was visible…now its whole chest. Its flippers beat the air. It was abnormally huge. Its eyes were glued to Thorgunna's linen.

A farmhand sneaked outside, returned with a heavy stick and clubbed the seal over the head with all his force. The seal's whiskers twitched. It grunted, then lunged at the farmhand, catching him with its claw, drawing blood. The farmhand screamed and staggered out of the room. Panicking, everyone else followed him.

But young Kjartan crept back in, all alone, wielding a sledgehammer. Fearlessly, he battered it down on the seal, as if driving a nail into a piece of wood. At last the seal began to sink. Clunk! Now only its head and shoulders were visible… Wham! Now only the top of its eyes… Thump!

Like a nightmare, the seal was gone but its memory lingered. The crack in the floor closed up. Everything fell still.

Kjartan was the hero of Frodriver. But his glory did not last long. For the following morning, some neighbours came banging at the door, calling:

'Farmer Thorodd's been drowned! And all five of his companions. They've been found washed up on the foreshore just below the Ness.'

On the first evening of the funeral feast, as the meal was being served in the main room, the door suddenly opened by its own accord. A strong draught blew in, cold as a grave.

Then the ghosts arrived.

At their head was Farmer Thorodd: watery-pale, translucent, blank-faced, trailing fronds of seaweed. Behind him stumbled his five drowned companions. And behind these, Thorir Wooden-Leg led another band, dark as shadows, dry as lava, thickly coated in mud.

Thurid leaped to her feet, trembling violently. 'Thorodd?' she whispered. 'Can you see me?'

He didn't answer.

The ghosts made themselves at home. The sea-ghosts sat down on one side of the fire; whilst the mud-ghosts took their seats opposite them. The funeral guests clung to each other and crept away to the back room, closing the door firmly behind them and turning the key in its lock.

The same thing happened every night of the funeral feast. Each time the guests were about to partake of their meal, the ghosts arrived and lorded it over the main fire. The guests were forced to retreat to the back room and shiver round a smaller fire, their food balanced on their knees.

Meanwhile, all through the day, the dried fish cupboard was alive with eerie sounds. Some of the farmhands went in and climbed on top of the pile. They saw a weird tail writhing in it, half-cow and half-seal. When they tried to grab it, it vanished at once, leaving great chunks of skin torn from their hands. Afterwards, they all fell ill and died.

By the time the last funeral guest had departed, there were just seven servants left at Frodriver Farm, out of twenty-three at the beginning. The rest had either died or fled.

By luck, Thurid's brother was that great man, Snorri the Priest. Young Kjartan went to seek his help, and Snorri told him exactly what to do.

First, they burned all Thorgunna's bed linen, every last thread of it.

Then a group of older men summonsed all the ghosts, by name, to a mock court. A jury was appointed and testimonies heard. The ghosts were accused of trespassing on Frodriver Farm; and of robbing its inhabitants of their health and lives.

All the ghosts attended when called. None denied the allegations. All were declared guilty.

When each ghost heard the verdict, it rose and said in a hollow echo of his former voice, 'I submit. I will go.'

And after that, the hauntings ended for good.

For notes on this story, see page 374.

THE WITCH QUEEN'S CURSE

Did you hear what happened when Hrut Herjolfsson went to Norway and met Queen Gunnhild, King Harald Greycloak's mother?

Apparently she rules the king with a rod of iron. She insisted that Hrut and his uncle stay in her own hall. And at the end of the first night, after the two of them had been feasting and drinking with her, she said, 'You're going to sleep in my bed-closet tonight, Hrut.'

'Huh? You mean me and my uncle?' said Hrut, pretending to be thick. He'd heard all the rumours about Queen Gunnhild being a frustrated old tart, and was trying to put her off.

'Don't be silly, my dear,' she simpered. 'I mean *you* and *me* – nobody else.' And then she took his hand, led him to her private cubicle, slammed the door shut behind them and locked him in with her.

Poor fellow: Gunnhild's old enough to be his mother. But Hrut didn't dare resist her. You see, he'd gone to Norway to claim an inheritance that a rival was trying to get his hands on. He knew that the only way to be sure of winning it, was by getting King Harald and his mother on his side. So he had no choice but to give her what she wanted.

He paid a terrible price for it.

Once he'd sorted out the inheritance, he tried to disentangle himself from the affair. He told Gunnhild he was suffering from acute homesickness, and the only cure was to return to Iceland. Of course Gunnhild took it as a personal insult.

'You can't fool me,' she said, 'You've got another woman out there, haven't you?'

'No I haven't,' he protested.

This was actually a lie, and Gunnhild saw through it straight away.

'Why don't you admit it?' she said. 'You don't think I'm good enough, I'm too old to satisfy you, eh? – and you've got some voluptuous young beauty waiting for you back home. You're just like all the other wily young Icelanders who come to my son's court: you've been using me, leading me on, purely to try and make a fortune.'

What could Hrut say? He kept arguing his innocence and piling on the flattery. At first she seemed to believe him, because she gave him a gift – a stunning gold arm-ring – and then she wound her arms round his neck as if they were married, and started canoodling with him in full public view. But suddenly she drew away and her tone changed.

'Whoever the bitch is, I'm going to ruin it for you both,' she hissed. 'I put this spell on you, Hrut: I *curse* you. You will suffer in the same way as you are making me suffer. You will never fully enjoy the woman you have set your heart on.'

Hrut tried to laugh off the business and forget it. He sailed back to Iceland and, once he'd settled down again, married the beautiful girl who had, indeed, been waiting for him all that time. It was Unn, Mord Fiddle's Daughter; and they'd been betrothed since before Hrut went away.

On the surface they seemed like an ideal couple. As far as anyone could see, Hrut treated her really well and was very generous to her. Yet Unn clearly wasn't happy with him, and lots of people noticed that she was constantly on the verge of tears. No one could understand why.

At last, Unn confided in her father. She told him that Hrut had a very embarrassing personal problem, so that they'd never managed to consummate the marriage, not even once.

And so she divorced Hrut. Just as Queen Gunnhild's curse had predicted, he never did enjoy the woman he'd set his heart on.

For notes on this story, see page 375.

THE HAUNTED FARM

At first, nobody was sorry when Killer-Hrapp died. But then the hauntings started.

You'll have guessed from his name, that Hrapp was a brute. He'd fled to Iceland from the Hebrides, because victims of his abuse had started demanding compensation. He bought a farm in Laxardale – Hrappstead, he called it. Unfortunately, as soon as he'd settled in, he started harassing his new neighbours, just like he'd done in his previous home.

The trouble didn't stop until Hrapp grew old and died. Everyone looked forward to his funeral. But there wasn't one.

'What's his widow done with the body?' they asked.

'The poor soul was scared out of her wits by him,' came the answer. 'So even once he was dead, she felt compelled to follow his instructions. She had to have an extra deep grave dug – not outside, but under the door that leads into their main room. And she had to have his corpse placed *upright* in it, so he can still keep watch over the house.'

All the neighbours were very unnerved. And not without cause, for soon afterwards, most of Hrapp's servants died in bizarre circumstances; and the rate of illness and death amongst locals soared sky-high.

In the end, the district chieftain, Hoskuld, intervened. On his orders, the body was dug up and moved a long way off, far from any farmland or roads.

After that, the hauntings seemed to stop, so Hrapp's son tried to take over the farm. But almost as soon as he'd set up residence there, he went insane. A few months later, he too met an untimely death.

Next, a fellow called Thorstein bought the place. On the day that he planned to move in, he and his kin travelled to Hrappstead from their old home by boat. Unfortunately, on the way a gale blew up and swept them into a tidal race. They fought against it bravely, but it was a hopeless battle. For a supernatural creature was overseeing the maelstrom: shaped like a seal but unnaturally big, with an uncanny, almost human face. Thorstein's men tried to kill it, but their harpoons just snapped as they touched its skin. Nevertheless, they almost managed to reach the shore below Hrappstead – but at the very last moment, a freak gust of wind capsized the boat. Everyone on board was drowned.

Most people reckoned that the seal was Hrapp's ghost.

After that, Hrappstead stood empty for a long, long time. It became totally derelict.

One of Chieftain Hoskuld's sons was that celebrated fellow, Olaf the Peacock. Since getting married, Olaf had been looking out for a really good estate to farm. He often heard people saying what a shame it was that Hrappstead was going to waste, with its rich pastures and extensive woods, not to mention the excellent salmon fishing and seal hunting

300

nearby. When Olaf went to look around it, he was so impressed that he ignored its sinister history and bought it on the spot. To sever its connection with past ghosts, he changed its name to Hjardarholt.

For a while his family and workers were very happy there.

However, one evening a cowherd approached Olaf, looking dishevelled and very agitated. 'I'm never going near the byre after dark ever again master,' he said. 'You know that Killer-Hrapp who used to live here? Well, I tell you, his ghost is lurking inside it! Unless you give me some different work, I'm leaving.'

'Calm yourself, man,' said Olaf. 'I'll come over to the byre with you right away so you can show me...'

'Didn't you hear me, master? I refuse.'

'Even if the ghost is really there,' said Olaf, 'it can't do any harm if two of us approach it together. And I'll bring a weapon to protect us.'

He armed himself with a spear. Very reluctantly, the cowherd followed him back to the byre; but at the threshold, he stopped short and started trembling violently. Olaf snorted impatiently, seized the fellow's arm and forced him to go inside.

Within moments, the cowherd came running out again, screaming and spluttering: 'I knew it, I told you! The ghost's still in there... Tried to catch me... Managed to wrestle it... don't know how I got free... I've had enough! No more arguing, I'm off.'

With that, he fled. Olaf stared after him. Then he turned back to the byre, and stepped cautiously inside.

Behind him, the door swung almost shut, letting in only a

narrow sliver of light. He made out the shapes of cattle standing dead still in the gloom, as if bewitched into stone.

Suddenly they were blanked out by the figure of a gigantic man. He was naked and battle scarred from head to toe, his malevolent face twisted into an ugly snarl.

Now even Olaf found himself overwhelmed by panic. But he swallowed it boldly, clutched his spear and thrust it at the apparition.

Killer-Hrapp grappled it. With an ear-jarring crack, the spear snapped in two. Olaf still clung on tightly to the broken shaft – but the spearhead was lost, enclosed by Hrapp's limpid hands. Olaf lunged forward to try and retrieve it…

But at that very moment, the ghost vaporised like a puff of steam, and vanished.

The next day, Olaf went to see his father, Chieftain Hoskuld, and pestered him until he revealed exactly where he'd buried Killer-Hrapp's body, all those years ago. Olaf went to the spot with a band of men, and dug up the corpse.

It hadn't decayed at all.

Even more astonishing, deep in the ground next to the body, they found the very spearhead that the ghost had snatched from Olaf in the byre.

Olaf burned Hrapp's corpse on a blazing pyre. Then he had the ashes carried out to sea and dropped into the deeps.

After that, there were no more hauntings.

For notes on this story, see page 377.

DREAMING OF SORCERY

It seemed a bit strange when two elderly sisters arrived in Vatnsdal out of the blue, without any man to support them. Still, never mind, it takes all sorts, and people tried to make them welcome. Chieftain Thorstein Ingimundarson even let them stay in his own hall over the winter; and the following spring, he arranged for each sister to be set up in a small house of her own.

The women's names were Thorey and Groa. Of course, everyone wanted to know more about them. Where had they come from? Who were their parents? Why were they alone? What had brought them to Vatnsdal? The sisters themselves were very reticent. And even though Chieftain Thorstein had accommodated them for months, he could only reveal that a ship had carried them to a harbour near the top of Vatnsdal, and they had decided to settle in the valley because they'd been travelling around for ages and were sick and tired of it.

However, the chieftain's wife, Thurid was a bit more forthcoming. 'I'll tell you why we've been so obliging to them,' she whispered. 'It would have been dangerous not to. That Groa's a witch.'

That put the shivers up the valley!

As soon as she'd settled into her new house, Groa

announced that she was going to hold a feast. She invited Chieftain Thorstein and Thurid, and all Thorstein's siblings and their kin. The other valley dwellers were glad they weren't included: for no one wanted to enter a house of sorcery. It was a major topic of conversation.

'Of course, Thorstein and Thurid have to go: they'd be taking a huge risk if they snubbed Groa by turning down her invitation,' people said.

'At least she never did him any harm while she and her sister were staying with him all that time. They're wise to keep on humouring her.'

But a few days before the feast was due to be held, Thurid confided to her friends that Chieftain Thorstein had been suffering from bad dreams.

'Every time, it's the same,' she said. 'He seems to see himself – you know, his double – standing over him: himself over himself. He dreams that the double whispers to him, "*Don't go to the witch's feast, don't go to the witch's feast!*" And then he wakes up in a terrible sweat. I said to him, "That's your *fylgja*, Thorstein, your guardian spirit." He said, "Do you think that means my fate's sealed? Isn't it claimed that a *fylgja* usually shows itself when a person's due to die?" He was acting quite calm about it; but *I* wasn't feeling calm, I can tell you! "Hopefully," I said, "it's just giving you a warning. If you heed it, you might still be all right." So I begged him to agree that we'd give Groa's party a miss. But he hasn't yet made up his mind.'

Everyone waited on tenterhooks to see what would happen.

On the morning of the planned feast, a big group of travellers was seen arriving at Chieftain Thorstein's house –

his brothers and sisters with all their kin. However, they didn't stay there long, but soon all rushed out again, mounted their horses and rode at full speed back the way they had come. Apparently, Thorstein had spun a story that he couldn't go to the feast because he'd been struck by a terrible illness. It wasn't appropriate for his kin to attend without him.

Someone must have carried a message to that effect to Groa. Because at sunset, the witch opened the door of her house and stepped outside, muttering to herself angrily: 'That chieftain's too canny. I never anticipated he'd dare to wrestle with his own destiny. How can I thwart him?'

She stood very still on the spot for a long moment. Then, abruptly, she started walking round and round her house, all the while facing backwards. Finally she stopped, turned to the mountain, drew out a red cloth wrapped around something that gleamed like gold, and waved it furiously.

'Ach!' she screamed. 'Let whatever is fated come to pass!'

Then she stomped back inside and slammed the door.

The next moment, there was an ominous rumble. Suddenly a clutch of rocks loosened from the cliff – came rolling down – and landed on top of her roof with a thunderous crash.

Witch Groa, and the servants inside there with her, were all instantly killed.

For notes on this story, see page 378.

'Now are the words of the High One spoken…
Good luck to whoever recited them,
good luck to whoever knows them…
good luck to all who have listened!'
— *Havamal, **Poetic Edda***

NOTES

THE ORIGIN OF THE STORIES: MAGIC MEAD
(story p. 20)

'The origin of stories' is a theme found in a number of world cultures, indicating the high esteem in which narrative traditions are commonly held.

Snorri tells this tale in some detail in the *Prose Edda*, beginning with the question: 'How did this craft that you call poetry originate?' The answer opens with a war between the two tribes of **gods**, the Aesir and the Vanir; and a peace settlement which they seal by each side spitting into a vat. From this spittle, they create the sage Kvasir, and send him travelling through the world, spreading knowledge. He is treacherously killed by the **dwarfs**, who then mix his blood with honey, brewing a supernatural mead with power to transform all who taste it into either a poet or a scholar. It ends up under the guard of **giantess** Gunnlod Suttungsdaughter, deep inside the mountain, as retold here.

Snorri presents the next section as a separate but linked story. **Odin**, disguised as a man called Bolverk, sets out on a journey, meets nine **slaves** mowing hay and sharpens their scythes for them. The slaves are so impressed by his whetstone that they fight each other to death, trying to decide which of them should buy it from him. Odin then lodges overnight with their master – who turns out to be the **giant** Baugi, brother of Suttung. Odin volunteers to take over the slaves' work in return for a drink of Suttung's Magic Mead. After a summer of hard labour, he claims his promised payment; and when he fails to get it, he resorts to supernatural tricks. He persuades the unwilling Baugi to secretly bore a hole into the mountain, then transforms himself into a snake and crawls through it. Inside, he finds Gunnlod guarding the brew. Snorri says prosaically: 'He lay with her for three nights and then she let him drink three draughts of the mead'. Of the mead spilled at the end of the story, Snorri concludes: 'Anyone who wanted it took it, and that is what we call the rhymester's share. But Odin gave Suttung's mead to the gods and to those people who are skilled at composing poetry.' He uses this story to explain why **kennings** (metaphorical expressions) for poetry include 'Odin's booty' and 'the gods' drink'.

The episode – heavily charged with erotic symbolism – in which Odin bores into the mountain to seduce Gunnlod, is also recounted in a section of the **Eddic poem** *Havamal*. Here the event is supposedly described by Odin himself, who admits that in return for the drink, all he gave Gunnlod was a broken heart. These verses inspired my own retelling.

Other stories of love between gods and giantesses tend to be similarly one-sided. The Eddic poem *For Skirnis* (Skirnir's Journey), tells of the god **Frey's** love for a young giantess called Gerd. His servant, Skirnir, is despatched to proposition her. When normal encouragements fail to win her over, Skirnir resorts to bullying threats. The poem ends with the promise of Frey having his way with Gerd nine nights later, but does not reveal what actually happens. The myths generally portray giants' courtships of **goddesses** as totally beyond the pale.

IN THE BEGINNING *(story p. 25)*

The story of the creation is found in three sources. The most coherent occurs early on in the *Prose Edda*. There are also rather vague partial accounts in two **Eddic poems**: *Vafthrudnismal* (The Sayings of Vafthrudnir) and *Voluspa* (The Prophecy of of the Seeress). The first two sources take the form of question-and-answer dialogues, which thus seemed an authentic approach to use in my own retelling. They all include long lists of names, most of which I have omitted here for greater fluency and clarity.

In his account of the creation, **Snorri** opens with the question; 'Who is the highest and most ancient of **gods**?' to which the answer is given as '**Odin**'. Next, Snorri raises the questions 'What was the beginning? And how did things start? And what was there before?' to launch his descriptions. He frequently quotes actual verses from *Voluspa*. As well as the names included in my retelling, other significant ones (in order of occurrence) mentioned by Snorri are:

Niflheim – a mysterious place created before the earth, and source of the eleven poisonous rivers in the story.

Muspell – a bright, hot, fiery, impassable region in the south.

Surt – guardian of the frontier of Muspell, holder of a flaming sword.

Ginnungagap – a void between the frozen north and Muspell in the south, where the **giant** Ymir is formed from the meeting of northern cold and southern heat.

Audhumla – the cow created from frost, which feeds Ymir with her milk.

310

Like other medieval writers, Snorri tries to give this story historical authenticity by claiming that the gods, despite their supernatural qualities, were actually real people. Drawing on the classics, he even asserts that, after setting up the first human beings in **Midgard**, the gods 'made themselves a city in the middle of the world which is known as **Asgard**. We call it Troy'.

Voluspa tells of the gods building Asgard, making treasures and tools and playing board games. Whereas Snorri credits Odin's two brothers with helping him to breathe life into the first man and woman, here Odin's assistants are the gods Hoenir and Lodur (possibly the same character as **Loki**).

In contrast, *Vafthrudnismal* is a much more light-hearted poem. Its framework is a visit by Odin to the mighty giant Vafthrudnir, during which they engage in a quiz contest about both the creation and RAGNAROK (p. 109). It features many oft repeated refrains for example:

'Tell me one thing, if your wit is up to it'

and

'Much have I travelled, much have I tried, much have I tested the powers'.

Its good-natured dialogue confirms how Ymir's body parts were used to create the earth, its rocks, the sky and the sea; the origin of the moon, the sun, day and night and the seasons; and the emergence of the first giants and gods.

The sketches of the deities come mainly from the *Prose Edda*. More detailed information can be found in the GLOSSARY, and also within the actual stories.

THE DWARFS' TREASURES (story p. 30)

This story comes from the *Prose Edda*, where **Snorri** uses it to explain why a common **kenning** for gold was 'Sif's hair'. More interestingly for modern readers, it describes the provenance of **Thor**'s hammer, which features in a number of other myths – most notably the next story in this collection, THE THEFT OF THOR'S HAMMER (p. 41).

One might speculate that such an entertaining tale was used to introduce the younger generation to the character of **Loki**, and also familiarise them with the implements used by the most important **gods**. Since it is an 'origin' story, I have placed it here early in the history of **Asgard**. Yet Loki's lips are not described as being sewn together in any of the other surviving myths. This suggests that there was no logical chronology, and that each was a stand-alone story.

The magic ring, Draupnir, appears to be the same treasure which lies at the heart of the story cycle, THE CURSE OF ANDVARI'S RING (p. 114), and is also mentioned in THE DEATH OF BALDR (p. 99), where the source describes it as an arm-ring.

The myth seems to have been popular in the early 11th Century, since a Danish carving has survived from that time, apparently depicting Loki with his lips sewn together. Intriguingly, it seems to relate directly to the work of the **dwarfs** in the story, for it has been identified as a hearth stone with a hole in which to insert the nozzle of a pair of bellows.

THE THEFT OF THOR'S HAMMER *(story p. 41)*

This story is found in only one source, *Thrymskvida* (Thrym's Poem) in the *Poetic Edda*. Nevertheless, because it is a simple yet rip-roaring yarn, it is one of the best known of the Norse myths. However, there is much dispute between translators and scholars as to how authentic it is to the **Viking Age**. One claims that it assumed its present form c. 900 AD; another asserts that it was not composed until long after the Viking period; a third compromises by suggesting it is a mixture of very old features, reworked under 12th Century influences.

The **Eddic poem**, with its sacrilegious tone, pokes fun at **Thor**. This suggests that its surviving form might be from the Christian era; for in **pagan** times Thor was widely sacrificed to, and respected as a great protector of the people. In the highly masculine warrior culture of the Vikings, Thor's assumed effeminacy would have been considered a serious matter, not a humorous one, particularly for the most virile of all the **gods**. *Laxdaela Saga* demonstrates that a husband cross-dressing was grounds for **divorce** (see THE LOVE TRIANGLE, p. 215); whilst *Kristni Saga* records how a trite accusation of homosexuality provoked a double murder. Thus the present retelling retains the plot but softens the satirical humour that defines the Eddic poem.

The characteristics of Mjollnir are taken from the *Prose Edda*. The hammer seems to have been a powerful symbol of the **pagan** religion, for Viking Age decorated pendants believed to depict miniature 'Thor's hammers' have been excavated throughout Scandinavia; they were usually made of silver. A similar design appears on a number of **rune-stones**.

Loki's claim that **Freyja** is promiscuous comes from the Eddic poem *Lokasenna,* which describes the trickster at the centre of a ritualised contest of outrageous **insults** amongst the **gods** and **goddesses**. Loki also accuses several other goddesses of similar behaviour, and it is impossible to know whether this was an authentic depiction of pagan beliefs about her.

HOW ODIN WON THE RUNES *(story p. 48)*

To students of Norse mythology, the story of how **Odin** obtained the **runes** by sacrificing himself on a tree is an iconic one. Yet the only surviving source is a small section of a poem – twenty-five short stanzas – in the **Poetic Edda** called *Havamal* (The Sayings of the High One). Some scholars believe it to be a genuinely **pagan** composition, dating back to the 9th Century, though not all agree.

The story is narrated in what is taken to be the voice of Odin himself. Like many other parts of the *Poetic Edda*, it is rather obscure – either esoteric or assuming that its audience already knows the story well enough to enjoy an artistic interpretation of it.

I explored several different translations and their accompanying notes, and decided it would be unrealistic to attempt a literal retelling. Instead I have absorbed the original spirit, guessed its intention and used fresh verses to bring it back to life in a form reminiscent of the *Poetic Edda,* including the framework of a dialogue-quiz.

Although poetry in the pagan era of the **Viking Age** was purely oral, it was a complex art with structures comparable to or even exceeding the literary verse of later times. A number of academics have analysed its various forms. *Havamal* is written in a style known as *ljodahattr* – a 'metre of chants' which has the feel of a magical charm. A runic inscription in this metre has been found on an early 8th Century Norwegian gravestone. Typically it features repetition, alliteration and the use of first person narrative, often in six-line stanzas, each one split into two complementary halves.

In *Havamal,* the story runs as follows: Odin speaks of being wounded by a spear and then hanging from a tree for nine nights, sacrificing himself to himself. It says very little about the tree, describing it only as 'that windy tree...that rose from roots that no man ever knows'; scholars generally interpret it as the world tree, **Yggdrasil.** He complains that 'they' – unidentified – gave him neither food nor drink, implying he was not alone. He peers down, grabs 'the runes' with a scream and 'sinks back'. He is then mysteriously invigorated by nine songs from his grandfather and a swig of mead. The poem now turns to the imperative, urging its audience to find runes and meaningful symbols, then asking if they know how to cut, read, stain, test, invoke, sacrifice, despatch and slaughter. It advises not to sacrifice too much, offering the well-known proverb 'a gift always looks for a return'. There then follow eighteen verses back in the first person. These claim knowledge of various spells which include general healing, repelling attacks, the destruction of 'hag-riders', victory in battle, raising the dead, success in love and a final one 'which I never tell'; however, the narrator does not go into any detail about what the spells entail.

FISHING UP THE WORLD SERPENT *(story p. 51)*

In surviving versions of this myth, the medieval writers tend gently to mock **Thor** and his predilection for swatting **giants**. However, my retelling reverts to the presumed original purpose, which must surely have been to demonstrate this commonly worshipped **god**'s unassailable strength. It is based upon the straightforward storyline recounted in the *Prose Edda*. The only detail I have omitted is the claim that Thor disguises himself as a young boy when he initially approaches Hymir. **Snorri** concludes the tale with the statement:

'They say that Thor struck off [Jormungand's] head by the sea-bed… But I believe the contrary to be correct: that the **World Serpent** is still alive and lies in the encircling sea.'

The same story is told more elaborately in the **Eddic poem** *Hymiskvida* (Hymir's Poem). This has a folk tale feel, suggesting that embellishments were added at a later date. Hymir's catch of two whales comes from here. The poem opens with the sea-giant Aegir telling Thor to bring him giant Hymir's league-deep cauldron so that he can brew ale in it for the gods. Initially Aegir accompanies Thor on the quest, though he later disappears from the scene. Thor, now described as 'the lad' – presumably in accordance with Snorri's claim – reaches Hymir's hall where he meets the giant's hateful, nine hundred-headed grandmother and his 'all-golden' wife. The latter helps protect Thor from the giant and serves up a meal in which Thor eats two whole oxen. Instead of punching Hymir into the sea, Thor helps him carry both whales and boat back to his house. There he undergoes a further test of strength, being challenged to smash an apparently unbreakable glass; the giant's wife advises him to strike it against Hymir's own head. This done, Hymir finally gives Thor the cauldron, but calls up an army of other giants to attack him as he leaves. Thor kills them all with his hammer and carries the cauldron back to **Asgard** where it is used for the gods' drinking parties

Hymiskvida is structured within a frame story similar to A JOURNEY THROUGH GIANTLAND (p. 83), for it claims that Thor and Aegir travel to Hymir's house via a farm, from which they abduct two children. The poet seems aware of borrowing from a different tale, adding the disclaimer that 'someone more aware of the lore of the gods can tell [this] better'.

The cauldron element may have been borrowed from non-Norse stories. Supernatural cauldrons appear in a number of ancient Celtic tales. The Vikings had important settlements in the Celtic lands of Ireland (most notably in Dublin) and the Scottish highlands and islands; and many people of Celtic descent, especially women, settled in

Iceland during the **Viking Age**.

The **World Serpent**, Jormungand, was one of three monstrous children whom **Loki** fathered with a **giantess**. 'Thor fishing up the World Serpent' was a popular subject for Viking Age artists, with carvings of its main scene still in existence. In England there is one on a 10th Century stone carving in Cumbria. Others can be seen on Viking Age **picture stones** at both Ardre and Altuna in Sweden; and Hordum, Denmark.

THE EIGHT-LEGGED HORSE *(story p. 56)*

The story comes from the *Prose Edda*. As in many of the more light-hearted myths, **Loki** here is presented as an inveterate troublemaker who, without any apparent motive, delights in placing the **gods** in severe danger; then rescuing them at the last moment.

Sleipnir is mentioned as **Odin**'s steed in several other myths. The *Prose Edda* says that even one of the **giants** admires his 'marvellously good' horse, and Odin replies 'I'll wager my head that there's no horse as good to be found anywhere in **Giantland**.' In the **Eddic Poem**, *Baldrs Draumar* (Baldr's Dreams), Odin rides Sleipnir down to the land of the dead; whilst in the *Prose Edda*'s version of the same story, it is Odin's son Hermod who rides him to the same destination. Here an example of Sleipnir's exceptional power is cited, for he is described as jumping right over the infernal region's gates.

Pictures of an eight-legged horse can be seen on two Swedish **picture-stones**. One, found at a farm near Ljugarn, shows an image of Sleipnir's rider being offered a drinking horn by a woman, possibly a **valkyrie**. The other, from Ardre, may date back as far as the 8th Century, and also depicts Odin on his mount.

THE MIGHTY WOLF *(story p. 66)*

This story comes from the *Prose Edda*, where **Snorri** states that Fenrisulf is one of **Loki's** three offspring with the **giantess** Angrboda, the other two being **Hel** and the **World Serpent**, Jormungand. The **gods** are disturbed to hear that these monsters are being raised in **Giantland**, especially as certain prophecies predict that the three will cause great mischief and disaster, due to the natures of both their parents. **Odin** despatches Jormungand 'into that deep sea that lies around all lands': he reappears in the stories FISHING UP THE WORLD SERPENT (p. 51) and A JOURNEY THROUGH GIANTLAND (p. 83). Hel is thrown into Niflheim, the primeval place of freezing mists which appears in the creation story (see IN THE BEGINNING, p. 25).

The *Prose Edda* describes Tyr as exceptionally brave, valiant and clever, with power over battle victories: it recommends that men of action should pray to him. Skirnir, who fetches the **dwarfs'** fetter, is **Frey**'s servant. In a seemingly incomplete **Eddic poem** called *Skirnismal* (Skirnir's Sayings), he acts as a go-between when Frey falls in love with a **giantess** called Gerd.

The scene in which Tyr puts his hand into Fenrisulf's mouth is depicted in an early 10th Century carving in Cumbria, England.

THE APPLES OF YOUTH *(story p. 72)*

The story comes from the *Prose Edda*. Here, **Snorri** describes two other elements in the compensation paid to the **giantess** Skadi. Firstly, she is allowed to choose one of the **gods** as her husband; but only by looking at the candidates' feet, the remainder of their bodies being concealed from her. She fixes on a beautiful pair of feet, expecting them to belong to the handsome Baldr (see THE DEATH OF BALDR, p. 99); but instead finds herself paired off with Njord. Unfortunately they are not compatible, since Skadi likes to live in the mountains whilst Njord prefers the coast. Secondly, **Odin** takes the eyes from her dead father and throws them into the sky to form two new stars.

Snorri relates it as a 'story within a story', told at a feast held in **Asgard** to honour a magician called Aegir (possibly the same as the sea-**giant** Aegir who appears in the *Poetic Edda* version of FISHING UP THE WORLD SERPENT (see notes to that story, p. 316). The storyteller is called Bragi, apparently the husband of Idun, and renowned for his wisdom, command of language and knowledge of poetry. Afterwards, Bragi also narrates the MAGIC MEAD myth (p. 20), then launches into a discourse on poetry.

The characters of **Loki**, Idun, Bragi, Aegir, Skadi and Njord are also brought together in the curious **Eddic poem** *Lokasenna* (Loki's Insults), which is constructed around a formal exchange of outrageous **insults**.

The concept of a magic substance which confers everlasting life on those who eat it occurs in other cultures, particularly in ancient stories from China, where it is commonly known as the Elixir of Immortality.

A JOURNEY THROUGH GIANTLAND (story p. 83)

The story comes from the **Prose Edda**. Here, **Snorri** tells it partly as an explanation for the phenomenon of tides in the sea; for at the end of the story the Giant King tells **Thor**:

'When you drank from the horn, and thought that it
diminished so little...it was a great wonder, which I
never thought possible. One end of the horn stood
in the sea, but you did not see that. Next time you
go to the sea-shore, you will discover how much
the sea has sunk by your drinking; that is now called
the ebb.'

Explanations of natural phenomena are a common purpose of myth. However, although the principle characters of this story are mythological – **gods**, and their arch opponents the **giants** – their entanglement with ordinary humans and the ironic humour that dominates the story give it the feel of a folk tale told for entertainment, rather than a sacred story. Certainly the activities that Thor, **Loki** and their young human **slaves** share with the Giant King and his cronies during their adventure have a very human dimension: contests of physical prowess, feasting and heavy drinking are all recorded as being popular **Viking Age** activities. Moreover, it seems incongruous that Thor, the most physically powerful god of all, the focus of so many prayers for help, is portrayed as helpless against the giants; and that the latter should be represented as so much wiser and more cunning than the gods. Loki too is out of character, for virtually uniquely amongst the surviving stories, instead of causing trouble, he is portrayed as being unequivocally on the gods' side.

All this suggests that the story, in its present form at least, dates from after the **conversion to Christianity**. It is interesting to compare it with the story of Thor in FISHING UP THE WORLD SERPENT (p. 51) which ancient carvings prove definitely dates from the **pagan** era. There, Thor is shown as more than capable of both defeating a giant and hauling the **World Serpent** out of the lake, whereas in the present tale his power seems to have diminished. During the years in which the old and new religions were in conflict, there must have been an ideological preference for keeping alive tales that showed the weaknesses of the old deities and the limitations of their power.

THE DEATH OF BALDR (story p. 99)

This story is told in some detail in the *Prose Edda*, partly to explain the origin of fishing nets and earthquakes. In the *Poetic Edda*, it is referred to in *Baldrs Draumar* (Baldr's Dreams); and a description of **Loki**'s punishment also occurs at the end of the **Eddic poem** *Lokasenna* (Loki's Insults). In the latter, it is inflicted for a rather different crime – that of insulting many of the deities with outrageous profanities. It is interesting to compare it with the temporary and less gruesome penalty imposed on Loki at the end of THE DWARFS' TREASURES (p. 30), in which his lips are stitched together.

Stories of failed attempts to bring people back from the dead are told in cultures throughout the world. The best known one, of course, is the Greek myth of Orpheus, but there are similar tales from as far away as Japan and Native America. This Viking story is unusual in that failure is not the fault of the attempted rescuer, but maliciously caused by a third party, Loki. The idea of someone being made almost – but not quite – invulnerable to any wound is reminiscent of the Greek myth about Achilles' Heel.

Draupnir, the magic golden ring which **Odin** commits to the pyre and is later returned to him, is the one given to him in THE DWARFS' TREASURES; and also seems to be the centre piece of the THE CURSE OF ANDVARI'S RING cycle of stories (p. 114 ff).

RAGNAROK *(story p. 109)*

The main source of this dramatic and haunting prophecy is a detailed account in the *Prose Edda*. Here **Snorri** openly draws on – and, indeed, quotes from – the poem *Voluspa* (The Prophesy of the Seeress), which forms the first entry in the *Poetic Edda*.

Voluspa is believed to date back to the 11th or possibly the 10th Century. Its narrative switches between the first person and the third person, with the tense likewise moving between past and present. It gives the impression of having developed from a series of dreams actually experienced and recounted long ago by a particular wise woman (or perhaps several women) who claimed the gift of second sight. It opens with the prophetess addressing **Odin** himself. The same poem also refers to the creation (see IN THE BEGINNING, p. 25) and a number of other myths which were presumably familiar to the original audience. There is additional information in the quiz dialogue of the **Eddic poem**, *Vafthrudnismal* (The Sayings of Vafthrudnir).

For my retelling I have simplified the sources, rearranged the order of some events and omitted the less familiar names to make the story both clearer and more logical. The most haunting images used come from *Voluspa,* whose form has also inspired my narrative.

Snorri's detailed description includes some fascinating snippets of **Old Norse** superstition. For example it mentions that when the earth floods from the **World Serpent** going ashore, the biggest ship in the world, called Naglfar:

'will be loosed from its moorings… It is made of dead people's nails, and it is worth making sure than no one dies with untrimmed nails, since such a person contributes much material to the ship Naglfar which **gods** and men wish would take a long time to finish.'

Later he predicts that the Wolf will swallow Odin:

'And immediately afterwards, [Odin's son] Vidar will come forward and step with one foot on the lower jaw of the wolf. On this foot he will have a shoe for which the material has been collected for all time: it is the waste pieces that people cut from their shoes at the toe and the heel. Therefore anyone who wishes to help the gods must throw these pieces away.'

Snorri's vision of what will happen to those who die in Ragnarok seems to have been influenced by Christianity, for he speaks of 'heaven' and distinguishes between the fates of the 'good and virtuous people' who will go to live in a red-gold hall with plenty to drink; and the 'oath-breakers and murderers' who are destined for a hall made of poisonous snakes.

Similar horrific prophecies of the end of the world, and its eventual rebirth, can be found in many world mythologies. The best known is perhaps the Bible's Apocalypse found in the Revelation of John, the last book of the New Testament. Hinduism describes the world destroyed by flood and fire, and a sage preserving the seeds of all living creatures ready for the birth of a new age. The Aztecs of ancient Mexico believed that the world had ended and been reborn several times, on each occasion with the death of the sun followed by the birth of a new one.

KENNINGS *(text p. 112)*

Kennings are a stylistic convention of **Old Norse** poetry, in which a person or thing is not named, but referred to by one of their attributes, deeds or legends. In many surviving verses attributed to **skalds** of the **Viking Age**, this was taken to extraordinary extremes, with virtually every statement composed as a metaphor. It must have been a real challenge for audiences to recall the relevant stories quickly enough to understand the verses they were listening to.

Snorri devotes long sections of the *Prose Edda* to numerous examples, attributing them to named Viking Age poets. Most are very obscure and require detailed knowledge of mythical and legendary characters and events in order to make sense of them. Here are translations of two short examples of kennings in use, with their presumed meanings:

'The oppressor of the kinfolk of evening-faring women
Yawned with his arm's mouth
Over the heavy red lump of tong-weed.'

> *Meaning:*
> **Thor**
> Put his fist
> Over the iron.

('evening-faring women', are **giantesses**, their kinfolk are the **giants** and Thor is the enemy of giants).

326

'The pale ice-ring flew swiftly
Beneath the soles of the rock-guarder...
The rock-lord did not have to wait long after that
For a swift blow
From the tough multitude-smashing friend
Of Hammer-Face-Troll.'

> *Meaning:*
> The shield
> flew swiftly at the giant...
> The giant did not have to wait long after that
> for a swift blow from Thor's hammer.

SIGURD THE DRAGON SLAYER *(story p. 116)*

This must have been a very popular story during the **Viking Age** and also the centuries that followed; for it is preserved in several medieval texts, and is widely represented in ancient carvings.

There is a full account in the *Prose Edda*, where **Snorri** uses the story to explain the origin of the **kenning** that calls gold 'Otter-payment'. He adds that gold is sometimes also known as 'the **gods'** forced payment' or 'strife metal'. The longest version forms part of an important 13th Century book called *Volsunga Saga* (The Saga of the Volsungs). The story is also the subject of three **Eddic poems.** Scenes from it were carved into **rune-stones**, stone crosses and wooden church buildings; some of which survive in England, the Isle of Man and Sweden.

Volsunga Saga sets the story of Sigurd killing the dragon in a wider, quasi-historical context, implying that the main characters were real people who lived several hundred years before the beginning of the Viking Age. All the surviving texts entangle them with supernatural characters from the **pagan** myths. Both *Volsunga Saga* and the *Prose Edda* claim that Sigurd's grandfather, Volsung, was the great-grandson of **Odin** himself. This is in line with a convention followed by many medieval writers, who tried to rationalise forbidden pagan beliefs by claiming that the gods were really ancient heroes, elevated to supernatural status by creative storytellers.

My retelling is mainly based on Snorri's account. This opens with three gods – Odin, **Loki** and Hoenir – travelling through the human world. They come to the waterfall where Loki stones a salmon and an otter; then have an altercation with Hreidmar and his sons, as described here. Hoenir plays no active role so it is not clear why he is included in the cast.

The **dwarf** Andvari, though appearing only briefly, is a key player, since it is he who originally supplies the cursed ring. Its powers to constantly reproduce itself are identical to Odin's dwarf-smithed ring, Draupnir (see THE DWARFS' TREASURES, p. 30). One of the Eddic poems, *Reginsmal* (Regin's Sayings) gives a wording for the curse Andvari places on it:

> 'It shall drive two brothers to their deaths, push
> eight princes to killing and strife. No one wins
> joy from my wealth.'

Loki, true to form, applauds this ominous curse and promises to pass it on.

Volsunga Saga tells the entire story from Sigurd's viewpoint, beginning with his illustrious ancestors. The *Saga* is named after Sigurd's grandfather, Volsung. Like the *Prose Edda*, it claims that his original ancestor was Odin himself. His descendants are collectively known as the Volsungs. The original Volsung has a supernatural birth, being six years in the womb and born already well grown. He becomes the mighty **King** of 'Hunland', somewhere in Europe (according to Snorri, in France). A huge tree called the Barnstokk grows in the centre of his palace, its branches stretching out through the roof. With his wife, Hljod – daughter of a **giant** – he has eleven outstanding children. The most significant are male and female twins called Sigmund and Signy.

Volsung gives Signy in marriage to a rival king called Siggeir, despite her premonition of catastrophic consequences. During the celebrations, an incognito visitor – obviously Odin – enters the hall and thrusts a magnificent sword into the Barnstokk. Echoing contemporary King Arthur stories, Sigmund is the only man able to withdraw it and claim it as his prize. Siggeir, consumed with envy, treacherously kills Volsung. Sigmund goes into hiding, largely thanks to the cunning of his sister Signy, who is a shrewd and ruthless heroine.

She plays a key part in the ensuing fantastical episodes which involve shape-shifting, incest and child murder. She deceives Sigmund into sleeping with her and gives birth to their son. Father and son later become werewolves for a while, kill Signy's other children, escape a gruesome slow death and finally burn Siggeir alive in his own hall. Signy kills herself by walking into the same fire, saying that her work is done.

Sigmund becomes a rich and powerful king. He marries and has two more sons. There are further **feuds**, battles and deceptions. His first wife dies, and Sigmund marries a woman called Hjordis. However, a love rival declares war on him and in a fierce battle, Sigmund's sword is broken by Odin and he is mortally wounded. The pregnant Hjordis flees abroad, taking the broken fragments of sword.

Their son, Sigurd, is born some months later in the court of King Hjalprek of Denmark. He is **fostered** by Hjalprek's blacksmith, Regin, who helps Sigurd obtain a superb horse, called Grani – supposedly descended from Sleipnir, Odin's steed (see THE EIGHT-LEGGED HORSE, p. 56). He tells him the story of Otter's murder and Fafnir's transformation into a dragon. Sigurd is outraged, and promises to kill Fafnir as well as avenging his own father's death. Regin twice attempts to make his protégé a sword, but both break as soon as Sigurd tests them. Finally, he forges a new weapon from Sigmund's broken one, and names it Gram, in accordance with Sigmund's wishes. Sigurd uses Gram to avenge his father's death, with Odin making another cryptic appearance. Having achieved victory, his adventure with the dragon begins.

As Sigurd digs the pit to hide in, Odin is on hand to give him advice. The dialogue between Sigurd and the dying dragon is also found in the **Eddic poem** *Fafnismal* (The Sayings of Fafnir). Sigurd's tactic in withholding his name is a common folk tale device, based on the premise that the man who knows his enemy's name has supernatural power over him. Unfortunately, Sigurd is easily persuaded to give away his secret a few sentences later. All three accounts include the episode in which tasting dragon flesh enables the hero to understand the speech of birds – another common folk tale motif.

Sigurd's adventures continue after he rides away with the treasure. It seems that once this may have been a separate story, perhaps part of a cycle. However, both the main sources join them together – rather awkwardly, for the narrative now gradually morphs into an epic hero tale which attempts to root itself in real history. See the next story, CRUEL AND SWEET IS A WOMAN'S REVENGE.

CRUEL AND SWEET IS A WOMAN'S REVENGE
(story p. 130)

In both the **Prose Edda** and *Volsunga Saga*, this story follows on from the previous tale, retold here as SIGURD THE DRAGON SLAYER (p. 116).

My retelling is mainly based on the *Prose Edda*, with extra elements provided by *Volsunga Saga*. The latter contains much more detail but also a number of illogicalities and non sequiturs, so I have slightly rearranged the order of certain episodes to ensure that the complete story makes sense. **Snorri** says that 'most poets have composed poetry based on these stories', and no less than twelve of these poems have come down to us in the **Poetic Edda**, providing a variety of interesting perspectives. Judging by their subject matter and approach, some were almost certainly composed by women.

I have omitted four elements that appear in the sources, mainly to preserve the flow of the plot.

Firstly, when Brynhild and Sigurd share a bed in her fiery fortress, it is claimed they do not actually make love, for he lays his unsheathed sword between them. This may reflect the Christian author's need to portray Sigurd, the 'ideal hero', as a guardian of Brynhild's chastity; there is a similar motif in the Arthurian legend of *Tristram and Isolde*. The idea of a hero changing shape in order to make love to an unwitting woman is also Arthurian, appearing in the medieval legend of that British **king**'s conception.

Secondly, before Atli kills Hogni, there is an almost comical diversion in which a counsellor suggests cutting out the heart of a **slave**, with the intention of persuading Hogni to reveal the whereabouts of the treasure. Hogni nobly but unsuccessfully tries to prevent this slaughter of an innocent man. Eventually, the slave's heart is presented to Gunnar to terrorise him into giving up the treasure; but Gunnar rejects it because the heart is 'quaking' – something his brother's heart would certainly never do.

Thirdly, before Gudrun kills Atli, there is a grisly episode in which she murders their two sons then serves the unwitting Atli their blood in goblets made from their skulls, alongside their roasted hearts. This was clearly a favourite horror theme in ancient Europe, for there is an almost identical episode in VOLUND THE SMITH (p. 234); it may have been derived from the much older Greek myth of Atreus in which the hero kills his brother's three children and serves their flesh to him at a banquet.

Finally, the full story does not end with Gudrun's killing of Atli. In the sources, she walks into the sea and tries to drown herself. However, she is washed up at the court of a king called Jonakr, whom she marries; and they have three sons. The family tragedy continues when Gudrun's daughter, Svanhild, is betrothed to a neighbouring king, but is tricked into becoming the mistress of her fiancé's son. In punishment, the son is hanged, and Svanhild is trampled to death by horses. Gudrun sends her sons to avenge Svanhild's death, but they all die tragically on this mission.

The story is a curious mixture of historical legend and supernatural fantasy. Some of the characters were almost certainly real people who lived around the 4th to 5th Centuries AD. The most important is Atli, more familiarly known as Atilla the Hun. The Huns were skilled horsemen and archers who originated from central Asia. By the 5th Century they had conquered an empire extending from Europe to Persia and possibly far beyond. An interesting link to this story is that the Hunnish capital was known as 'The Ring', since it comprised a circular city of tents, wooden buildings and wagons. Atilla was the Hunnish monarch from the year AD 435, having previously ruled for a year alongside his brother, and was one of the main foes of the Western and Eastern Roman Empires. He died in 453, and though there are varying accounts, a woman may indeed have been involved in his final moments in some way. A Greek contemporary of his, Priscus, described him choking to death from a nosebleed as he celebrated his latest of many marriages. Eighty years later another Roman historian claimed that he was 'pierced by the hand and blade of his wife' – which perhaps evolved into the **Viking Age** version.

The episode of Gunnar in the snake-pit seems to have been a popular subject of ancient Germanic art, continuing into the 9th and 10th Centuries, the peak of the Viking Age. Surviving works show the scene carved onto the cart from the Oseberg ship burial in Norway, a stone cross in the Isle of Man and several **picture-stones** found on the Swedish island of Gotland.

RIDDLES *(text p. 144)*

Riddles are commonly associated with the Anglo-Saxons, yet they also occur in a number of the Vikings' **Eddic poems**, usually as a device to reinforce sacred lore.

These more prosaic examples all come from the 13th Century *Hervarar Saga ok Heidreks*. King Heidrek announces that any man who wrongs him will be spared execution if he can pose a riddle that Heidrek cannot solve. One of his followers, Gestumblindi, commits a crime and in desperation sacrifices to **Odin**. In response, Odin comes to him in the form of Gestumblindi's double and they exchange clothes. Odin, posing as Gestumblindi, puts a series of riddles to the king. Heidrek successfully answers them all – until the final one: 'What did Odin say in Baldr's ear before he was borne to the funeral pyre?' (See THE DEATH OF BALDR, p. 99). Obviously, none but Odin can answer this, so Heidrek both guesses his opponent's true identity and agrees to free the real Gestumblindi. Odin poses an identical riddle in the final verse of the Eddic poem *Vafthrudnismal* (Vafthrudnir's Sayings).

Some scholars believe that the verse riddles contained in this **saga** come from much older oral traditions; and that the saga itself has roots in **Viking Age** Norway, possibly based on stories about 4th and 5th Century central European kingdoms.

IN PRAISE OF SLAVES, PEASANTS AND NOBLES *(text p. 148)*

This is based on a rather strange **Old Norse** poem called *Rigsthula* (Rig's List). The only surviving version is in the *Codex Wormianus*, a 14th Century Icelandic manuscript which also contains the ***Prose Edda***. There is scholarly disagreement as to the age of *Rigsthula*. Some claim it is a medieval invention; whilst others use archaeological evidence to argue that its oral roots genuinely lie in the **Viking Age**, possibly in 10th Century Denmark.

Rigsthula tells of a god travelling through the human realm and visiting three homes. A 14th Century prose introduction says that it comes from 'old stories' and that the god is Heimdall. Both the translations I used question this and assert that his characteristics and behaviour make him more likely to be **Odin**. Whatever the truth, in this adventure he is called 'Rig', which may be connected linguistically to an old Irish world meaning '**king**' (there was an important Viking kingdom in Ireland).

The first home Rig visits is on the seashore and belongs to Great-Grandpa and Great-Grandma. They offer him a humble meal of broth and thick, heavy bread; then Rig shares their bed for three nights, lying between them. Nine months later Great-Grandma bears a swarthy child called Slave. He grows up to marry a gangly, sunburned girl whose name is often translated as Wench. They bear numerous children, the forebears of all **slaves**.

Next Rig arrives at a house where Grandpa and Grandma are sitting inside at their handiwork. The meal they serve him is 'fine and filling, fairly spread', ample and tasty. Again, for three nights Rig sleeps between the couple and nine months later Grandma bears a child called Peasant, who is 'red-headed and ruddy with roaming eyes' and grows up robustly to manage his own small farm. He marries Daughter-in-Law, and they have numerous children from whom are descended all the generations of peasants.

Finally, Rig arrives at a hall where Father and Mother are sitting together, displaying all the characteristics of good breeding. They serve Rig a fine meal, then they too willingly share their bed with him. Nine months later, Mother gives birth to **Earl**, wraps him in silk and has him brought up amongst warriors. At one stage he meets Rig, who personally teaches him to read and carve **runes** and claims him as his own son. Earl comes to rule eighteen estates and, as expected of a nobleman, is generous in handing out wealth. He marries a 'slim-fingered, white-skinned, wise maid' called Brisk by one translator, Capable by the other. All their children are sons. The youngest boy, Kin, is blessed with supernatural talents: he can read runes, blunt blades, calm waters, understand birdsong, quench fires and soothe sorrows. He has the strength and vigour of eight men. He wins a rune contest against Rig, who thus gives him the right to take his name. Riding through the woods, he stones some birds, and is reprimanded for this by a wise crow who says he would be better off going to battle...

And, frustratingly, here the surviving manuscript ends, leaving the tale incomplete.

Rigsthula is often quoted as a serious work which proves belief in a rigid class system, and portrays the different social strata as they really were. However, the poem has a light-hearted feel, especially with the colourful – almost comical – names ascribed to representatives of each group, who are all portrayed as caricatures. For example, it depicts slaves as deformed and repulsive; yet the **sagas** show that many slaves were, in fact, high-born people captured in raids, or their descendants; and that many were freed to make their way very successfully in the world.

Deciding how to retell *Rigsthula* was somewhat problematic, particularly as it seems to have a distinct medieval overlay. Does it have some mystical meaning, or is it simply a muddle of different influences? I took inspiration from one translator who suggests that it may be derived from a praise poem for a Viking king – possibly a 10th Century Danish monarch, either Gorm the Old (died c. 935) or Harald Bluetooth (died c. 985) . Perhaps it was used at a feast at which the aristocratic host was happy to spread his bonhomie to all present, including local yeoman families benevolently invited to the occasion, and even the slaves and servants whose labours made the event possible. Unable to make useful sense of the frame story of the wandering god randomly spreading his genes through society, I have concentrated solely on the colourful descriptions of the three classes. The names of the children and their characteristics are taken exactly from the original, dipping into two translations.

KING GEIRROD THE MAGNIFICENT *(story p. 151)*

This folk tale with mythical characters comes from a single source, *Grimnismal* (Grimnir's Sayings) in the **Poetic Edda**.

The actual story is narrated in prose, presumably jotted down from folk memory by the scribe who committed the ancient poems to paper. It seems intended to give a salutary message that rulers should behave honourably. This is complemented by fifty-four rather esoteric verses which only vaguely relate to the plot. Instead, they mainly describe mythical lore, including over fifty different names of **Odin**, some of them relating to other myths. One translator claims that these verses date from the first half of the 10th Century; however, the prose story in its present form is clearly medieval.

As in parallel tales, *Grimnismal* features Odin disguising himself to visit the human world and meddling in human affairs. Unusually, here his wife Frigg participates as well. The prose text describes the divine couple sitting together in

Asgard on Odin's throne, *Hlidskjalf,* watching over the world and arguing about the two young princes. Frigg favours Agnar and Odin Geirrod, and they have a wager over which of them will fare better. The soothsayer who offers the mysterious warning is named in the poem as Frigg's maid, Fulla.

There is no evidence that any of the royal characters were real people. However, the verses mention 'the land of the Goths' – suggesting that the story was one of many absorbed by the Vikings from central Europe.

AMLETH *(story p. 160)*

This story is clearly one of the ancient tales that inspired Shakespeare's *Hamlet.* Although there are many differences, the name of the hero and his mother (Gertrude in Shakespeare) are virtually the same. Shakespeare also followed the main plot of the hero's uncle killing his father and marrying his mother; Amleth's feigning of madness; and his uncle sending him to England in a thwarted attempt to have him murdered.

Most surviving **Viking Age** stories have their roots in Icelandic oral tradition and literature, but *Amleth* comes from Denmark and is recorded in **Saxo Grammaticus'** 13th Century Latin book *Gesta Danorum* (History of the Danes). Saxo's version has a very leisurely medieval style, full of extended anecdotes about Amleth's pretended insanity, and sophisticated linguistic jokes. Its motifs of burning people alive inside a building, and the changed message, both bear distinct echoes of CRUEL AND SWEET IS A WOMAN'S REVENGE (p. 130). For more about burnings, see NJAL THE PEACEMAKER AND HIS ANGRY SONS (p. 183 and Notes p. 344).

Hilda Ellis Davidson, editor of the translation I used, says that it is not known from where Saxo sourced this story. She cites a similar name to Amleth which occurs in an unrelated 9th Century **skaldic verse**, but suggests that the story's origins may lie in a Scandinavian folk narrative or an episode in a lost **saga**. Saxo says that Fengi, and the brother he murdered, ruled over Jutland under what seems to have been a high **king** of Denmark, naming the latter as Rorik – Gerutha's father. Other commentators claim that this might be a 6th Century Danish king called Rorik 'Ring-scatterer' who is mentioned in passing in a number of other sources. Further adventures of Amleth are recounted in the next section of *Gesta Danorum*, but Davidson says these are more likely derived from Latin rather than Scandinavian sources.

A SLAVE WOMAN'S STORY *(story p. 168)*

The stories now move from myth and legend to accounts of supposedly real people. This one forms several chapters of *Laxdaela Saga*. The events described here, if true, took place during the early to mid 10th Century.

There is a tendency to think of all Vikings as

Scandinavian, alongside the assumption that the people who settled the previously uninhabited country of Iceland from the 9th Century onwards were Norwegians. However, recent research has shown that during the 'settlement' period of Iceland, some fifty per cent of the female population and twenty per cent of the males in fact had Celtic blood. It is speculated that, like Melkorka, many were Irish or Scottish **slaves** who were forced to adopt the **Old Norse** language, names and way of life.

In *Laxdaela Saga*, Melkorka's son Olaf later becomes known as Olaf the Peacock and is feted as a great chieftain. His own eldest son, Kjartan is one of the principal characters in the **saga**'s central love story, retold in this collection as THE LOVE TRIANGLE (p. 215) The saga author clearly recounted Melkorka's story to provide an ancestral context to Kjartan's deeds and misfortunes; but it is interesting enough to stand alone as a record of the implications that pirate raiding and slavery had on one woman's fortunes.

In the saga, Olaf's trip to Ireland to claim his heritage is preceded and followed by visits to the court of King Harald Greycloak and Harald's mother, Queen Gunnhild, in Norway. There, it is claimed, the ageing 'king-mother' develops a flirtatious liking for him – similar to, though less extreme than, the one experienced by Hrut in THE WITCH QUEEN'S CURSE (p. 296). Gunnhild furnishes him with a ship and large crew in which to sail to Ireland, and later provides the ship in which he returns to Iceland. Since this episode is repeated with different heroes in other sagas – indeed, Kjartan has a similar adventure with a later king and a royal lady – it seems to be a literary addition rather than an authentic part of the historical story.

The translators of *Laxdaela Saga* say in a footnote that Myrkjartan is a Norse variant of the Irish name Muircheartach. They say that, at the time of this story, no high king of Ireland was called by that name, though it was the name of several Irish petty kings.

AUD THE DEEP-MINDED *(story p. 176)*

Aud's story is recounted fully in **Landnamabok** and more briefly in other sources. In some texts she is named Unn, but her story is exactly the same. An interesting aspect of her settlement in Iceland is the revelation that women were allowed to claim ownership of land there in their own right, even though they were entitled to less than men. The system for allocating landholdings is described in *Landnamabok*, which says that **King Harald Finehair** devised it when immigrants to Iceland appealed to him to mediate disputes between them.

The first chapters of *Laxdaela Saga* are concerned with the tale of Aud/Unn, including a colourful description of her death. It says that her body was carried to a previously prepared burial mound, and she was laid in a ship inside it with much treasure, before the mound was sealed. Some of *Laxdaela Saga's* most important characters are descended from her, several generations removed (see THE LOVE TRIANGLE, p. 215). The translators date her arrival in Iceland as c. 915, around forty-five years after the first settlers arrived in the country, and eighty-five years before Iceland's official **conversion to Christianity**. Breidafjordur, where she and her followers made their home, is on the west coast.

Aud's son, Thorstein the Red, won his kingdom in partnership with **Earl** Sigurd the Mighty of the Northern Isles: this is also briefly described in the early 14th Century chronicle of the Orkney Islands, *Orkneyinga Saga*. Together they conquered half of Scotland, which Thorstein ruled as king until his death. Aud's two brothers settled in Iceland long before she arrived there. *Landnamabok* records that her ships were wrecked when she reached Iceland. However, she declined one brother's offer of lodgings because he was only willing to accommodate half her shipwrecked companions; the other brother was generous enough to take in the whole party.

Aud the Deep-Minded is still remembered in modern Iceland as a great matriarch. Several places are supposedly named after her activities, for example, Kambness in Breidafjordur is where she lost a comb; and Dogurdarness - 'Breakfast Promontory' – is named after a morning meal that she ate with her companions while they were exploring their new home.

Her propensity for emancipating **slaves** is also mentioned in one of the sagas about **Vinland**, *Eirik's Saga*, which says the people Aud freed included 'many well-born men, who had been taken captive in the British Isles by Vikings.' Amongst them is a man of noble descent called Vifil, who is the grandfather of Gudrid, one of the main female characters in the Vinland Sagas. (See the stories WINELAND, p. 254 and GHOSTS IN GREENLAND, p. 282).

The retelling here imagines how Aud's story must originally have been passed on, through gossip spreading around Iceland and through successive generations, until it was finally written down in *Landnamabok* around two hundred years later.

NJAL THE PEACEMAKER AND HIS ANGRY SONS *(story p. 183)*

This tragedy forms the climax to one of the greatest of all the Icelandic **sagas**, *Njal's Saga*. It was written around 1280, but set in the late 10th Century, against the background of Iceland's **conversion to Christianity**. The translators of the edition I used as my source say it was based on oral tradition and some written records. Njal's house was named Bergthorsknoll, after his wife Bergthora (many place names were named after women); a modern farm of the same name is located near the coast of southern Iceland, just north of the Vestmannaeyjar archipelago.

Njal's Saga is a rich and complex historical novel with numerous strands and subplots, and a colourful cast of characters covering several generations. Some of the characters also appear in other major sagas. Its main theme is an endless series of killings and revenge killings. Njal attempts to break this mould by using his ingenuity and profound knowledge of Icelandic **law** to replace the ongoing slaughters with negotiation and financial reparation; but he is unable to hold violent forces at bay for ever, and he himself ends up their most illustrious victim.

There are two cryptic references in **Landnamabok** which suggest that Njal Thorgeirsson was a real man and that he was indeed burned alive in his own home. It mentions the 'ancestors of Burned Njal', who include 'Thorgeir…his son Njal was burned in his house'.

Setting fire to houses while the inhabitants were inside seems to have been a horrifyingly common form of revenge in the **Viking Age**, for there are a number of other references to similar events in *Landnamabok*. A translators' footnote states:

'These "burnings in", though recognised in blood **feuds**, were the most barbarous cruelties… The doors and windows of the house were fastened from the outside, hay was placed against the house round about, and set on fire, and the inmates when trying to escape were butchered or driven back into the flames.'

Such mass murders were not limited to Iceland. *Egil's Saga* describes King **Harald Finehair** of Norway burning an enemy and his kinsmen. Burnings in Sweden are mentioned in *Landnamabok*; and in the semi-mythical *Ynglinga Saga* in **Heimskringla**. Elsewhere in the present book CRUEL AND SWEET IS A WOMAN'S REVENGE (p. 130), set in central Europe and Denmark's AMLETH (p. 160) both feature legendary house burnings.

The first part of *Njal's Saga* is concerned largely with a malicious woman called Hallgerd, whose first two husbands are murdered, giving her a formidable reputation.

Eventually she marries Gunnar Hamundarson, who ignores everyone's advice not to get involved with her. Gunnar is a stereotypical saga hero: tall, strong, rich and handsome, a brilliant warrior and sportsman, who wins both treasure and fame by adventuring in mainland Scandinavia. His best friend is the main protagonist of the saga, the lawyer Njal Thorgeirsson.

The saga describes Njal as follows:

'He was so skilled in **law**, that no one was considered
his equal... His advice was sound and benevolent,
and always turned out well for those who followed
it. He...solved the problems of any who came to him
for help.'

A blood feud develops between Gunnar's wife, Hallgerd, and Njal's wife, Bergthora. In a grim echo of the vendettas usually practised by **Viking Age** men, the women arrange a series of killings of and by each others' servants. Njal constantly tries – but fails – to halt the women's feud by arranging financial compensation. Nevertheless, he and Gunnar keep reaffirming their friendship despite the hostilities of their wives – until Gunnar himself is killed in an unrelated feud.

Meanwhile Njal's two younger sons, Grim and Helgi, are travelling in Norway, where they run into Thrain, an old enemy of theirs. As part of the women's blood feud, Thrain had been involved in the murder of the Njalssons' **foster**-father. Thrain contrives a situation that makes the Norwegian ruler, Earl Hakon, believe the Njalssons to be guilty of a major crime. They are captured and put in chains. Although eventually they are freed and paid compensation by the Earl, this nurtures their hatred of Thrain. Eventually, in a dramatically described battle on the ice, the Njalssons kill Thrain.

Njal pays Thrain's **kin** generous reparation on behalf of his sons. He also takes in Thrain's young son, Hoskuld, to raise as his foster-child, favouring him over his own children, even pulling complex legal strings to have Hoskuld made a chieftain. It is Njal who arranges Hoskuld's marriage to a woman whose uncle later organises the burning.

During the final showdown at the **Althing**, the amount of financial compensation that Njal raises to try and compensate for his sons' crime – six hundred ounces of silver – is truly exceptional; by comparison, other reparations for killings described in the same Saga amount to either one hundred or two hundred ounces. It seems extraordinary that Flosi decides to turn down this phenomenal payment merely because of a childish **insult**; yet Viking Age stories widely demonstrate that a wounded reputation was considered as damaging as a severe physical injury.

After the burning of Njal and his kin, there are further long drawn-out battles, fought both at court and with weapons. The saga ends with a final reconciliation.

Njal's Saga is a carefully crafted literary construction. Even if the feuds and other episodes it describes really did take place, as Knut Liestol points out in *The Origin of the Icelandic Family Sagas*, it 'has much that is incredible and even impossible'. We will never know how much of the characterisation – if any – is based on the genuine personalities of the historical characters.

A TALE OF GRETTIR THE STRONG *(story p. 193)*

This is one of the most entertaining episodes from the 14th Century *Grettir's Saga*, a fantastical collection of tall stories about the exploits of a charismatic anti-hero who lived during the 11th Century. Its central character, Grettir 'the strong', is twice mentioned briefly in **Landnamabok**. Despite these historical credentials, Grettir's adventures – being full of ghosts, monsters and sorcery – are almost certainly either pure invention or greatly exaggerated versions of real events.

Grettir is a powerfully built young trouble-maker, with a talent for composing offensive poetry – identical qualities to the heroes of two other **sagas**, *Egil's Saga* and *The Saga of Gunnlaug Serpent-Tongue*. He comes from a good family, but regularly falls out with his father, even getting into violent fights with him. At the tender age of fourteen, he kills an older man as they ride to the **Althing** – where he is sentenced to three years' **outlawry**. His father persuades a reluctant friend to take him to Norway on his ship, and during the voyage Grettir matures a little, discovering that hard work wins more friends than insolence and threats.

The crew abandon him on an island, ruled by the same Chieftain Thorfinn of this retelling. Grettir greatly impresses him by daringly entering a grave mound, winning a battle against the monster that guards it, and retrieving the large hoard of treasure buried inside. Thorfinn promises to give Grettir his own sword if he performs another outstanding deed. The trouncing of the berserkers, as described here, wins him both the promised reward, and great fame.

Berserkers were warriors associated with **Odin.** They

were said to work themselves up into frenzies of supernatural strength that made them invulnerable to any weapon, and could supposedly shape-shift into bears or wolves. Although some **kings** kept special troops of berserkers in their armies, they could be very dangerous and were often despised as thugs and troublemakers.

Grettir travels around Norway, his acclaim winning him easy hospitality. His reputation for extraordinary strength and bravery grows, yet he continues to make enemies. Single-handedly, he kills a great bear that was ravaging a flock of sheep, but in the process enrages and then kills an arrogant rival. A chain of retaliatory violence ensues, which Grettir only escapes by returning to Iceland – where he revives an old grudge and enters yet another cycle of violence.

The saga now moves to another major episode about a haunted farm. Grettir overcomes the offending ghost in a violent struggle. However, the ghost curses him to bring ill luck and misfortune down upon himself, and to suffer hallucinations that make solitude unbearable. The curse has its intended effect, provoking more violent impulses and a fear of travelling alone at night.

He returns to Norway, murdering a man, unintentionally setting fire to an occupied house and killing a youth who **insults** him. Banished by the king, he goes back to Iceland for the final time. Here further disputes and violence, this time within his family, result in the slaughter of his brother. Grettir achieves vengeance for this, but as a result is condemned once more to outlawry.

He lives rough in the Icelandic wilderness for several years, alienating locals by stealing weapons, horses, food and clothing. At one point he wins slight redemption by killing a pair of trolls which had been troubling a farm. His reward for this deed seems to be bedding the farmer's wife, for the saga relates that she later gives birth to Grettir's son, a big strong lad called Skeggi, though he dies at the age of seventeen.

After this, Grettir's power wanes as the curse laid on him years earlier takes serious hold. Accompanied by his faithful fifteen-year-old brother and a vagrant, he retreats to the island of Drang, situated in a fjord four miles off the coast of northern Iceland, and lives there for several years. Then an elderly sorceress lays curses and spells against him on a tree trunk, which finds its way to Grettir, causing him a serious infected wound. As he lies dying, a band of men storm the island to attack him. He puts up a final brave fight, despite his illness, but is beheaded.

The saga contains much repetition, countless outlandish events and some strongly comical episodes. In the story retold here, neither the wife nor daughter are named – unusual in a saga, for exact names and genealogies were normally considered highly important. All this suggests that, whatever the foundation of truth, Grettir's adventures were assembled from various oral legends and folk tales which grew ever bigger and more astonishing over the years.

GISLI THE OUTLAW'S LAST STAND *(story p. 201)*

This story forms the last few episodes of *Gisli Sursson's Saga*. Written in either the late 13th or early 14th Century, the **saga** is based on the lives of people of the mid to late 9th Century. Gisli, Thordis, their two brothers, Thordis' first husband Thorgrim, her second husband Bork the Stout, and Aud are all mentioned in **Landnamabok;** as is Ingjald, who is described as 'a backer-up of Gisli Sursson'.

The saga describes a very complex and tragic series of incidents which lead up to Gisli being **outlawed**. Gisli is an ambiguous character: hot-blooded, resolute and unforgiving; yet hard working, always anxious to adhere to his perverse code of honour and to protect those **kin** who are loyal to him. His skills as a warrior and a survivor would have won him much admiration in the **Viking Age**.

Opening in Norway, the saga presents Gisli as a young man of over-high principles. He kills his sister Thordis's suitor on suspicion that he has seduced her, then falls into further violent conflict over two rival suitors. As a result, the family is burned out of their house. His patronymic, Sursson, was his father's nickname, acquired when he extinguished this fire using barrels of *sur* – whey.

To escape the trouble, the entire family emigrates to Iceland. There Gisli and his siblings seem to settle down. He becomes close to his brother Thorkel, and to Thordis and her first husband Thorgrim. When he marries Aud, he also bonds closely with her brother Vestein. The four men intend to seal an oath of mutual blood brotherhood. Here the saga gives an interesting description of the ancient ceremony involved, presumably preserved in oral memory from the

Viking Age. The proponents pile up turf rectangles to form an arch, then stand in pairs underneath this, face to face. Each draws blood, mixed together as they swear on the **gods** to practise everlasting loyalty, and to avenge each other as necessary. Spectators predict that, given the men's temperaments, this is a hollow ceremony and that the four will soon fall out. Sure enough, before the ritual is even complete, Thorgrim refuses to ally himself with Vestein; provoking Gisli in turn to decline allegiance to Thorgrim.

This discord combines with Gisli's divided loyalties between his siblings and his two brothers-in-law, and a contrived scene in which two of the women are implicated in possible marital infidelity. The result is a chain of retaliatory murders in which the killers attempt to hide their identities, yet leave enough motives and clues to be indicted. It culminates in Gisli being **outlawed**. Like his fellow outlaw, Grettir the Strong (see the previous story, A TALE OF GRETTIR THE STRONG, p. 193), Gisli's bleak situation is made worse when he is cursed by an evil sorcerer, making it impossible for well-wishers to succeed in helping him.

The harsh, masculine morals of *Gisli's Saga* are complemented by an equally robust cast of female protagonists. The most exemplary is Aud, who stands by her husband throughout his sentence of outlawry, staunchly risking her own life to both shelter and defend him right through to the final battle. She is opposed by the vengeful Thordis, who has more than enough reason to hate her brother Gisli, having lost both a lover and a husband to his sword. The grisly description of Gisli's death is typical of the sagas, which commonly include copious details about noteworthy battles and the combatants' wounds.

WORDS OF WISDOM *(text p. 208)*

Despite popular belief that the **Viking Age** was defined solely by violence, the surviving literature shows that Viking people also followed a strong ethical code and placed high value on sober, down-to-earth behaviour.

Some of the proverbs here come from *Havamal* in the *Poetic Edda,* sometimes combining the essence of two separate verses. Others are quotes from two **sagas**: *Grettir's Saga* and *Njal's Saga.*

OF LOVE AND GODDESSES *(text p. 212)*

The information about these **goddesses** comes from a short, cryptic passage in the *Prose Edda.* Some scholars question whether they are all genuine individuals, or whether some are confused identities with the major goddesses, Frigg and **Freyja**. Unfortunately few stories specifically about the goddesses have survived to throw light on this. Nevertheless, **Snorri**'s descriptions suggests that they once played an important role in the spiritual lives of women; indeed, he describes them as being equally powerful and holy as the **gods**. Moreover, Frigg and **Hel** play key roles in THE DEATH OF BALDR (p. 99); whilst Idun holds all the deities' fates in her keeping in THE APPLES OF YOUTH (p. 72).

THE LOVE TRIANGLE *(story p. 215)*

This story forms the central plot of *Laxdaela Saga* (The Saga of the People of Laxardale), written by an anonymous 13th Century Icelandic author. The oldest complete surviving manuscript is part of a mid-14th Century work known as *Modruvallabok*, which also contains ten other sagas.

The main characters are briefly mentioned in *Landnamabok*, to which it is believed that **Ari the Learned** made a contribution. Ari was the great-grandson of Gudrun from the saga, so much truth may have been preserved, as Gudrun's story was passed down through oral family tradition before her scholarly descendant perhaps helped to write it down. Most interestingly, *Landnamabok* lists Gudrun's brothers and says 'they were **outlawed** on account of the slaughter of Kjartan Olafsson.' It also mentions Gudrun, her four husbands and children, and Kjartan's wife Hrefna. It is possible to date the saga fairly accurately, since Kjartan and Bolli's experiences with **King Olaf Tryggvason** in Norway, including Kjartan's baptism, are described in the quasi-historical *Kristni Saga*, which names the year of **conversion to Christianity** as 1000.

The main events take place in Breidafjord, the coastal region of North-West Iceland that was originally settled by a woman known in *Laxdaela Saga* as Unn – which is an alternative name for AUD THE DEEP-MINDED (p. 176). Kjartan and Bolli were descended from her; whilst Gudrun was descended from her brother, Bjorn the Easterner.

All the place names mentioned in the saga can still be found on a modern Icelandic map. Kjartan and Bolli grow up on Olaf the Peacock's farm Hjardarholt, in Laxardale off

Hvammsfjord. Osvif and Gudrun live along Svinadalur above the same fjord, at a place called Laugar (meaning 'baths' - after the hot springs there). Svinadalur is also the location where Kjartan is ambushed and killed. Osvif owns more land in Saelingsdale. During the hostilities, Kjartan thwarts Bolli's attempt to buy land nearby at Saelingsdalstunga, Bolli eventually moving there after his **foster**-brother's death. The interlude in Norway takes place in Trondheim, the original Norwegian capital, said to have been founded by King Olaf Tryggvason in 997.

Kjartan's initial courtship of Gudrun at the hot springs reflects the fact that Iceland is an actively volcanic country with numerous natural thermal springs scattered throughout the land; socialising whilst bathing in them is still a popular activity.

The saga offers interesting insights into how marriage was viewed in the **Viking Age**. It shows young women (Thurid as well as Gudrun) pressed by their parents to marry unsuitable men against their will; but it also indicates the ease with which such unhappy wives could obtain **divorce** and remarry. As in *Njal's Saga* (see NJAL THE PEACEMAKER AND HIS ANGRY SONS, p. 183), Viking Age Iceland is portrayed as a highly ordered society dominated by both economics and the **law**, with strict procedures governing divorce, land purchase and so on. Some elements are disconcertingly familiar to modern readers: Gudrun's 'prenuptial contract' with Thorvald; Kjartan 'gazumping' Bolli's attempted purchase of a new farm, and Kjartan and Bolli adventuring abroad before they settle down. However, it also portrays a very superstitious society; like some other sagas, it makes much of the major characters having premonitions of the disasters ahead through vivid and disturbing dreams.

There is a very similar story in *The Saga of Gunnlaug Serpent-Tongue*. Here the hero is a rebellious, uninhibited youth who is also a very talented poet, his compositions and recitals infuriating and delighting in equal measure. At the age of twelve he has a row with his father and runs away, finding sanctuary with a neighbour descended from the famous **skald**, Egil Skallagrimson (hero of the eponymous *Egil's Saga*). He falls in love with his new foster-sister, Helga. When he comes of age, he goes off travelling – asking for Helga's hand on his return. Since he is so unsettled, her father refuses a formal betrothal but promises her to Gunnlaug if he returns within three years. Gunnlaug now travels throughout the northern world, impressing kings and **earls** everywhere and earning great riches. However, he misses the deadline by a few months and Helga's father, outraged by his irresponsibility, forces her to marry a rival. When Gunnlaug returns to Iceland, he challenges this man to a deadly dual, leaving Helga both widowed and heartbroken at the loss of her childhood sweetheart.

VOLUND THE SMITH *(story p. 234)*

This haunting folk tale is from *Volundarkvida* (Volund's Poem) in the **Poetic Edda.** Some scholars believe it was composed by a Norse poet working in the Danelaw (Danish Viking occupied area of England) between 900 and 1050. The hero seems to have been widely known in northern Europe, for he is also mentioned in several Anglo-Saxon poems including *Beowulf*. Two very ancient carvings which appear to depict scenes from from the story are still in existence. One is a **picture-stone** from the island of Gotland in Sweden, dating from either the 8th or 9th Century. The other is a small Anglo-Saxon whale-bone chest from the early 8th Century, currently held in the British Museum.

Volundarkvida opens with the haunting scene in which Volund and his brothers encounter the three **valkyries** on the shore of the lonely lake by which they have built their halls. The feather cloaks which they cast off indicate that the story has been influenced by the motif of 'swan maidens' – supernatural women who shape-shift between human and bird (or sometimes animal) form – which is common in folk tales all over the world. However, unlike most swan maiden stories, these women are portrayed as willing brides to the men who find them, and they are able to leave to resume their work for **Odin** on the battlefields at their own volition. As a **Finn**, Volund would be assumed to have an affinity with such supernatural creatures.

The original poem does not explain why Volund was chosen as a prospective, though unwilling, husband for Bodvild. So, without changing the plot in any way, my retelling attempts to make better sense of it by rearranging the order of events very slightly and giving Bodvild a more proactive role.

HELGI & SIGRUN *(story p. 242)*

This story is constructed from four ancient texts, which in turn seem to have been put together from fragments of a number of much older poems, some possibly dating from the early 10th Century. The variety of sources suggests that it was once a very well-known tale with several versions in circulation. In this spirit, I have blended together plot elements and imagery from all the sources to bring this heroic legend back to life.

The three oldest sources are in the **Poetic Edda**. Two share the title *Helgakvida Hundingsbana* (The Poem of Helgi, Slayer of Hunding): one is subtitled *The First Poem* and the other *The Second Poem*. The other poem is *Helgakvida Hjorvardssonar* (The Poem of Helgi son of Hjorvard). The anonymous scribe who wrote these out interspersed the verses with many short paragraphs of prose, summarising events in an attempt to fill in missing sections of plot. A similar tale is also included in *Volsunga Saga*. As represented in my retelling, these sources provide interesting insights into the mythical **norns** and **valkyries**; into the practice of **sacrificing** to **Odin,** and the use of **insults** as a preliminary weapon of war.

There seem to be two different heroes called Helgi, both of whom had relationships with valkyries. The two *Helgakvida Hundingsbana* poems, as well as *Volsunga Saga,* all claim that Helgi was a son of Sigmund the Volsung (and thus a brother to the famous Sigurd of THE CURSE OF ANDVARI'S RING cycle – p. 114 – though Sigurd is never mentioned in the Helgi poems.) They tell of Helgi winning fame by exterminating Hunding and his sons – formidable rivals, though little is revealed of them – and then battling to rescue Sigrun from her forced betrothal. On the other hand, *Helgakvida Hjorvardssonar* says that Helgi was the son of a Norwegian **king** called Hjorvard, and his valkyrie was called Svava. This story is rather different from my retelling and is dominated by supernatural characters and rituals. It describes the hero and his brother both being tempted by a **troll-wife**, and a curious ceremony involving the swearing of oaths over a special Yuletide cup. This Helgi is also killed in battle. The tale ends with the statement that Helgi and Svava are both born again – a theme conveniently taken up in *Helgakvida Hundingsbana: The Second Poem*, which says that 'Sigrun was Svava reborn'.

According to one translator, Helgi was originally a Danish popular hero – the same described in some detail by **Saxo Grammaticus** as the conqueror of both Hunding and Hodbrodd. He speculates that the story spread into Norway and thence to Iceland, at some point creatively confusing Helgi's parenthood to make him part of the famous Volsung dynasty.

VERSES FROM THE COURT POETS *(p. 250)*

These poems are all based on translations of **skaldic verse** from *Heimskringla*. Scholars believe that the skalds named in this book were almost certainly real men, and that their poems are fairly true to the original compositions.

The first verse is by Tjodolf, employed by **King** Harald Hardrada (The Hard Ruler) who was killed in 1066 – the twentieth year of his reign – during a failed attempt to conquer England. **Snorri** says it was composed to celebrate the launching of a great ship, in which Harald sailed out to wage battle against King Svein of Denmark.

The next two poems are from the reign of King Olaf Haraldsson (reigned 1014-30), also known as St Olaf, who employed a number of different skalds.

The first, known as *Bjarkamal*, is by an anonymous poet. Snorri describes the skald Thormod reciting it in a loud voice to waken the king's slumbering army on the morning of a major battle, and King Olaf rewarding him for this effort with a heavy gold ring.

The following verses, by Sigvat, were composed to prove his loyalty to King Olaf after a visit to King Knut in England. Snorri says that on his return, King Olaf looks at him in silence and indicates that he had heard rumours of Knut trying to persuade him to change masters. Sigvat's composition obviously has the desired effect, because he is allowed to return to his old seat and is soon restored to the king's favour. Snorri claims that Sigvat spoke more easily in verse than in normal language.

The final and oldest example is about King Hakon the Good (934-60) and is attributed to Eyvind Skaldaspiller. It is taken from a very long poem which he composed immediately after Hakon's death. The verse here describes his final battle; subsequently the poet imagines Hakon's triumphant passage to the mythical **Slain Hall.**

WINELAND *(story p. 254)*

The name 'Wineland' is widely considered to be the correct translation of the **Old Norse** name *Vinland*.

Two different short **sagas** tell of the **Viking Age** discovery of Vinland, which has been identified as being in North America. It appears that they were written independently of each other; yet that they were based on the same oral accounts, which evolved differently over many years of retelling. The oldest is *Graenlendinga Saga*, which survives in a 14th Century manuscript, believed to be copied from a lost 12th Century manuscript. *Eirik's Saga*, probably composed in the mid-13th Century, survives in two Icelandic manuscripts of the 14th and 15th Centuries.

Grænlendinga Saga is generally considered the more reliable source. It claims that the story of the Vinland voyages originates from Karlsefni himself – which has inspired my own retelling to use his perspective.

Eirik's Saga contains considerable extra detail, particularly about Karlsefni's expedition to Vinland. However, much of it has a rather fanciful feel. For example, it claims that the Skraelings once escaped by mysteriously sinking into the ground, and includes a supposed sighting of a glittering, one-legged 'uniped'.

The oldest known written reference to Vinland was recorded by **Adam of Bremen** in 1075, sixty-five years after the believed date of Karlsefni's voyage:

'He also spoke of yet another island of the many
found in that ocean: it is called Wineland because

vines producing excellent wine grow wild there.
That unsown crops also abound on that island we
have ascertained not from fabulous reports but from
the trustworthy relation of the Danes.'

There are also cryptic references to Vinland in *Landnamabok*, which cites Karlsefni as a historical person, and *Islendindingabok.*

Despite this, and the evidence of the sagas, until the mid-20th Century, scholars were sceptical as to whether the voyages to Vinland had actually taken place. However, in 1960 a Norwegian husband-and-wife team, explorer Helge Ingstad and archaeologist Anne Stine Ingstad, set out to prove that they did.

The Ingstads assumed that the two sagas had accurately preserved information from the first travellers; and that they in turn had precisely described their routes and sailing times to guide those who followed in their wake. The sagas imply that Vinland lay south-westwards across the sea from Greenland – i.e. along the Atlantic coast of modern Canada. They describe two places which the Norse travellers passed en route: *Helluland* (Flat-Stone Land) whose description matches some of coastal Baffin Island; and *Markland* (Forest Land) which is consistent with part of Labrador.

Sailing past these areas, and aided by a 16th Century Icelandic map of the North Atlantic ocean, the Ingstads arrived at the northernmost tip of Newfoundland, a place today called L'Anse aux Meadows, where a local fisherman showed them some unusual grassy mounds. They excavated these between 1961 and 1968. This was followed by further work by the national heritage organisation, Parks Canada, during the 1970s. Eight 11th Century houses were unearthed there, alongside a forge and four workshops, all built in the Viking style with turf walls, pointed roofs and earthen floors; plus a stone oil lamp, a set of scales and evidence of iron working. This offers conclusive proof that Viking Age travellers really did reach North America. L'Anse aux Meadows is now a UNESCO World Heritage Site and a National Historic Site of Canada.

There is also evidence of very ancient settlement by indigenous Native American people in the same area, giving credence to the so-called 'Skraelings' of the Sagas. Taking account of known migrations, some scholars believe that the Skraelings may have been part of the Algonquian language group.

The Ingstads produced a fascinating book, *The Viking Discovery of America*, which attempts to distinguish the facts and fantasies of the two sagas, and links them to the actual excavations. Their only problem in proving the Vinland voyages was that the climate of Newfoundland does not support wild vines. They attempted to overcome this by suggesting that translating the name Vinland as 'Wineland' is the result of a transcription error, and that its name should more correctly be translated as 'pasture-land'.

However, more recent studies have refuted this. They speculate that L'Anse aux Meadows was just one of several Norse settlements in North America; that the name 'Vinland' referred to a huge area around the modern Gulf of St Lawrence; and that the settlers used L'Anse aux Meadows as a base to search for resources much further afield. In support of this, archaeological finds around L'Anse aux Meadows include butternuts and butternut wood worked with metal tools. Like wild grapes, butternut does not grow there: its nearest location is roughly nine hundred miles south-west of L'Anse aux Meadows in modern New Brunswick, suggesting that the pioneers also reached this area.

The travellers to Vinland all set out from Greenland. From the late 10th Century, this remote country attracted many Viking farmers.

Greenland lies roughly two hundred miles due west from Iceland and, according to *Landnamabok*, was first sighted in the year 900 by an Icelandic sailor blown off course by a storm. No one returned there until 978, when a party landed on its wild east coast and survived a stressful winter there involving atrocious weather and a murder. A few years later, **Eirik the Red** explored its much more inviting south-west coast. In the summer of either 985 or 986 he persuaded hundreds of hopeful migrants to move there with him, calling it Greenland because 'he said that people would be much more tempted to go there if it had an attractive name'. They set off in twenty-five ships, of which only fourteen arrived, the others being either blown back or lost at sea.

Ninety-five per cent of Greenland is totally uninhabitable, since the interior is covered by a vast, unbroken ice-cap. However, the settlers were able to establish flourishing farms in two areas along the south-west coast. On narrow coastal strips of fertile land, they kept sheep, cattle, horses, pigs and goats. The fjords and rivers contained abundant fish and there was excellent game hunting in the northern wilderness.

One community was, rather misleadingly, known as The Eastern Settlement. Its location was near the modern town of

Qaqortoq. Most of the saga characters were based here; and archaeologists have discovered evidence of one hundred and ninety Norse farms in the area, though some may be of a later date. The most prominent is Brattahlid, centre of much action in the two sagas. It was originally built by Eirik the Red on the bank of a fjord named after himself, Eiriksfjord. The site includes four barns with room for around forty cattle, and a church built by his wife, Thjodhild.

The Western Settlement was some two hundred miles further northwards on the same coast, near what is now the Greenlandic capital of Nuuk. Around ninety farms have been identified there.

At the time of the Vinland voyages, there were probably between six hundred and one thousand Greenlanders including children. At a later date this rose to about three thousand. Greenland was an outpost of Icelandic culture, **converting to Christianity** shortly after Iceland, and linked to the older country by strong **kinship** ties. After the end of the Viking Age, it gradually declined, partly due to the impact of a worsening climate, and the Norse colony is thought to have died out completely around the year 1500.

The exploration of Vinland began around the year 1000 AD – only fifteen years after the first migrants had established themselves in Greenland – and may have continued intermittently for up to twenty years. This is verified by carbon dating of the finds at L'Anse aux Meadows.

The first parts of both *Graenlendinga Saga* and *Eirik's Saga* are taken up by the story of Eirik the Red, reformed brawler and **outlaw**, and one of the best-known historical characters from the Viking Age. However, he plays no active role in the exploration of Vinland. His son, Leif 'the Lucky', is said to have acquired his nickname from his 'great magnanimity and goodness' – either for bringing Christianity to Greenland, or for rescuing some shipwrecked Norwegians.

One of the most important characters, particularly of *Eirik's Saga*, is Gudrid. Her grandfather, Vifil, is said to be one of the **slaves** freed by AUD THE DEEP-MINDED (p. 176) when she settled in Iceland. Gudrid's willingness to accompany two husbands – first the ill-fated Thorstein, and then Karlsefni – on their journeys to Vinland suggests that Viking Age women could be as eager for adventure as the men, apparently unperturbed by the dangers of traversing the often deadly sea. There is an interesting ghost story connected with her, retold here as GHOSTS IN GREENLAND (p. 282).

Like Gudrid, Eirik the Red's only daughter, Freydis, is an enthusiastic pioneer in the newly discovered country. In *Grænlendinga Saga,* she is portrayed as true heir to her father's pugnacious qualities: it describes her as 'an arrogant, overbearing woman' and claims that her expedition to Vinland is dominated by bad will, arguments, deceit and murder. By contrast, *Eirik's Saga* paints Freydis as a valiant, if rather strange, heroine. It says she is a member of Karlsefni's expedition to Vinland, during which there is a Skraeling attack on the Norse settlement. Everyone flees, ungallantly leaving the pregnant Freydis behind; bizarrely, she beats a sword against her bared breasts and thus manages to frighten the Skraelings away. Whichever version one believes, it seems that the real woman was certainly formidable.

A JOURNEY TO THE EAST (story p. 263)

This story forms the plot of a **saga** called *Yngvar inn Vidforla*, ('Yngvar the Far Travelled') which was probably written in the early 13th Century. It is said to be a translation of a slightly earlier Latin manuscript which has now been lost. The saga itself states that:

> 'Ketil went back to Iceland, settling there amongst his **kin**, and he was the first to tell of these events…
> We have heard this story told [i.e. presumably recited] but in writing it down we have followed a book composed by the learned monk Odd, which he based on the authority of well-known people'.

It seems rather like a work of fantasy, with its **giants**, dragons and demons; yet there almost certainly was a real explorer called Yngvar who led an expedition to Russia, for the adventure is commemorated on between twenty-two and thirty ancient **rune-stones** (the 'Yngvar rune-stones') that have been found in Sweden (different experts give different numbers of stones). They were carved in memory of men who sailed alongside the hero. A typical inscription reads that the stone was raised 'in memory of [man's name] who was killed in the east with Yngvar'. The men seem to be of different ages, for some rune-stones were raised in memory of lost fathers and others to honour lost sons. The saga implies that Yngvar embarked on his expedition with thirty ships. Such a large number seems unlikely for a river voyage of exploration through such remote landscapes; however, there may well have been more than one, since one of the runic inscriptions mentions a man who owned his own vessel. The most poetic inscription says, 'they travelled valiantly far for gold, and in the east gave [food] to the eagle'.

Although written in Iceland, the flavour of *Yngvar inn Vidforla* is very different from the earthy family **feuds** that dominate most Icelandic sagas; and it is unusual for the action to be centred on Sweden and especially Russia. Moreover, the giants and dragons which pepper it seem to have more in common with broader European folk narratives than specifically Norse legends. The demons are obviously based on Christian lore, or may even be an import from more distant Asian mythologies.

The saga states that Yngvar died at the age of twenty-five in 1041. Some scholars claim that the saga describes an actual Norse expedition along the Volga River to the Caspian Sea, which culminated in a battle against the Saracens in the same year. However, there does not seem to be anything in the text to really support this. The name of the river along which Yngvar's expedition sails is never given and the Caspian Sea does not appear in the text. The only eastern sea mentioned by name – but not actually visited – is the Red Sea, with the comment 'and that's where we think the world ends'. It seems likely that the saga author had perhaps heard of a real hero called Yngvar who led an expedition into the east. Since this was unknown territory to Icelanders, presumably he then developed the story with events and places that were pure imagination.

The last chapters of the saga are concerned with the adventures of Yngvar's son, Svein. They are very medieval in tone, and full of Christian propaganda, as he struggles to overcome the 'heathens' that he encounters, and feature not only another dragon but also some Cyclopses blatantly imported from Greek mythology. It concludes with Svein marrying Queen Silkisif and building a great cathedral in her city.

PAGAN PRAYERS AND SPELLS *(p. 272)*

Amongst the old **pagan** beliefs preserved in the *Poetic Edda* and *Prose Edda* there are a number of mystical incantations. Sometimes they are also referred to in the **sagas**.

The first comes from *The Saga of St Olaf* in **Heimskringla** and is based on a verse by the **skald** Sigvat. It is not in his own words – he was a Christian – but supposedly reports what he heard when he and two companions were travelling in Sweden. He says that they came to a house where a woman was blocking the doorway and forbade them to come in, because her people were busy making a sacrifice to 'the elves' – presumably household spirits. Sigvat adds that she 'thrust me away as if I were a wolf'. The saga is set in the early 11th Century when much of Sweden was still pagan.

This is followed by a short prayer from *Oddrunargratr*, the **Eddic poem** quoted on p. 211 as an introduction to TALES OF LOVE AND HATE. The context is a very female occasion: a young woman called Oddrun has just helped her friend Borgny give birth to her child, born out of wedlock; so it is not surprising that Borgny appeals to the **goddesses** to watch over her supporter as a way of expressing her thanks.

Next comes a verse from the Eddic poem, *Hyndluljod*. The poem opens with the goddess **Freyja** waking up her friend, a **giantess** called Hyndla, and asking her to help on a romantic errand. It seems strange that Freyja should have a giantess for a friend, and even stranger that it is the goddess herself who intends to make the sacrifice to a **god**. Nevertheless, perhaps it gives a flavour of how appeals to the pagan deities were worded.

The extracts now move on to spells and charms.

The first of these comes from *Egil's Saga*, and is attributed to its eponymous hero, the contentious poet, Egil Skallagrimsson. A man has complained about Egil's drunken, slanderous verses to the equally controversial Queen Gunnhild (see THE WITCH QUEEN'S CURSE, p. 296). They add poison to Egil's next drink but, guessing what they are up to, Egil stabs his hand, uses the same knife to carve the drinking horn with **runes** and rubs his blood into them, before chanting his incantation. It is clearly effective, for at once the horn splits, spilling the poisoned drink onto the floor.

The next is from a long section of the Eddic poem *Havamal* in which **Odin** imparts all kinds of useful advice to a mysterious confidant called Loddfafnir. It is supposedly in the high god's own words.

Finally, there are two verses from the Eddic poem, *Sigrdrifumal*. This is about the legendary Sigurd from THE CURSE OF ANDVARI'S RING cycle (p. 114 ff). It features a **valkyrie** called Sigrdrifa – a substitute for Brynhild who appears in other versions of the stories – and the extract here is supposedly in her own words as she shares her wisdom with Sigurd, mentioning both men's and women's concerns. Tyr, mentioned in one of the verses, is the god who attempts to tame Fenrisulf in THE MIGHTY WOLF (p. 66).

THE KING'S AMULET *(story p. 276)*

This story comes from *Vatnsdaela Saga* (The Saga of the People of Vatnsdal). Vatnsdal (Water Valley or Lake Valley) is a long valley in northern Iceland, south of the town of Blonduous; there is a lake at its mouth and two more lakes nearby. The **saga** follows several generations of inhabitants centred on a family of local chieftains all descended from the original settler there, Ingimund Thorsteinsson, who is believed to have lived in the early 10th Century. The same story is told more briefly in *Landnamabok*.

According to the saga, Ingimund established a dynasty of chieftains in the valley, and the temple he built to **Frey** was a hundred feet long. The rest of *Vatnsdaela Saga* comprises a number of similar, self-contained yet all related short stories – another of these is retold in DREAMING OF SORCERY (p. 303).

The sailing time from Norway to Iceland is taken from *Landnamabok*. **Viking Age** ships were completely open to the weather, and passengers were crammed in beside goods and livestock, so such a voyage must have been not just dangerous but also most uncomfortable. In the early Viking Age, the woods described by the wizards did indeed extend much further over the Icelandic landscape than the sparse, scrubby remnants that can be seen there today.

In the saga, Ingimund's occupation as a pirate raider is described without shame and in a very positive light. Despite the distress caused to its victims, the sagas describe many other prominent men routinely engaging in this activity, in order to swell their coffers – including **kings** such as **Harald Finehair** himself, Eirik Bloodaxe, and both the father and son of AUD THE DEEP-MINDED (p. 176).

In the sagas the **Lapps** (also known as **Finns**) are usually associated with the magic arts. Their traditional drums, made of wood and reindeer hide and engraved with esoteric figures, were claimed to enable those with shamanistic gifts to go on 'out-of-the-body' spiritual journeys – a practice in common with other traditional arctic cultures.

However, skills of prophesy were not exclusive to them. One of the sagas about **Vinland**, *Eirik's Saga,* contains a vivid description of a fortune-telling session in Greenland, at a time of great famine. Here the prophetess is a young Norse woman known as 'the little sybil', raised in a family where her nine late sisters had shared the same talent. Before beginning work for the householder, she is given a special meal of goat's milk gruel and animal hearts, and must sleep in the house overnight. In order to perform her ritual the following day, she calls for a group of women to stand in a circle around her, while one of these sings a 'warlock song' that she had learned in Iceland from her **foster**-mother. Following this, the prophetess says that the invisible spirits have now arrived, and makes a series of predictions, both general and personal. Most of these, the saga writer adds, turn out to be true.

GHOSTS IN GREENLAND *(story p. 282)*

This tale seems to have been in wide circulation, for it appears in both the **sagas** about the discovery of **Vinland**, *Graenlendinga Saga* and *Eirik's Saga*. In typical saga fashion, all that the ghost of Thorstein Eiriksson predicts for his wife comes true (see WINELAND, p. 254).

The two accounts are broadly similar. However, *Eirik's Saga* claims that the two Thorsteins were already friends who jointly owned a farm in the Western Settlement, and that Gudrid and her husband visited Thorstein the Black intentionally. *Graenlendinga Saga* follows the plot retold here, but names Thorstein the Black's wife as Grimhild.

The shipwrecked couple's unsuccessful voyage gives a vivid glimpse into the perils and uncertainties of sea travel during the **Viking Age**, despite exceptional ships and highly developed navigational skills.

THE BIG WOMAN FROM THE HEBRIDES
(story p. 286)

This tale forms several chapters of the mid-13th Century *Eyrbyggja Saga*, which is set in the Snaefellsnes peninsula in western Iceland. Some of its elements – a character from the Hebrides instigating the hauntings, the association of ghosts and seals – also appear in other **Viking Age** tales of the supernatural (see THE HAUNTED FARM, p. 299). An interesting detail is the use of legal procedures to subdue the evil spirits. If the anonymous author is to be believed, even the rituals of Christianity were not considered sufficient for exorcism; as in other sagas, it portrays Viking Age Icelanders as having high regard for the power of the **law**.

Although Snorri the Priest only plays a minor role in this episode, overall in *Eyrbyggja Saga*, he is one of the principle characters. An important chieftain, he also appears in *Laxdaela Saga*, *Njal's Saga* and *Grettir's Saga*. The sources describe him as being wise and shrewd but with a dangerous taste for vengeance. He is believed to have lived from 963 – 1031, making it possible roughly to date this story. It is not clear why Snorri, as the brother of Thurid, had not intervened before. But then this episode is essentially a folk tale, and illogicality is often a quality of such narratives.

Skalholt, where Thorgunna ordered her body to be buried, became the site of Iceland's first bishopric and first official school in 1056.

THE WITCH QUEEN'S CURSE *(story p. 296)*

This short episode is taken from the beginning of *Njal's Saga* (see NJAL THE PEACEMAKER AND HIS ANGRY SONS, p. 183).

Another **saga**, *Egil's Saga*, contains several further anecdotes about Queen Gunnhild's proficiency in witchcraft. This presents Gunnhild as a malicious character who dominates her husband, **King** Eirik Bloodaxe. It claims that she never forgives **insults**, and takes revenge on her enemies by attempting to have them poisoned. She also appears in *Laxdaela Saga* (see THE LOVE TRIANGLE, p. 215), which recounts how the ageing queen flirts with the young Olaf the Peacock, though here there is no mention of her actually seducing him.

According to *The Saga of Harald Finehair* in **Heimskringla**, Gunnhild is the daughter of a petty king called Ozur Tote of Halogaland, northern Norway. Her father sends her to a remote place to learn witchcraft from two brilliant **Finns**. Their supernatural skills include following tracks like dogs, and killing with a mere glance anyone who dares to approach them. Added to these fearsome traits, they have lecherous designs on her, so she is delighted to be rescued by King Harald Finehair's favourite son, Eirik Bloodaxe. The somewhat fanciful story says that Eirik's followers arrive at her hut while the Finns are away, and she hides them there, scattering ash from a sack both inside and around the hut, presumably as a form of magic. The Finns, drawn by the men's scent, return but fail to find where they are concealed. After a meal, Gunnhild lies in bed with the Finns one on each side, placing her arms around their necks. The Finns twice fall asleep, only to be awakened by Gunnhild, but the third time she fails to wake them (implying that she had cast a spell of her own on them which has now taken effect). She pulls a large sealskin bag over each Finn's head, binding them firmly below the two men's hands. At a signal, Eirik's men leap from their hiding place, kill the Finns and drag them from the bed. That night there is a tremendous thunderstorm. The following day, Gunnhild is taken by ship to meet Eirik and later marries him.

A more prosaic account, in the Latin language text *Historia Norwegiae* (History of Norway) possibly originating in the 13th Century, claims that she was the daughter of 'the notably foolish' King Gorm the Old of Denmark, and describes her as 'a vicious and most iniquitous woman' with 'excessive arrogance'.

Whatever her true ancestry, Gunnhild clearly had a formidable temperament. A later saga in *Heimskringla* says that after the death of King Hakon Haraldsson (in 960), several sons of Eirik Bloodaxe ruled Norway, though the eldest, Harald Greycloak is officially listed as the king. Instead of a patronymic, Harald took his mother's name, being known as Harald Gunnhildarson – defying usual convention and reflecting her power and status. The same saga says that Gunnhild 'was called the king-mother and mixed herself much in the affairs of the country'; and that 'Gunnhild, the king-mother, and her sons often met, and talked together about the government of the country'. Gunnhild's malevolence and supernatural influences seem to have been passed down to her sons, for *Heimskringla* claims that:

'While Gunhild's sons reigned in Norway the seasons were always bad, and the longer they reigned the worse were the crops; and the peasants laid the blame on them. They were very greedy, and used the peasants harshly.'

THE HAUNTED FARM *(story p. 299)*

This story is spread over several disjointed chapters in *Laxdaela Saga*. Later in the same **saga,** a family of Hebridean sorcerers kill the heroine's second husband, as retold in THE LOVE TRIANGLE (p. 215). Indeed, those Scottish islands seem to have been regarded as a breeding ground for people with supernatural powers – see THE BIG WOMAN FROM THE HEBRIDES (p. 286). The latter, like the present story, also features a ghost which shape-shifts into a seal.

A note by the translators says that in Icelandic folklore, ghosts were not considered to be mere spirits, but 'undead' corpses capable of actual physical violence. Other sagas include ghost stories in which apparitions not only haunt farmhouses but also keep gruesome watch over burial mounds and the treasure within.

DREAMING OF SORCERY *(story p. 303)*

Like THE KING'S AMULET (p. 276), this brief but haunting tale comes from *Vatnsdaela Saga.* Chieftain Thorstein is the son of the former story's hero.

The **saga** says that afterwards, Groa's sister Thorey was driven out of the district. The place where Groa's house had stood was believed to be haunted and no one else was ever willing to live there.

The same story of Groa and Thorey is briefly recorded in **Landnamabok**, which also contains reports of sorcerers, male as well as female, some with skills of shape-shifting and prescience. It reports on a woman called Geirvid, summonsed for causing the death of a man from an illness 'which he had caught when he went to learn the art of magic from her'; although the legal action against her collapses because her son mysteriously 'took the oath upon the altar ring'. Sorcery sometimes had benign effects rather than evil ones; for example, another woman called Thurid earned her nickname 'Sound-Filler' back in northern Norway where she grew up, because during a year of famine there, she 'brought it about by wizardry that every sound was filled with fish.'

There are further short 'witch' stories in *Vatnsdaela Saga.* One tells of a malicious woman called Ljot, whose bully of a son causes trouble by harassing a local girl. At the end of the ensuing violent **feud**, Ljot appears, walking backwards with her head thrust between her legs and her eyes darting about hideously. She threatens to 'change the whole lie of the land there', adding that 'all of you will run wild and driven crazy with fear out among the wild animals'. However, before she can work her spell, she dies 'in her rage and sorcery'.

Another concerns a man with the colourful name of Thorolf Sledgehammer, an unpleasant thief who lives alone with twenty huge black cats, said to be fortified by bewitchment. When the chieftain goes to his house to challenge him, the wailing cats block the doorway as Thorolf fills the house with acrid smoke. The chieftain's brother sets fire to the house and Thorolf suddenly leaps out, seizes another of the chieftain's men and drags him into a bog, where both vanish for ever.

Fylgjur (plural of the **Old Norse** *fylgja*) were spirits connected with belief in unavoidable destiny, usually warning of impending death. They also appear in a number of other **sagas**.

GLOSSARY

Adam of Bremen

11th Century German chronicler whose book *Gesta Hammaburgensis Ecclesiae Pontificum* (Deeds of the Bishops of of Hamburg) contains interesting information about Viking **pagan** religious practice, particularly a supposed temple at Uppsala in Sweden – although there is some doubt as to whether it is genuinely based on factual observation.

Althing

The **Viking Age** national **assembly** of Iceland, directed by the **Lawspeaker**. It met every summer in the open air at *Thingvellir* (Assembly Plain) in south-west Iceland, around forty-five kilometres north-east of modern Reykjavik. It discussed current legal cases, and passed new legislation. Most importantly, the **Lawspeaker** recited aloud one-third of Iceland's current **laws** each year; thus covering all the laws every three years. The Althing is Europe's oldest national assembly: it first convened in 930, and the modern Icelandic parliament still goes by the same name.

All free men were eligible to take part, travelling from all over Iceland, and often accompanied by their families, for it was the major annual social event and a hothouse for gossip – a fact widely attested by many **sagas**. Accommodation was in booths made of turf, boulders, wood and fabric.

Ari the Learned (Ari Thorgilsson)

Author of the oldest surviving history of Iceland, lived c. 1068 – 1148. Wrote *Islendingabok*. Probably also helped to write *Landnamabok*, and possibly an authority on Norwegian **kings**. Descended from AUD THE DEEP-MINDED (p. 176), and the great-grandson of Gudrun Osvifsdaughter from *Laxdaela Saga* (see THE LOVE TRIANGLE, p. 215).

Asgard

The realm of the **gods** and **goddesses**. The *Prose Edda* describes it as a city where all the deities have their halls. Mentioned in a number of myths.

assembly (Old Norse *thing*)

A community meeting, to which virtually all free men could contribute. A forum for complaints, decisions and legal matters. **Viking Age** Iceland was divided into four Quarters, with three assemblies in each, and also had a national assembly called the **Althing**.

conversion to Christianity

The change from **paganism** to the Christian religion plays an important part in many **sagas**. It also had a major influence on surviving **Viking Age** narratives, since medieval writers modified the old stories to fit in with the Christian ethos.

DENMARK
Christianity probably practiced from the early 9th Century. A **rune-stone** at Jelling refers to **King** Harald Bluetooth (reigned c. 958 – 986) as the person who officially converted the country, around 960.

NORWAY
Some 10th Century rulers were baptised but did not impose their faith. King **Olaf Tryggvason** is credited with systematically and brutally converting the whole country c. 1000. The conversion was officially confirmed by Olaf Haraldsson, who destroyed all the pagan sites, making Christianity compulsory c. 1024.

SWEDEN
Pagan for most of the Viking Age, gradually
converted to Christianity during the 11th Century,
with pagan beliefs and rites allowed to continue
alongside the new faith for some time. While other
Norse countries became mainly Roman Catholic,
Sweden's leanings eastward linked it to the
Orthodox church.

ICELAND
The Norwegian king, **Olaf Tryggvason**, sent
missionaries there. Formally converted in 1000,
with the entire population baptised, as described in
Islendingabok, Kristni Saga and various sagas. At a
meeting of the **Althing,** initially pagans and
Christians agreed to each keep their own religion
and **laws**; but **Lawspeaker** Thorgeirr Thorkelsson
persuaded against this, fearing violence would
result. Some pagan practices such as sacrifice were
allowed to continue in secret for a few more years.

GREENLAND
Christianity introduced from Iceland shortly after
that country's conversion.

divorce

In many **sagas**, divorce plays a significant part in the plot,
often contributing to ongoing blood **feuds**. During **pagan**
times, it could be initiated by either partner simply declaring
before witnesses that the marriage was dissolved, followed
by financial settlement and arrangements for custody of any
children.

There seem to have been many grounds for divorce,

including: violence by one party against the other; non-consummation or sexual neglect; cross-dressing; general incompatibility; and adultery on the wife's part – though men were allowed to keep a mistress, and in the sagas illegitimate children often flourish.

After divorce, a woman's dowry (her share of her birth-family's wealth, which she brought to the marriage) was returned to her and her 'bride-price' (the husband's payment to her **kin** for her hand) remained her property. Gudrun in *Laxdaela Saga* (see THE LOVE TRIANGLE, p. 215) contrives a pre-nuptial agreement with her first husband, guaranteeing her financial independence in the event of divorce, which she is quick to make use of. The sagas imply that there was no social stigma for divorced women, who often remarried.

dwarfs

Mythical characters, according to **Snorri** also known as 'dark-elves', and inhabiting either rocks or soil. They seem to have been exclusively male. Stories depict them as exceptionally skilled smiths, especially working with gold, and capable of fashioning extraordinary treasures, often with magic properties; see THE DWARFS' TREASURES (p. 30) and THE CURSE OF ANDVARI'S RING cycle (p. 114). They are often portrayed as shrewd and dangerous, treacherous liars who kill willy-nilly.

earls

High-ranking men, particularly in northern Norway and the Scottish islands, who either ruled independently, or on behalf of a **king**.

Eddic poems
One of those collected in the *Poetic Edda*, with either a mythical or heroic theme. Generally written in a style that assumes the audience already knows the story or the key mythological facts.

Eirik the Red
Important character in the **sagas** about **Vinland**, leader of the pioneer Norse colony in Greenland. Norwegian by birth, he left his home 'because of some killings' and settled in Iceland, where his eldest son, Leif the Lucky, was born. After various further disputes and murders, Eirik was declared an **outlaw**, thus forcing him into exile. This stimulated him to explore Greenland, where he eventually established a flourishing colony. In later life he became both respectable and greatly respected.

feuds
Blood feuds play a major role in many **sagas**. They often continue for many years and involve several generations. They unfold according to informal conventions, involving repeated tit-for-tat reprisals, with the initial catalyst often irrelevant or forgotten. The stories portray vengeance as a duty of **kinship**, though often the feuds are eventually settled financially, either in or out of court.

Finns
The usual name in the **sagas** for the nomadic people of Arctic Scandinavia, the cross-border area straddling northern Norway and Sweden as well as Finland, today known as Lapland. Finns or '**Lapps**' appear in a number of

sagas, usually as sorcerers or fortune tellers. Their descendants are the modern Sami people.

fostering
Both boys and girls were commonly fostered by another family, as demonstrated by the **sagas**. This was regarded not as a stigma but an honour, and fostering usually took place while the natural parents were still alive. Foster-relations had the same rights and obligations as blood-relations. An 11th Century **rune-stone** in the Isle of Man declares: 'It is better to leave a good foster-son than a bad son.'

Frey
A major **god,** brother of **Freyja.** Rules weather and thus crops, and rules over human wealth. Owns a golden boar which runs faster than a horse and sparkles with light; a magic ship which always attracts a fair wind and folds up to fit in his pocket; and a sword capable of 'fighting by itself', which he gives up for the love of a **giantess**. Like his father, Njord (who plays little role in the surviving myths), there is evidence that Frey was widely worshipped during the **pagan** era: several **sagas** mention temples and sacrifices dedicated to him.

Freyja
A major **goddess**, sister of **Frey.** The *Prose Edda* says 'She is the most approachable one for people to pray to…She is very fond of love songs. It is good to pray to her concerning love affairs.' She drives a chariot pulled by two cats. In contrast to her romantic aspect, she is also associated with war, for she shares warriors slain in battle with **Odin,** taking

the half that he discards. She was once married to a mysterious man called Od, but he left her to go travelling, causing her to weep red-gold tears. They had a daughter together, the goddess Hnoss; and **Snorri** also lists another daughter of Freyja, called Gersemi.

giantesses
Presumably the same as **troll-wives**. Some are described as very beautiful: in one myth the light from a giantess's arms is described as shining over the sea and sky, brightening the world. They appear in a variety of roles and have an ambiguous relationship with the **gods**; sometimes opposing them but more often being seduced by them, helping them and bearing their children. In fact, **Snorri** lists the giantesses Gerd (lover of **Frey**), Skadi (wife of Njord) and Jord (mother of **Thor**) amongst the **goddesses**.

Giantland (Old Norse *Jotunheim*)
Mythical realm of the **giants** and **giantesses**, also sometimes known as *Utgard* (the world outside). It lies across the sea, set apart from the human realm.

giants
Wise and cunning opponents of the **gods** – in many stories their arch enemies. Particularly hated by **Thor**, whose mission is to kill as many giants as possible. Many of the conflicts between gods and giants take the form of challenges of cunning or willpower rather than physical battles. Some giants have wives and children. As described in the myth IN THE BEGINNING (p. 25), the world and all its physical features were created from a giant's body.

The relationship between gods and giants is ambiguous, and the myths fail to explain why they are enemies. There is considerable cross-breeding between them, with most of the gods having either a giant or a **giantess** as a parent.

goddesses (Old Norse *Asynjur*, singular *Asynja*)
The *Prose Edda* says the goddesses are as holy and powerful as the **gods,** though few stories about them have survived. They live in **Asgard**.

They are variously listed as: Frigg (wife of **Odin**), **Freyja,** Saga, Eir, Gefiun, Fulla, Hnoss (Freyja's daughter), Sjofn, Lofn, Var, Vor, Syn, Hlin, Snotra, Gna, Rind, Idun, Sigyn, Nanna, Skadi, Ilm, Bil, Njorun, Sol, Thrud, Ran and Gersemi.

Strangely, three **giantess** are also included in the lists: Skadi (wife of Njord), Jord (mother of **Thor**), and Gerd (lover of **Frey**); yet Thor's wife, Sif, is omitted.

gods
The gods live in **Asgard**. According to the *Prose Edda* the gods were once divided into two groups.

The *Aesir* (singular *As*) comprised twelve gods: **Odin,** **Thor, Loki,** Baldr, Tyr, Bragi, Heimdall, Hod, Vidar, Ali (or Vali), Ull, and Forseti. Hoenir is also included amongst them in some myths.

The *Vanir* formed a separate group concerned with fertility, but little information has survived about this aspect. The only known members are Njord and his children **Frey** and **Freyja.**

In the *Prose Edda*, the MAGIC MEAD myth (p. 20) opens with a peace settlement to end a war before the two groups.

Harald Finehair (Harald Halfdanarson)

King who united the petty kingdoms of Norway into a single country, and ruled it from after 890 until 930. **Snorri** tells a romantic tale about this in *Heimskringla*: the young Harald proposed to a king's daughter called Gyda, who refused to marry him unless he became king of all Norway. Impressed by her spirited challenge, and grateful for the idea, Harald took a vow neither to cut nor comb his hair until he had achieved this goal. Within ten years, he had won both kingdom and bride; and his newly groomed coiffure earned him the epithet 'Finehair'. *Heimskringla* claims that he also had numerous other wives. He appointed **earls** to administer each province on his behalf.

According to a number of **sagas**, many Norwegians subsequently emigrated to the newly settled country of Iceland to escape his rule. *Islendingabok* claims that Harald 'was king for seventy years and lived into his eighties'.

Heimskringla (The Earth's Circle)

A collection of sixteen 'kings' **sagas**', possibly written by **Snorri**, relating the supposed history of the kings of Norway until the 12th Century. The early chapters are more legend than history; like the work of **Saxo Grammaticus**, they claim that the **pagan** deities were originally real people, later elevated to divine status. Its name is derived from the first two words of the text.

Hel

(1) **Goddess** of the underworld, daughter of **Loki** and a **giantess**, sister of the **World Serpent** and Fenrisulf (see THE MIGHTY WOLF, p. 66). The *Prose Edda* says she provides 'board and lodging to those who die of sickness and old

age.... She is half black and half the colour of flesh... rather sad and fierce looking.'
(2) Also used as a name for the underworld itself.

insults (Old Norse *flyting*)

The ritualised exchange of insults is portrayed in the literature as an important aspect of Norse culture. The main themes are cowardice and sexual deviancy. Sometimes the exchange provoked an actual battle, but it could also be a substitute for physical aggression. There are many examples in myths, heroic legends and **sagas**. A startling example is the **Eddic poem** *Lokasenna*, in which **Loki** insults the major **gods** and **goddesses** in the most outrageous terms.

Islendingabok (The Book of the Icelanders)

Written c. 1122 - 1133 by **Ari the Learned**. Briefly describes the original settlement of Iceland starting in the year 870 AD, and virtually completed sixty years later. To verify his account, Ari cites oral traditions, some passed to him by people he knew well, and later events from his own lifetime. It mentions: Irish monks as the original inhabitants; the establishment of the **Althing** and the country's **laws**; the settlement of Greenland by **Eirik the Red** and, in passing, the discovery of **Vinland** (see WINELAND, p. 254). Its main focus is Iceland's **conversion to Christianity**, as a pragmatic legal process. Includes lists of bishops and Lawspeakers, their genealogies and some significant new laws.

kennings

A stylistic convention of **Old Norse** poetry, in which a person or thing is not named, but referred to by one of their attributes or deeds. For example, a **giant** is a 'land-whale'; and ships are 'wave-horses'. Many of the mythological kennings are obscure to those not familiar with the stories from which they originate. Nevertheless, readers of the present book will understand why gold is known as 'Sif's hair' (see THE DWARFS' TREASURES, p. 30) and poetry is known as 'Kvasir's blood' (see MAGIC MEAD, p. 20).

kin, kinship
A person's role, loyalties and obligations were primarily defined by family. However, there were no set rules about which relationships should dominate, so that **feuds** often involved shifting alliances and conflicting loyalties through male and female parentage, marriage partners and in-laws, **foster**-relationships and even friendship.

kings
Kingship was hereditary and open to any in the direct male line, regardless of age or legitimacy, but presumably influenced by military prowess. The final choice of any new monarch was apparently made by a group of freemen and their leaders. **Kennings** for king such as 'protector of people' and 'guardians of men', indicate that monarchy involved responsibility for security, **law** and war. The benefits, alongside power, were control of all the kingdom's treasure, goods, estates and buildings. Originally the Viking lands comprised many small kingdoms, but eventually Denmark, Norway and Sweden each united into single realms. Iceland was a republic, with decisions reached by the consensus of all interested free men.

Kristni Saga (The Story of the Conversion)

An anonymous Icelandic text, preserved in a 14th Century manuscript. Like **Islendingabok**, it describes Iceland's **conversion to Christianity** as a political rather than a spiritual process. Includes a detailed description of Kjartan Olafsson being taken hostage by **Olaf Tryggvason**, as described in THE LOVE TRIANGLE (p. 215), and mentions the discovery of **Vinland.**

Landnamabok (The Book of Settlement)

Describes the settlement of Iceland and the establishment of farms there. Within interminably long lists of men, women genealogies and relationships, there are hidden gems of information particularly about **pagan** religious beliefs and temples, though some scholars question the accuracy. Mentions some **saga** characters and includes snippets of information about **Viking Age** practices such as belief in witchcraft and burning enemies alive inside their own homes. Some claim that **Ari the Learned** either wrote it, or at least contributed to it; but many scholars dispute this.

Lapps, Lappish

Another name for **Finns.** Ancestors of the modern Sami people of northern Scandinavia.

Law

The Viking lands were well-ordered societies. Laws were regularly recited at local **assemblies** and, according to the **sagas**, were taught to children at home. There are records of legal experts in Norway, Sweden and Viking areas of England. *Heimskringla* claims that the 9th Century

Norwegian **king** Halfden the Black 'made laws and kept them himself and made others keep them so that pride could not override the law', including a code of fixed penalties according to social rank. Laws played an important role in Iceland from its early settlement, although they were not recorded in writing there until the early 12th Century.

Lawspeaker

The highest authority in **Viking Age** Iceland, democratically elected, though only by chieftains. In no sense a ruler, but able to wield great influence. His responsibilities were to preside over the **Althing**, and to preserve and clarify the **laws**. These duties demanded that he learned all the country's laws by heart, and recited one-third of them every year at the Althing. He was assisted by a team of five or more equally knowledgeable 'lawmen'. He was initially elected for a term of three years, though some stayed in office for sixteen, nineteen and even twenty-six years.

Loki

Mythical character, the archetypal trickster – familiar in the stories of many cultures worldwide. The *Prose Edda* lists him amongst the **gods**, the surviving myths portray him as such, and he seems to live in **Asgard**; yet his father was a **giant** (the pedigree of his mother has not survived in any texts). Though the gods and giants are arch enemies, Loki mixes freely with both sides and is loyal to neither. He is a fascinating figure who can shape-shift and swap gender, and happily risks his own life and freedom by betraying others. According to **Snorri**:

'He is the originator of deceit, and the disgrace of all gods and men… Loki is fair and beautiful of face, but evil in disposition, and very fickle. He surpasses other men in the craft called cunning, and cheats in all things. He has often brought the Aesir into great trouble, and often helped them out again with cunning contrivances.'

Midgard (Middle Enclosure or Middle Dwelling Place)

Sometimes defined as the human world (the sense in which it is used in this book); or as the world of people and **gods**, excluding the **giants**. Elsewhere it refers to the mythical wall around the human realm.

norns

According to the *Prose Edda*, supernatural maidens who decide people's fates, which depend upon whether the Norns themselves are of noble or evil parentage. Variously descended from **gods,** elves and **dwarfs**.

Odin

According to the *Prose Edda*, the most ancient and important **god** who played a major role in creation. His grandfather was a supernatural man born from stones; his mother was a **giantess**; and at the beginning of time he consorted with **giants**. His wife is Frigg, and all the gods are their descendants.

Odin rules over all the worlds, seeing and understanding everyone's activities. He has numerous names including All-Father, Raven God and Father of the Slain. He gave away one of his eyes in return for a single drink from Mimir's Well, the source of wisdom and intelligence. He lives on wine alone, giving his allocation of meat to his two wolves, Geri and Freki. Two ravens, Hugin (Thought) and Munin

(Memory) sit on his shoulder, flying out each day to gather news. He owns two palaces. One, Valaskjalf, is roofed in silver and contains his throne, Hlidskjalf, from which he can see over all the worlds. The other is Valhalla (**Slain Hall**).

In a number of stories, Odin goes travelling through the human world and meddles in human affairs. Often he is not explicitly named, but is easily identified by his mysterious actions, his missing eye or by his aged appearance, grey beard and concealed face. He can shape-shift, and uses spells to control the elements, wake the dead, cause death, illness or bad luck, transfer a person's powers to another, control battles and foresee the future.

In real life, several passages in *Heimskringla* tell us that sacrifices were made to Odin and sometimes appeared to be rewarded. **Adam of Bremen** describes libations being offered to him at times of strife – for, he says, Odin rules war and gives warriors the strength to overcome their enemies.

Olaf Tryggvason

Norwegian **king** from 995 – c.1000, often credited with organising the compulsory **conversion to Christianity** in Norway, Iceland and other countries. Despite this achievement, **Adam of Bremen** claims 'he was skilled in divination... and placed all his hope in the prophecies of birds', earning himself the epithet 'Crow-Leg'. He appears in a number of **sagas**, often as a host to young Icelanders who travel to his court in search of adventure, fame and fortune.

Old Norse

The language of the Vikings, with several different dialects. It was used until the early 14th Century, after which modern

Scandinavian languages evolved. Modern Icelandic is particularly closely related to it and many English words are derived from it.

outlaws, outlawry

The laws of outlawry are best documented in Iceland. Outlaws had their property confiscated, were banished from their home country and could be killed with impunity. If someone was made a 'full outlaw', no one was allowed to offer him either help or shelter, and it was inevitable that he would be killed. Such a sentence could sometimes be reduced to exile for life. A 'lesser outlaw' had to spend only three years in exile; however, if he failed to go abroad within that time he was made a full outlaw. There were also 'district outlaws', banished from a specified area.

pagans, paganism

Before the **conversion to Christianity**, Vikings worshipped the **gods** and **goddesses** whose myths are preserved in the *Poetic Edda* and *Prose Edda*. Because the people were mainly illiterate, the only records of their religious practice were written either hundreds of years afterwards by scholars such as **Snorri**; or by near-contemporary outsiders such as **Adam of Bremen**, whose accounts were often second-hand and biased by his own Christian faith. No pagan temples or shrines survived the destruction which followed each country's conversion to Christianity.

It has been suggested that pagan belief and practice took many different forms, according to local culture in the various Viking lands. *Heimskringla, Kristni Saga, Landnamabok* and certain **sagas** refer to pagan temples; to sacred oaths sworn over a ring, and to sacrifices made to particular gods, particularly **Thor, Frey** and Njord. It is speculated that priesthood was a community rather than a professional role; and that sacrifices were offered to the gods in the hope of receiving good luck, victory in battle or some other favour in return. There is evidence that some rituals were performed in private homes, particularly relating to lesser spirits known as *landvaettir, disir* and elves; these may have been related to fertility and agricultural seasons.

picture-stones

Standing stones, often shaped like a keyhole, carved with stylised images, and sometimes including a short inscription in **runes**. They commonly depict ships and boats, people, weapons, battles or scenes from myths and heroic legends, alongside abstract patterns. A large number have been found on the Swedish island of Gotland.

Poetic Edda

Also known as the 'Elder Edda'. A collection of curious poems, transcribed from ancient oral tradition. Many scholars assert that some or most of them were either originally composed during the **Viking Age,** or are at least based on authentic Viking Age stories.

Their titles are sometimes translated as 'songs' or 'lays'; and indeed it has been suggested that they were composed to be sung rather than merely recited, or performed as mini-dramas. They are constructed according to complex stylistic rules, making much use of alliteration and specified numbers of syllables per line, but less use of rhyme. Twenty-nine of the poems are preserved in a ninety-page Icelandic manuscript known as *Codex Regius* (The Royal Manuscript), compiled by an anonymous scribe in Iceland, c. 1270 – 80. In modern translations these are usually supplemented by several related poems preserved in other medieval manuscripts.

The *Poetic Edda* provides much information about the Vikings' belief system. Many of the poems have a mythical theme, telling of **gods** and **goddesses**, **giants** and **giantesses**, **valkyries** and **dwarfs**; the creation and the prophesied end of the world. Others are about great legendary heroes and heroines, with a whole section relating to THE CURSE OF ANDVARI'S RING cycle (p. 114). A number take the form of dialogue – often a quiz between two supernatural characters – providing a platform for the revelation of sacred lore; some feature proverbs and other snippets of wisdom. One poem in particular, *Lokasenna*, derides many important deities in the most outrageous terms; some scholars believe that in the **pagan** era this may have been a valid form of sacred expression with a deeper purpose.

Prose Edda

A scholarly work by **Snorri**, written c. 1220 – 30, and the main source book of Viking mythology. Also known as 'The Younger Edda' or 'Snorri's Edda'. Based on oral tradition, it was an attempt to record all the surviving lore, stories and poetic conventions of the **pagan Viking Age**, although explored from a Christian perspective. Like **Saxo Grammaticus**, Snorri interpreted some of the myths as ancient history. It includes quotes from many of the poems transcribed a few decades later in the *Poetic Edda*.

The book is cleverly structured, divided into four sections. The Prologue claims that the **Old Norse** name for the **gods,** *Aesir* means they are 'men of Asia'. It introduces **Odin** as a **king** of Troy, as in the Greek myths, who visits Scandinavia and establishes royal dynasties there. Next follows *Gylfaginning* (The Tricking of Gylfi), in which a Swedish king disguises himself as an ordinary traveller, visits the gods and interviews three of them, who are mysteriously known only as High, Just-as-High and Third. They give him much detailed and very learned information about the mythological cosmos. The following section, *Skaldskaparmal* (The Language of Poetry) comprises a dialogue between the sea-**giant** Aegir and the god Bragi, who tells tales of the deities' exploits. This section also includes detailed explanations of poetic conventions such as **kennings**. The final part, *Hattatal* (List of Verse Forms) is a manual of poetry composition, based on praise poems composed in honour of a Norwegian king and **earl**.

runes

A simple form of writing, by carving linear letters into wood, stone, metal or bone. Runes were used mainly for memorial stones or for denoting ownership of objects. There were several different runic alphabets, all along similar lines. The most commonly used ones during the **Viking Age** had just sixteen letters which expressed the sounds F, U, TH, AW, R (two different letters), K, H, N, I, A, S, T, B, M and L, and are thus difficult but not impossible to translate.

rune-stones

Large, irregularly shaped standing stones cut with **runes**. Used as memorials to deceased **kin**; or to record activities, events, property ownership, inheritance, religious devotion and similar. On some the runes are carved within intricate patterns. Remnants of red, brown, blue and black pigment indicate they were once brightly painted. Thousands of **Viking Age** rune-stones have been found in Sweden, two hundred in Denmark and around forty in Norway; small numbers have also been found in other countries, including the Isle of Man. Also see **picture-stones**.

sagas

The main literary canon of medieval Iceland, the sagas are essentially historical novels, mostly written during the 13th Century, about the **Viking Age**. They are generally divided into Family Sagas and **Kings**' Sagas.

The Family Sagas (also known as Sagas of Icelanders) tell of supposedly real people: many are also mentioned in quasi-historical works such as *Landnamabok*. Most are centred on Iceland, though some of the action often takes place abroad. They are set mainly in the mid-10th to mid-11th Centuries, and resemble extended soap operas, covering several generations of a particular family and/or neighbourhood. Some scholars have offered convincing evidence that they were based on much older stories and traditions that originally circulated orally, greatly embroidered for dramatic effect; and indeed the saga writers themselves often use phrases such as 'it is said', or 'some say', as if they were citing oral traditions. Typically, they open at a time long before the main thrust of the story – sometimes over a hundred years earlier; and they include many deviations, sub-plots and stories-within-stories.

Certain stylistic themes and motifs recur in a number of Family Sagas. For example:
- Descriptions of both heroes and heroines as physically outstanding, intelligent and capable.
- Male protagonists start off as unpromising and 'difficult', but later become heroes.
- Male protagonists are very pugnacious, with an exceptional talent for composing acerbic poetry; this

earns them fame and fortune, but also leads them into trouble and violence.

- Young men go travelling before settling down – usually to Norway where an implausible number succeed in gaining favour with the **king**.
- The main plot is often interrupted, and its outcome affected, by the formal **conversion to Christianity**.
- Despite this, the supernatural is ever present, including sorcery, hauntings, symbolic dreams and prophecies fulfilled.
- Tragic heroines atone for blighted love affairs by becoming Christian hermits and/or nuns (the latter being impossible for a saga set in Viking Age Iceland, since the first Icelandic nunnery was not founded until the 12th Century.) Alternatively, both heroines and heroes conclude their adventures with a pilgrimage to Rome, where they die.

The Kings' Sagas are less well known. They mainly cover the monarchs of Norway, but sometimes also deal with Denmark, Sweden and Orkney. The most significant collection of these is *Heimskringla*.

Saxo Grammaticus
Danish scholar who wrote *Gesta Danorum* (Deeds of the Danes), c. 1216 – 1223. This purports to tell Danish history from prehistoric times to the late 12th Century, but also contains much material which is really myth and folk tale.

Shimmering Path (Old Norse *Bifrost* or *Bilrost*)
The route which links the worlds of **gods** (**Asgard**) and human beings (**Midgard**), though the traffic is all one way:

there are no stories in which people enter Asgard. The *Prose Edda* describes it thus:

> 'Have you not been told that the gods made a bridge from earth to heaven, which is called Bifrost? You must have seen it. It may be that you call it the rainbow. It has three colours, is very strong, and is made with more craft and skill than other structures.'

skalds, skaldic verse

Skalds were professional poets attached to the courts of **Viking Age kings**. If the **sagas** can be believed, the most highly prized skalds came from Iceland. Rather like modern poet laureates, their role was to compose poetry for special occasions; in addition, the sagas portray them often inventing a clever verse on the spot. Skaldic verse was originally completely oral, but seems to have been carefully preserved in memory until it was finally written down by medieval scholars such as **Snorri**. In *Heimskringla*, Snorri attributes particular poems to named skalds and often describes the circumstances under which they were supposedly composed. Scholars believe that such skaldic verses are fairly authentic to the Viking Age, though it is likely that the exact wording may have changed somewhat between the times of original composition and medieval transliteration.

Slain Hall (*Valhall*)

According to the *Prose Edda*, one of **Odin**'s two halls, with five hundred and forty doors, each one able to admit eight hundred warriors at once. It is here that Odin entertains warriors who have died in battle. Each day they go out to fight for sport, then return to Slain Hall to drink together in peace. The guests eat meat from a magic boar which is cooked each day but comes back to life each evening. They drink milk from the udder of a goat which grazes on the hall's roof – alongside a stag which has twelve great rivers dripping from its horns and flowing out through **Asgard**. An **Eddic poem** called *Grimnismal* says its rafters are made of spear shafts, its thatch of shields and mail coats are piled up along its benches; a wolf 'hangs' in front of its western doors and an eagle 'swings above'.

slaves, slavery

As in many other parts of the ancient world, slavery was an important institution during the **Viking Age**. Slaves, both male and female, were either seized in attacks and traded on as commodities, or born into servitude. Slave women dealt with many routine tasks in the house and dairy, and had the chance of achieving better status and conditions if they were chosen to be wet nurses, maids or concubines. Male slaves were generally assigned the heaviest, most unpleasant work, such as digging and dealing with dung, though they could be promoted to be overseers. Slaves could gain freedom by the generosity of their owner, by a third party willing to pay the owner compensation, or sometimes by their own endeavours. In Iceland, where increasingly small estates and a limited supply made slavery uneconomical, it was virtually obsolete by the 11th Century.

Snorri (Snorri Sturluson)

12th – 13th Century Icelandic scholar, author of *Prose Edda* and *Heimskringla*, and possibly some of the anonymous **sagas**. Born into a distinguished family, he became wealthy in his own right, held the post of **Lawspeaker** for two separate terms and was on friendly terms with the Norwegian royal family; yet he died a violent death.

Thor

One of the **gods**, son of **Odin** and the **giantess** Jord, married to Sif.

The *Prose Edda* defines Thor as the defender of both **Asgard** and the human realm, **Midgard**; and most importantly as the enemy of **giants** and **troll-wives**. He is powerful and strong and can overcome all living things. His most important possession is a hammer called Mjollnir, which he uses to smash the skulls of giants. It has many wondrous qualities: the *Prose Edda* says:

> 'He might strike with it as hard as he pleased; no matter what was before him, the hammer would not be harmed, and wherever he might throw it he would never lose it; it would never fly so far that it did not return to his hand; and if he desired, it would become so small that he might conceal it in his shirt'.

In order to grip the hammer, Thor dons a special pair of iron gloves, and he also wears a Girdle of Might which has the effect of doubling his normal phenomenal strength. He owns two supernatural goats which pull his wagon. Thor's hall, called Bilskirnir, is the biggest building ever made with five hundred and forty rooms (some translations call these floors or apartments).

Contrary to modern popular belief, no surviving records say that Thor was the god of sky or thunder; although **Adam of Bremen** claimed that he ruled over the air and thus both stormy and fair weather and crops.

Landnamabok contains many descriptions of men who were devoted to Thor, built temples to him, made sacrifices to him and generally relied on him to answer their prayers. Adam of Bremen says that Thor's followers gave him libations against plague or famine. His popularity is attested by the number of **saga** characters whose names include the component 'thor'.

troll-wives
Presumed to be another name for **giantesses**.

valkyries
Important female supernatural characters who appear in a number of **Eddic poems** and 10th Century **skaldic verses**, but are never fully explained.

The *Prose Edda* says that **Odin** sends valkyries into battle to allot death to particular warriors and oversee victory; on a more prosaic level, he also describes them as virtual waitresses in Odin's **Slain Hall,** serving drink and looking after the tableware and drinking vessels.

Some of the **Eddic poems** imply that certain mortal young women – usually **kings'** daughters – are able to choose to 'become' valkyries; and that they may switch between this state and their parallel lives as earthly princesses. However, no explanation is given of this and there is no evidence of any recruitment process run by their master, Odin, or of any tests they must pass in order to fulfill their chosen role.

In two **Eddic poems**, valkyries seem to be similar to the 'swan maidens' who have survived into modern European (and indeed worldwide) folklore: birds that can shed their feathers to transform into beautiful dancing women and then back again. In a third, they are described as wearing corselets spattered with blood. They ride horses – often in groups of nine – and carry shields, spears and helmets. They fly in troops and ride storms.

In *Volsunga Saga* (one of the sources of THE CURSE OF ANDVARI'S RING cycle, p. 114), Brynhild is portrayed as the mortal daughter of a king who is appointed to be a valkyrie by **Odin,** but this may be a medieval rationalisation. *Volsunga Saga* also calls them 'wish-maidens'. Near the beginning of this text, another valkyrie appears, said to be the daughter of a **giant**; she brings a magic apple from Odin to facilitate the conception of the hero Volsung.

Viking Age

The period of great Scandinavian expansion in Europe and across the north Atlantic, through trade, warfare, raiding and emigration. Generally considered to have lasted from the late 8th Century to the late 11th Century.

Vinland

Name given by Norse explorers from Greenland to the maritime area of modern Canada that they discovered and briefly settled – supposedly because they found wild grapes growing there. (See WINELAND, p. 254).

Voluspa

Important and esoteric **Eddic poem** describing the creation and end of the world. (See IN THE BEGINNING, p. 25 and RAGNAROK, p. 109). It possibly dates back to the late 10th Century.

World Serpent (Jormungand)

A monstrous creature that circles the ocean that was believed to surround the entire world. According to the *Prose Edda*, Jormungand is the offspring of the trickster **Loki** and the **giantess** Angrboda. He has two siblings: the ferocious monster Fenrisulf (see THE MIGHTY WOLF, p. 66) and **Hel**. He is raised in **Giantland**, amidst prophecies of disaster due to his parents' natures. In an attempt to avert this, **Odin** throws him into the middle of the ocean surrounding all lands, where he lies peacefully on the seabed biting his own tail. He is destined to play a major role in the end of the world (see RAGNAROK, p. 109).

Yggdrasil

A sacred ash tree, centre of the mythical cosmos, its branches spreading across the whole world and the sky. According to the *Prose Edda*, it has three roots. The first spreads into **Asgard**; underneath it is Weird's Well where the **gods** hold court. The second root extends into Giantland; underneath it lies Mimir's Well of Wisdom, from which **Odin** once drank, having given one of his eyes as a pledge. The third, its base constantly gnawed by a malign serpent, ends in Niflheim, the primeval wilderness of freezing mists and realm of **Hel**. An omniscient eagle sits in Yggdrasil's branches, with a hawk perched between its eyes; and a squirrel runs up and down the tree, carrying malicious messages between serpent and eagle. The dew that falls from it forms honeydew, said to be the food of bees. There is a parallel description in the poem *Grimnismal* in the *Poetic Edda*.

BIBLIOGRAPHY

ANCIENT TEXTS IN TRANSLATION

THE PROSE EDDA

Snorri Sturluson Edda, translated by Anthony Faulkes (London: J. M. Dent, 1987)

The Prose Edda by Snorri Sturluson, translated by Arthur Gilchrist Brodeur (New York: The American-Scandinavian Foundation, 1916, reproduced at www.sacred-texts.com)

The Younger Edda, also called Snorre's Edda or The Prose Edda, translated by Rasmus B. Anderson (Chicago: Scott, Foresman & Co., 1901, reproduced at www.gutenberg.org)

THE POETIC EDDA

Elder Edda: A Book of Viking Lore, translated by Andy Orchard (London: Penguin Books, 2011)

The Poetic Edda, translated by Henry Adams Bellows (Princeton University Press/New York: American Scandinavian Foundation, 1936, reproduced at www.sacred-texts.com)

Havamal: The Words of Odin the High One from the Elder or Poetic Edda, translated by Olive Bray and edited by D. L. Ashliman (London: Viking Club, 1908, reproduced by University of Pittsburgh at www.pitt.edu)

The Havamal, translated by W. H. Auden & P. B. Taylor
(reproduced at www.ragweedforge.com)

EARLY ICELANDIC AND SCANDINAVIAN HISTORY IN MEDIEVAL TEXTS

The Book of the Settlement of Iceland, by Ari Thorgilsson
the Learned, translated from the original Icelandic by Rev. T.
Ellwood (Kendal: T. Wilson Printer and Publisher, 1908,
reproduced by rarebooksclub.com, 2012)

Islendingabok / Kristni Saga (*The Book of the Icelanders / The
Story of the Conversion*), translated by Sian Gronlie (Viking
Society for Northern Research, University College London,
2006)

**A History of Norway and the Passion and Miracles of the
Blessed Olafr**, translated by Devra Kunin (Viking Society
for Northern Research, University College London, 2001,
reproduced at www.vsnrweb-publications.org.uk)

Saxo Grammaticus: *The History of the Danes Books I - IX*,
translated by Peter Fisher, edited with a commentary by
Hilda Ellis Davidson (Cambridge: D. S. Brewer, 1998)

Snorri Sturluson, *From the Sagas of the Norse Kings*,
translated into English by Erling Monsen and Dr A. H.
Smith (Oslo: Dreyers Forlag, 1967)

Snorri Sturluson, *Heimskringla or The Chronicle of the
Kings of Norway*, translated by Samuel Laing, based on
Heimskringla: A History of the Norse Kings (London: Norroena
1844 and 1907, reproduced at www.sacred-texts.com)

HISTORICAL DESCRIPTIONS AND COMMENTARIES WRITTEN BY OUTSIDERS DURING THE VIKING AGE

Adam of Bremen: *History of the Archbishops of Hamburg-Bremen*, translated by Francis J. Tschan (New York: Columbia University Press, 2002)

Ibn Fadlan and the Land of Darkness: Arab Travellers in the Far North, translated by Paul Lunde and Caroline Stone (London: Penguin Books, 2012)

MEDIEVAL SAGAS

Egil's Saga, translated by Bernard Scudder, in *The Sagas of Icelanders* (London: Allen Lane the Penguin Press, 2000)

Egil's Saga, translated by Hermann Palsson and Paul Edwards (London: Penguin Books 1976)

Eyrbyggja Saga, translated by Hermann Palsson & Paul Edwards (Edinburgh: Southside, 1973)

Gisli Sursson's Saga, translated by Martin S. Regal, in *The Sagas of Icelanders* (London: Allen Lane the Penguin Press, 2000)

Grettir's Saga, translated by Denton Fox & Hermann Palsson (University of Toronto Press, 1974)

Laxdaela Saga, translated by Magnus Magnusson & Hermann Palsson (London: Penguin Books, 1969)

Njal's Saga translated by Magnus Magnusson & Hermann Palsson (London: Penguin Books, 1960)

Orkneyinga Saga (The History of the Earls of Orkney), translated by Hermann Palsson & Paul Edwards (London: Penguin Books, 1981)

The Saga of the people of Vatnsdal, translated by Andrew Wawn, in *The Sagas of Icelanders* (London: Allen Lane the Penguin Press, 2000)

The Saga of the Volsungs, translated by Jesse L. Byock (London: Penguin Books, 1999)

Vikings in Russia: Yngvar's Saga and Eymund's Saga, translated and introduced by Hermann Palsson & Paul Edwards (Edinburgh: Polygon, 1989)

The Vinland Sagas: The Norse Discovery of America, containing *Grænlendinga Saga* and *Eirik's Saga,* translated by Magnus Magnusson & Hermann Palsson (London: Penguin Books 1965)

SKALDIC VERSE

Old Norse Poems translated by Lee M. Hollander (New York: Morningside Heights, Columbia University Press, 1936, reproduced at www.sacred-texts.com)

HISTORY, RESEARCH AND COMMENTARY

Jesse Byock: *Viking Age Iceland* (London: Penguin Books, 2001)

W. A. Craigie: *The Religion of Ancient Scandinavia* (London: Constable & Company, 1914)

H.R. Ellis Davidson: *Gods and Myths of Northern Europe* (London: Penguin Books, 1964)

Peter Foote & David M. Wilson: *The Viking Achievement - The Society and Culture of Early Medieval Scandinavia* (London: Sidgwick and Jackson Ltd., 1970, 1973)

James Graham-Campbell: *The Viking World* (London: Frances Lincoln, 1980)

James Graham-Campbell & Dafydd Kidd: *The Vikings* (London: British Museum Publications 1980)

Terry Gunnell: *Eddic Poetry*, in Rory McTurk, editor: *A Companion to Old Norse-Icelandic Literature and Culture* (Oxford: Blackwell Publishing, 2005)

Terry Gunnell: *The Drama of the Poetic Edda: Performance as a Means of Transformation*, in *Pogranicza teatralnosci: Poezja, poetyka, praktyka* (Warsaw, Instytut Badan Literackich Pan Wydawnictwo, 2011)

Terry Gunnell: *Viking Religion: Old Norse Mythology*, in Richard North & Joe Allard: *Beowulf and Other Stories: A New Introduction to Old English, Old Icelandic and Anglo-Norman Literatures* (Harlow: Pearson Education, 2007)

Helge & Anne Stine Ingstad: *The Viking Discovery of America: The Excavation of a Norse Settlement in L'Anse aux Meadows, Newfoundland* (New York: Checkmark Books, 2001)

Judith Jesch: *Women in the Viking Age* (Woodbridge, Suffolk: The Boydell Press, 1991)

Knut Liestol: *The Origin of the Icelandic Family Sagas*, translated from the Norwegian by A. G. Jayne (Oslo: Instituttet for Sammenlignende Kulturforskning, H. Aschehoug & Co. (W. Nygaard), 1930)

John Lindow: *Norse Mythology: A Guide to the Gods, Heroes, Rituals and Beliefs* (New York: Oxford University Press, 2002)

Andy Orchard: *Dictionary of Norse Myth and Legend* (London: Cassell, 1997)

R. I. Page: *Chronicles of the Vikings* (London: The British Museum 1995)

R. I. Page: *Norse Myths (The Legendary Past)* (London: The British Museum Press, 1990)

Judy Quinn: *The Gendering of Death in Eddic Cosmology*, in Anders Andren, Kristina Jennbert & Catharina Raudvere, editors: *Old Norse Religion in Long-Term Perspectives: Origins, Changes and Interactions* (Lund: Nordic Academic Press, 2004)

Julian D. Richards: *English Heritage Book of Viking Age England* (London: B. T. Batsford, 1991)

Else Roesdahl: *The Vikings*, trans. Susan M. Margeson and Kirsten Williams (London: Allen Lane the Penguin Press, 1991)

Peter Sawyer, ed.: *The Oxford Illustrated History of the Vikings* (Oxford University Press, 1997)

Gisli Sigurdsson: *The Medieval Icelandic Saga and Oral Tradition – A Discourse on Method*, translated from the Icelandic by Nicholas Jones (The Milman Parry Collection of Oral Literature, Harvard University Press, 2004)

Christopher Tolkien: **Introduction** to *Hervarar Saga ok Heithreks* (London: University College, Viking Society for Northern Research, 1956, reproduced at www.vsnrweb-publications.org.uk)

(Various authors): *The Viking* (London: Senate Publishing, 1999)

(Various authors): *Viking Voyages to North America* (Roskilde, Denmark: Viking Ship Museum, 1993)

WEBSITES

www.hurstwic.org

www.vikinganswerlady.com

Other books by Rosalind Kerven

Faeries, Elves & Goblins: The Old Stories (National Trust)

Arthurian Legends (National Trust)

English Fairy Tales and Legends (National Trust)

The Mythical Quest (British Library)

The Giant King: Looking at Norse Myths & Legends
(British Museum)

Enchanted Kingdoms: Looking at Celtic Myths & Legends
(British Museum)

King Arthur (Dorling Kindersley)

Aladdin & Other Tales from the Arabian Nights
(Dorling Kindersley)

The Rain Forest Storybook
(Cambridge University Press)

In the Court of the Jade Emperor: Stories from Old China
(Cambridge University Press)

Earth Magic Sky Magic: Native American Stories
(Cambridge University Press)

The Slaying of the Dragon: Tales of the Hindu Gods
(Andre Deutsch)